Artist's
Colour
Manual

Collins
Artist's
Colour
Manual

Simon Jennings

The Collins Artist's Colour Manual
was conceived, edited and designed at
Hill Top Studio, East Sussex, England.

*The right of Simon Jennings to be identified as
the author of this work has been asserted by
him in accordance with the Copyright, Designs
and Patents Act 1988.*

Research and Text,
Design and Art Direction
Simon Jennings

Text Editor
Geraldine Christy

Technical Consultant
Emma Pearce *Winsor & Newton*

Art Educational Consultant
Carolynn Cooke
Impington Village College, Cambridge

Consultant Editor
Sally Bulgin *Publisher, The Artist
& Leisure Painter Magazines*

Cathy Gosling
Editorial Director, HarperCollins

Studio Photography
Ben Jennings

Design and page make-up assistant
Amanda Allchin

Colour charts and research
Chris Perry
Rose Jennings

Index
Mary Morton

09 08 07 06 05
6 5 4 3 2

© HarperCollins Publishers 2003
© Photographs/artwork
Simon Jennings/Ben Jennings
© Paintings and artworks
the individual artists
(see pages 8–9)

The CIP record for this
book is available from
The British Library.

ISBN 0 00 7147031

Colour origination by
Colorscan, Singapore
Printed and bound by
Imago, Singapore

Artist's Colour Manual
Contents

Chapter 1
What is Colour?
10–45

Pigments in history	12
Pigment standards	16
Optical illusions	20
The four-colour process	21
Optical colour mixing	23
Colours of the spectrum	24
Additive and subtractive colour	25
The basic colour wheel	26
Colour in action	29
Choosing media	30
Oil colours	30
Watercolours	32
Acrylic colours	33
Gouache and egg tempera	34
Pastels and coloured pencils	35
Mediums	36
Media in action	39
Choosing palettes	40
Colour language	42
Interpreting colour	44

Chapter 2
Colour by Colour
46–93

Colour by colour	49
Blue	50
Turquoise	54
Violet	55
Red	56
Orange	60
Yellow	62
Yellow Ochre	66
Green Earth	67
Green	68
Brown and Red Earth	72
Black and darks	76
Grey	84
White	86
Metallic and special-effect colours	88
Flesh colours	90

Chapter 3
Creative Directions
94–153

Creative directions	96
Watercolour: straight and mixed	98
Subdued colours	102
Working without black	104
Fast colour for flesh	106
A seven-colour palette	110
Renaissance skin tones	112
Massive colour in oils	114
Rich colour from acrylics	118
Transparency and luminosity	124
Colour contained	128
Broken colour	132
Painting with non-art colours	136
Colours from the mail	140
Colours for free	144
Travelling colour	146
Colour on cloth	148
Smooth colour	150
Dry colour and line	152

Colour Index & Reference
154–192

Colour index	156
Guide to suppliers	180
Glossary of terms	182
Bibliography and further reading	187
Index	188

The Artist's Colour Manual
Sketchbooks 31 x 21cm (12¼ x 8¼in)
Simon Jennings
Examples of original manuscript, research notes
and colour experimentation for
The Artist's Colour Manual, 2001–03

*'Colour possesses me.
I don't have to pursue it.
It will possess me always,
I know it.
Colour and I are one,
I am a painter.'*

PAUL KLEE (1879–1940)

COLOUR

is essentially such a visual subject that perhaps it is rather strange that so many millions of words have been written about it. But that is no bad thing – and to add to them here are a few more, along with some stunning pictures, as well. Many thanks to all who have contributed to the Artist's Colour Manual, especially the eleven participating manufacturers who supplied invaluable technical information and scores of colours with which to experiment. I am also deeply grateful to the galleries that pointed me towards artists whose work demonstrates a unique relationship with colour, and finally to the individuals themselves who opened up their studios and provided me with first-hand information and access to their fabulous imagery. Their inspiration and enthusiasm demonstrated to me that 'hands-on, eyes-open' is the one and only way when it comes to understanding

COLOUR.

simon jennings, hill top studio (mmiii)

A book such as this is made possible by the goodwill and cooperation of many people and represents the work of many hands and minds. I am indebted to the following for their generous contributions, enthusiasm and support.

Main contributing artists
in alphabetical order:

Ray Balkwill, page 98

Joan Elliott Bates, page 102

Nick Bowering, page 104

Jessie Carr, page 136

Judith Chestnutt, page 140

Lucy Dunsterville, page 136

Sue Fitzgerald, page 118

Peter Graham, page 28

Desmond Haughton, page 110

Daphne Jo Lowrie, page 128

Chris Perry, page 148

John Reay, page 132

Tim Riddihough, page 106

George Rowlett, page 114

George Underwood, page 113

Marina Yedigaroff, page 124

Additional contributing artists
in alphabetical order:

Helen Banzhaf, page 148

Carolynn Cooke, page 152

Helen Dougall, page 148

Jackie Simmonds, page 39

Douglas Wilson, page 39

Art materials suppliers
The following manufacturers generously donated materials and equipment for review and sampling, and for use in colour charts and photography throughout this book.
In alphabetical order:

Daler-Rowney

Golden

Liquitex

Lukas

Maimeri

Old Holland

Royal Talens

Schmincke

Sennelier

Tri-Art

Winsor & Newton

(See pages 180–81 for contact details)

I am particularly grateful to the following individuals and companies for their support in organizing and obtaining materials and images for use in the *Artist's Colour Manual*:

Andrew Long, Winsor & Newton
George Frangeskou, Liquitex UK
Neil Hamer, Daler-Rowney
Arjan Knegt, Royal Talens
Ben Woolfitt, Tri-Art
Guenda Burgheim, Maimeri
Ute Hallerbach, Lukas
Christine Wiegold, Schmincke
Andrew Street, Schmincke UK
Paul Schulz, Golden

Jason Mackie, Global Arts
Unit 8, Leeds Place, Tollington Park, London N4 3QW.
Telephone 0207 281 2457
Email: mail@gas.demon.co.uk
For facilitating the cooperation of:
Old Holland in the Netherlands, **Sennelier** in France and **Golden** in the USA.

James Stock, Great Art
(Gerstaecker UK Ltd)
Normandy House, 1 Nether Street, Alton, Hants, GU34 1EA, UK.
Telephone 0845 601 5772
Email: welcome@gerstaecker.co.uk
www.greatart.co.uk

For technical and editorial support, advice and encouragement, my particular thanks to:

Emma Pearce
of Winsor & Newton, for reading the manuscript, corroborating the Colour Index International listings and writing the pigment history and pigment standards information at the beginning of the book.
(Emma Pearce's quotation p.12 is reproduced by kind permission of David Pyle.)

Sarah Miller
UK Education Manager at Winsor & Newton, for cheerfully answering questions and promptly dealing with my technical and general enquiries.

Carolynn Cooke
of Impington Village College, Cambridge, UK, for supporting the project, reading the manuscript and commenting on art-educational and curriculum issues.

Sally Bulgin
Publisher of *The Artist & Leisure Painter Magazines,* for enthusiastically supporting the project and ratifying the content.

Dr Francis Duck
of The Royal United Hospital, Bath, UK, for reading and corroborating the technical and scientific content of the physics of colour and the colours of the spectrum information.

Geraldine Christy
for editing my manuscript and research notes, and contributing to the writing, and for rewriting additional contributions, and looking after the details of text, type and language and preparing the text matter for press.

Chris Perry
for enthusiasm and general all-round support and particularly for diligent work in the preparation of colour samples and pigment declarations for the colour index.

Additional contributions
Additional research, writing and editing contributions: Emma Pearce (Pigments general), Brenda Howley (Choosing media), Rose Jennings (Blue and general research), Sally-Anne Schilling (Blue), Kate Gwynn (Red), Susanne Haynes (Yellow), Chris Perry (general research), and Ashley Howard (additional editing).

Colour samples and swatches
All the colour samples and swatches were created specifically for this book by Simon Jennings, Rose Jennings and Chris Perry, with the exception of the diagonal colour chart samples used in Chapter 2, 'Colour by Colour'. These samples, on pages 48, 49, 50, 54, 55, 60, 62, 66, 67, 68, 72, 84 and 85, were kindly supplied by Schmincke and show colours from their Mussini resin-oil range. The colour swatches on page 98, 'Watercolour: straight and mixed', are by Ray Balkwill.

Special photography
All special photography, studio set-ups and rostrum photography was by Ben Jennings. Thank you.

Page make-up
Thanks to Amanda Allchin.

The following Galleries assisted in contacting artists for participation in this project, and I am grateful for their help:

Len Hodds (Gallery Manager) and Robin Prewer of
The Buckenham Gallery
81 High Street,
Southwold, Suffolk, UK.
Telephone 01502 725 418
Email:
len@buckenham–galleries.co.uk
www.buckenham–galleries.co.uk

Michael Richardson
(Michael Richardson Contemporary Art)
Art Space Gallery
84 St Peter's Street,
London N1 8JS.
Telephone 020 7359 7002
Email: artspacegallery@msn.com
www.artspacegallery.co.uk

Bourne Gallery
33 Lesbourne Road,
Reigate, Surrey, UK.
Telephone 01737 241 614
Email:bournegallery@aol.com
www.bournegallery.com

The Alresford Gallery
36 West Street, Alresford,
Nr. Winchester, Hampshire SO24 9AU
Telephone 01962 735286

Picture credits/Image sources
All images are identified in the following listing by chapter and page number (p.), followed, in italics, by either description or abbreviated title, or column (col.) position, from left to right.

Chapter 1
p.12 *Abbé Breuil, Young Bison*/Avalon Press, 1948; *Portrait of a Woman*/British Museum; *Michelangelo, Madonna, Child and St John with Angels*/National Gallery, London. p.13 *pigment samples*/Sennelier; *Mauve*, Simon Garfield (book jacket)/Faber & Faber, design by Pentagram (portrait of William Henry Perkin courtesy of the National Portrait Gallery, London). p.15 *Science of Art images*/Winsor & Newton. p.16 *watercolour pans*/Sennelier. pp16–17 *main image*/Great Art (Gerstaecker). p.17 *pigments, left*/Sennelier; *pigments, right*/Winsor & Newton. p.19 *pigment jars*/Sennelier. pp.20–21 *dot screen*/Simon Jennings archive. p.22 *Masterpiece, Roy Lichtenstein*/©DACS. p.23 *Le Chahut, Georges Seurat*/Kröller-Müller; *Sigmar Polke, Girlfriends*/Tate Modern. p.24 *Newton and the Prism, after George Romney*/from *Life of George Romney*, William Hayley,1809; *Dark Side of the Moon Album Cover*/George Hardie, Storm Thorgeson; *John Everett Millais, The Blind Girl*/Birmingham Museums & Art Galleries. pp24–25 *Patrick Gries, The Hand of Nature*/Fondation Cartier pour l'art contemporain, Paris. p.26 *diagrammatic colour*/Daler-Rowney; *sketchbooks*/Simon Jennings. p.27 *Orange jug*/Simon Jennings. pp28–29 *all paintings*/PeterGraham. p.31 *col.3*/Schmincke. p.32 *cols 3–4*/Sennelier. p.38 *Sudden storm over Thames, Rotherhithe Pier*/George Rowlett; *Red Tulips*/Marina Yedigaroff (photograph Richard Heeps); *Morning mist*/Ray Balkwill; *Shoreline*/Judith Chestnutt. p.39 *Carnevale di Venezia*/Jackie Simmonds; *Lemon*/Douglas Wilson; *Check headband*/Tim Riddihough, cols 3–4, centre photos/Sennelier. p.40 *col.3*/Winsor & Newton; *col.4, top*/Winsor & Newton, *col.4, bot.*/Daler-Rowney; *col.5, mid. and bot.*/Winsor & Newton. p.41 *col.1, top*/Winsor & Newton; *col.2, palettes*/from *Art Class*/HarperCollins; *col.4, top*/Winsor & Newton, *col. 4, bot.*/Schmincke. p.42 *col.4, colour sketches*/Simon Jennings. p.43 *Hymn, photograph*/*Science, On the Way to Work*, Hirst & Burn/Faber & Faber; *Young Scientist Toy*/Joustra/Humbrol Ltd. p.44 *colour sketch*/Simon Jennings.

Chapter 2
p.51 *col.1, Benedetto di Bindo, c.1400, Madonna.of Humility* (diptych detail)/Philadelphia Museum of Art; *col. 4, Iznik tile*/from Turkish Ceramics, Tashin Öz; *col.4, Dutch tile/Traditional Dutch Tile Designs*,The Pepin Press, Amsterdam, from the collections of the Royal Tichelaar Makkum. p.52 *cols.2–3, pigments*/Sennelier, *col.4 pigment*/Sennelier. p.53 *col.1, pigment*/Sennelier; *col.3, tube*/Schmincke; *col.4, IKB*/Simon Jennings, *col.4, Franz Marc, Blue Horse 1* (detail)/Stadtische Galerie im Lenbachhau, Munich. p.57 *col.1, fire bucket*/Phil Hind; *col.2, Giotto, Kiss of Judas* (detail)/Scala, Scrovegni Chapel, Padua. p.58 *col.2, preparing madder*/Winsor & Newton; *col.3, dried madder*/Winsor & Newton; *col.4, crimson and carmine*/Winsor & Newton. p.59 *col.1, factory*/Lukas. p.60 *col.1, factory*/Maimeri, Giovanni Manzoni; *col.2, Antonio Mensaque, Oranges*/National Trust. p.61 *col.2, colour swatches*/Great Art (Gerstaecker). p.63.*col.2, bot.*/Winsor & Newton. p.65 *col 1, yellow pigments*/Maimeri, Giovanni Manzoni; *col.2, Lemons*/Simon Jennings; *col.3, bot.*/Simon Jennings Archive. p.66 *col.4, top*/Simon Jennings Archive; *col.4, bot. pigments*/Maimeri, Giovanni Manzoni. p.67 *col.4, Earth*/Simon Jennings Archive. *p.68 col.3, Scheele engraving*/Chroma-tography, 1869. p.69 *col 4, bot. colour swatch*/Great Art (Gerstaecker). p.70 *col.2 and col.4, top*/Maimeri, Giovanni Manzoni; *col.3, bot.*/Great Art (Gerstaecker). p.71 *Green sketch*/Simon Jennings, *Vincent van Gogh, Night café*/Yale University Art Gallery. p.72 *col.3, bot.*/Maimeri, Giovanni Manzoni. p.77 *col.2, top*/*Observer*, Simon Jennings Archive, *col.3, Vines*/How To Books, Simon Jennings Archive. p.79 *Kasimir Malevich, Black Suprematist Square*/Tretyakov, Moscow; *Rembrandt, Self-portrait*/National Gallery London; *After Ad Reinhardt* (facsimile)/Simon Jennings. p.81 *col.4, pigments*/Royal Talens. p.83 *Our Lady of Czestochowa*/Polish National Tourist Board. p.85 *Homage to Grey* (facsimile)/Simon Jennings. p.86 col.1, *White lead stacking*/G. Dodd, British Manufacturers 1844; *col.1 bot.*/Winsor & Newton; *col.3*/Winsor & Newton; *col 4*/Daler-Rowney. p.87 *col.2, Resists*/Simon Jennings. p.88 *Antique Bronze*/Simon Jennings Archive. p.89 *Framed Madonna* (facsimile)/Simon Jennings Archive. p.90 *col.1, Flesh experiments*/Simon Jennings. p.92 *Vincent van Gogh, Italian Girl*/Musée d'Orsay, Paris.

Chapter 3
p.96 *col.3, from top*/Ray Balkwill, Joan Elliott Bates, Nick Bowering; *col.4, from top*/Tim Riddihough, Desmond Haughton, George Underwood. p.97 *col.1, from top*/George Rowlett, Sue Fitzgerald, Marina Yedigaroff. *col.2 from top*/Daphne Jo Lowrie, John Reay, Jessie Carr and Lucy Dunsterville; *col.3, from the top*/Judith Chestnutt, Simon Jennings, Simon Jennings; *col.4, from top*/Chris Perry, Simon Jennings, Simon Jennings. p.98 *col.1, artist at work*/Ray Balkwill, *cols. 3–4, colour charts*/Ray Balkwill. p.99 *paintings*/Ray Balkwill. p.100 *studio details*/Ray Balkwill, *col.4, painting detail*/Ray Balkwill. p.101 *painting*/Ray Balkwill. p.102 *Sir William Coldstream*/Simon Jennings Archive. p.103 *painting and detail*/Joan Elliott Bates. p.104 *col.4, Linear detail*/Nick Bowering. p.105 *all images*/Nick Bowering. p.106 *Red man standing*/TimRiddihough. p.107 *Check headband*/Tim Riddihough. p.108 *col.1, bot.*/Tim Riddihough. p.109 *all images*/Tim Riddihough. p.111 *main image and detail*/Desmond Haughton. p.112 *Michelangelo, Madonna, Child and St John with Angels*/National Gallery, London. p.113 *all images*/George Underwood. p.115 S*unlit Walmer Beach, Deal Pier, Bathers and Crab Boat*/George Rowlett; *col 4 Sudden storm over Thames, Rotherhithe Pier*/George Rowlett. pp116–117 *Sudden storm over Thames, Rotherhithe Pier* (detail)/George Rowlett. pp118–119 *Cardinal Grapes and Silken Shawl* (and detail)/Sue Fitzgerald. pp120–121 *Two Dragons*/Sue Fitzgerald. p.122 *col.1, detail*/Sue Fitzgerald. p.123 *col.2, bot. painting* (detail)/Sue Fitzgerald, *col.3 painting* (detail)/Sue Fitzgerald. p.125 *Chrysanthemums*/Marina Yedigaroff (photo Richard Heeps). p.127 *Red Tulips*/Marina Yedigaroff (photo Richard Heeps). p.129 *Siblings*/Daphne Jo Lowrie. p.130 *all images*/Daphne Jo Lowrie. p.131 *cols 2–3, paintings* (and details)/Daphne Jo Lowrie. p.133 *Lowestoft Beach*/John Reay (photo Dean Annison). p.134 *col.1*/John Reay. p.135 *main image*/John Reay (photo Dean Annison). p.131 *preparatory sketch*/Jessie Carr and Lucy Dunsterville. p.140 col.1, *Colour sample*/Judith Chestnutt. p.141 *Shoreline*/Judith Chestnutt. p.142 *col.4, top and middle*/Judith Chestnutt. p.143 *col.1, Colour samples*/Judith Chestnutt, cols. 3–4, *Wastepaper collages*/Simon Jennings. pp144–145 *all images*/Simon Jennings. pp146–147 *main image and details*/Simon Jennings. p.148 *col.1 and cols.3–4, Vessels*/Helen Banzhaf; *foot of page, Set Aside*/Helen Dougall. p.149, *all images* Chris Perry. p.150, *all images* Heinz Edelman/TVC, King Features. p.151 *Building Fascias*/Simon Jennings. p.152 *col.2, centre images*/Carolynn Cooke. pp152–153 *all other images*/Simon Jennings.

WHAT IS
COLOUR?

CHAPTER 1

'Today's artists work with colours produced by an industry which has spent two centuries getting better and better and better, whilst most people in this world have to work with things that have got worse and worse.'

EMMA PEARCE
(IN 'WHAT EVERY ARTIST NEEDS TO KNOW ABOUT PAINT & COLORS' BY DAVID PYLE)

Young Bison
(Altamira, N. Spain)
From a watercolour by the Abbé Breuil
Prehistoric Painting/Brodric/Avalon Press 1948

Today's artists are lucky in being constantly provided with pigments that are more permanent and offer an ever-widening choice of handling properties. In less than 200 years the finest quality ranges have improved from around 30 per cent permanent to 99–100 per cent, as well as providing two or three times the number of colours.

Although many early pigments are now replaced by more reliable ones, many are not. Incurable romantics may find it pleasing that the first pigments remain some of the finest available to the artist.

☛**See also**

CI International	18–19
Choosing media	30–35
Colour by colour	50–93
Creative directions	96–153
Colour Index	156–179

The first colours
More than 15,000 years ago cavemen began to use colour to decorate cave walls. These were earth pigments, yellow earth (ochre), red earth (ochre) and white chalk. In addition they used carbon black (Lamp Black) by collecting the soot from burning animal fats. These colours were all that were needed to produce the sensitive and exquisite drawings and stencils that we are still able to see today.

The Egyptians
There is evidence that by 4000BC the Egyptians were manufacturing colours. The earth colours were cleaned by washing, which increased their strength and purity, and new pigments were being derived from minerals. Perhaps the most famous is Egyptian Blue, first produced around 3000BC. This was a blue glass made from sand and copper, which was then ground into a powder. It was replaced in the sixteenth century by Smalt, itself finally superseded by Cobalt Blue in the early nineteenth century.

The Egyptians also utilized malachite, azurite and cinnabar by crushing and washing each mineral. Cinnabar was prized as the first known bright red.

Vegetable dyes were also developed by the Egyptians, who found a way of 'fixing' the dye onto a transparent white powder to produce a pigment. This process is called lake making and it is still used today to produce rare colours.

Excavated at Hawara in 1888
Portrait of a Woman, AD100–120
Encaustic on limewood
British Museum, London

The Chinese
Although the discoveries and knowledge of the Chinese civilization ran parallel with other ancient societies, the Chinese were well in advance of the rest of the world with many inventions, including paper. Pigments were no exception and Vermilion was developed in China around 2000 years before it was used by the Romans. Vermilion was made by heating mercury and sulphur, producing an extremely opaque, strong red pigment that had almost entirely replaced Cinnabar by the eighteenth century. By the end of the twentieth century Vermilion itself was replaced by a range of cadmium colours, which provide greater permanence.

The Greeks
The Greeks also added to the artist's palette, notably by manufacturing white lead, the first fully opaque white (known today as Flake White or Cremnitz White). The manufacturing process took several months and involved stacking lead strips in a confined space with vinegar and animal dung. This method (with a few refinements!) was used until the 1960s and produced arguably the finest pigment of all for the artist's palette. The physical structure and reaction with oil give a superbly flexible and permanent paint film. The Greeks also made red lead, which was used for priming metal until the 1990s, when lead pigments were banned for use by the general public.

The Romans
For the most part the Romans inherited the palette of the Egyptians and Greeks. Pompeii is one of the main historical sources, dating to AD79, and Vermilion has been identified on many Pompeiian wall paintings. One of the most important colours was Tyrian Purple, which was also one of the most costly. The colour is prepared from a small colour-producing cyst within a whelk. Huge quantities of whelks were required – P. Friedlander, in 1908, collected just 1.4 grams of pure dye from 12,000 molluscs. Spoil heaps of shells can still be seen on the sites of ancient dye works around the Mediterranean. Its high price ensured that Tyrian Purple was reserved as a dye for the togas of Roman dignitaries, and it became a symbol of power and status.

The Renaissance
Little changed in the first millennium AD with regard to colours and it was the rebirth of artistry that fuelled new pigment development from the fourteenth century. The Italians further developed the range of earth pigments by roasting siennas and umbers to make the deep rich red of Burnt Sienna and the rich brown of Burnt Umber. Earth colours featured heavily in their painting technique, Terre Verte (Green Earth) being the principal underpainting colour for flesh.

Michelangelo Buonarroti (1475–1564)
Madonna, Child and St John with Angels, c. 1506
Oil on wood panel (detail)
National Gallery, London

Renaissance developments

The Italians improved the lake-making processes of the Egyptians and developed Naples Yellow, another opaque lead-based pigment. However, it was the development and use of genuine Ultramarine that perhaps personifies the paintings of the Renaissance.

Lapis lazuli was first used as a pigment by simply grinding it, but even the best stone can have up to 90 per cent impurities and it was the discovery of how to extract the blue that enlightened the Renaissance palette. The bright, deep blue produced had excellent lightfastness and was the most expensive pigment known to man. This high value was the reasoning behind gracing the Madonna in blue.

The beginning of modern pigments

By the eighteenth century the world was not only enjoying greater trade between continents, and therefore more industry than previous centuries, but also beginning to see the benefits of modern scientific chemistry. In 1704 a German colour maker named Diesbach was manufacturing red lake pigments, which required the use of potash as an alkali. He ran out of his supply and used some that was contaminated with animal oil. Instead of making red he made purple and then blue – the first chemically synthesized colour, Prussian Blue, had been produced! Prussian Blue remains a popular colour to this day and is also known for its novel ability to fade in daylight, yet recover its strength in darkness!

Early nineteenth century

The Industrial Revolution at the beginning of the nineteenth century produced both new processing possibilities and new opportunities for trade in every quarter of life, including artists' pigments. Scientists were driven by the demand for new, more permanent, colours and were able to utilize new minerals and chemistry to invent many of the colours that we think of today as 'traditional'.

Cobalt pigments

Cobalt Blue was discovered in 1802 by Thénard. It was a wonderful transparent, granulating mid blue of great permanence. It is used widely in ceramics and loved by artists for its moderate tinting strength, as well as for its fast-drying and watercolour characteristics.

Cobalt Green, though first made in 1780, did not enter common usage until after Cobalt Violet first appeared in 1860, with Cobalt Yellow (Aureolin) becoming available in 1862. The colour Cerulean Blue is also a type of cobalt and was available as early as 1805.

By combining cobalt oxide with aluminium, phosphorus, tin, zinc or a number of other metals, a variety of colours is produced. The cobalt pigments have always been expensive and the search continued for a less expensive dark blue pigment for the artist's palette. In the 1820s a national prize of 6000 francs was offered in France to anyone who could discover a method of artificially making Ultramarine at a cost of less than 300 francs per kilo. Both the French and Germans competed, but it was J.-B. Guimet who succeeded in 1828. Known as French Ultramarine ever since, the pigment is chemically identical to genuine Ultramarine, but physically finer and is without the impurities of the lapis rock.

Chrome pigments

The isolation of new elements in the late eighteenth century also played a part in providing new colours. In 1820 deposits of chrome in the USA facilitated the easy manufacture of Chrome Yellow, a highly opaque, low-cost colour available in a variety of hues. Although chrome colours had a tendency to darken they remained popular until the 1990s because of their good covering power and economical price. Chemically the colours are lead chromes and as such they fell foul of the legislation against lead pigments at that time.

Zinc pigments

Similarly, the isolation of zinc in 1721 eventually gave rise to zinc oxide by the end of the eighteenth century. This was used as an artists' white in preference to lead white as it was less hazardous and more permanent, particularly in watercolour. However, it lacked opacity until 1834 when Winsor & Newton developed a method of heating the oxide to increase its opacity. This new type of zinc oxide was called Chinese White.

Cadmium pigments

In 1817 the metal cadmium was discovered by Stromeyer, but it was not until 1846 that cadmium yellows were introduced to the artist's palette. Immediately popular for their great permanence, range of hues, moderate tinting strength and high opacity, Cadmium Yellow remains the mainstay for artists in this area of the spectrum. Cadmium Red was not available until after 1910.

Genuine Emerald

Genuine Emerald Green was first documented in 1822 and was highly toxic. Consisting of copper aceto-arsenite, it provided a bright clean emerald colour until the 1960s. It is most famous, however, for its potentially fatal effects. It is thought that Napoleon died as a result of arsenic poisoning from the wallpaper in his prison home on St Helena. Emerald Green was a very popular wallpaper colour, but unfortunately in damp conditions arsenical fumes were released.

The first modern organic pigments

In 1856 William Henry Perkin was a student at the Royal College of Chemistry. In his improvised laboratory at Greenford, Middlesex, he was attempting to synthesize quinine when he unexpectedly produced a purplish dye from oxidizing impure aniline with potassium bichromate. Mauvine, the first organic (based on carbon chemistry) colour was born. This led to the distillation of coal tar, which produced a huge range of new pigments over the decades to come. Mauvine as a dye was an instant success and became the most fashionable dress colour for Victorian ladies.

Impressionism and portable colours
The explosion of new pigments during the nineteenth century, the invention of the metal tube and the arrival of the railways all combined to facilitate the rise of the Impressionist movement. Bright new colours in portable, stable tubes and a method of easy travelling led to a period of painting that has become one of the most recognized in the history of art.

Alizarin Crimson
Alizarin Crimson is arguably the most important organic pigment of the nineteenth century. It was introduced in Germany in 1868, providing a blue-shade crimson of strong tinting strength and high transparency. It was immediately to become a core colour in the common palette. At that time, and until the 1960s, it was the most permanent crimson available. However, in pale washes it is susceptible to fading and modern quinacridones are more lightfast.

Synthetic iron oxides
The nineteenth century also saw the development of the Mars colours. These 'earth' colours are produced in a wide range of browns, reds, yellows and black, according to the levels of moisture and heat used. Originally they tended to be opaque, and they are much stronger than the natural earths. They have become important to artists of today since the deposits of good natural earths have become depleted.

The twentieth century
Pigment development continued apace into the new century.

'Hansa' yellows
During the first decade of the twentieth century the Hoechst company brought out the first of the 'Hansa™' yellows. Here was a synthetic organic pigment of good permanence, clear bright hue and high transparency. The colour is known as Lemon Yellow, but the Hansa group quickly gave rise to darker yellows and this pigment type is still important. The chemistry of this and other synthetic organic pigments is immensely complex. In words, Hansa is made by coupling diazotized amines containing nitroso and/or halide groups with acetoacetanilide or one of its derivatives! No longer can they be called a basic name relating to their origin, like cadmium or cobalt. Instead we see trade names, such as 'Winsor' Yellow or sometimes shortened names like Azo Yellow Medium. Reds were similarly developed and from the 1920s onwards these new pigments were offered as artists' materials.

Titanium White
The most important pigment of the century in terms of volume was Titanium White. Although the element had been identified in 1795, it was not until 1920 that an economical method of purifying the metal oxide was established. A non-hazardous, and the strongest, most opaque white available, Titanium quickly became the most popular white for artists.

Monastral Blue
In 1935 Monastral Blue was introduced by ICI. Known also as Phthalocyanine Blue, this offered a deep transparent blue of enormous tinting strength, yet moderate cost. Prized for its mixing abilities, it has also become the basis of many student-range blues as it can be reduced considerably and still offer a strong colour.

Quinacridones
A very important group of pigments originated in the 1950s. The first quinacridones were introduced to the artist's palette as Permanent Rose and Permanent Magenta. Until then the pink and mauve colour area had suffered from poor lightfastness; now crystal-clear hues were available without fading. Over the next 50 years many more colours became available, ranging from deep crimson to gold. This is achieved by juggling the chemicals involved. It is a quinacridone that is used as Permanent Alizarin Crimson.

Artists' pigments today
An average palette today of only twelve colours contains a selection of pigments from every historical era as well as every pigment type. Broadly defined, there are three pigment types.

Earth colours
Ochres, siennas, umbers and Mars colours.
Traditional colours
Cobalts, cadmiums, titanium and ultramarines, for example.
Modern colours
Phthalocyanines, quinacridones, perylenes and pyrroles, for example.

The Science of Art
(opposite)
In the 1990s Winsor & Newton commissioned these striking microscopic photographs of pigment sources.

Categories of pigment
Chemically, pigments are categorized by whether they contain carbon or not. This results in a more technical, but more accurate, definition of possible types.

Inorganic pigments
Earth, mineral (for example, cinnabar), synthetic (for example, cobalt).
Natural organic pigments
Rose Madder is an example in this category.
Synthetic organic pigments
The quinacridone colours fall into this category.

Can it get any better?
By the 1990s more pigment types of synthetic organic origin were appearing. Perylenes, pyrroles and new arylides (for example, Hansa yellows) have come into use. In some cases new hues are available, further extending the possibilities in watercolour or filling a perfect gap in portraiture, or providing even greater transparency for mixing or glazing. In other cases some good lightfast pigments were replaced by pigments that were even more lightfast. So we replace colours that last for a few hundred years with ones that last many hundreds of years! Today's artists are certainly fortunate to be living and painting in the twenty-first century.

Thanks to the automobile!
The car permanently has to endure the elements, whether rain, hail or sunshine, and pigments used for automobiles must withstand snowbound or desert conditions. Artists have everything to be thankful for that such lightfast pigments had to be developed. Without the car we would not have the reds, yellows and purples that we enjoy today.

Winsor Green, magnified x 240
Winsor Green, which is found in most Winsor & Newton colour ranges, is made from a single pigment. Despite the higher cost, single pigments give cleaner, brighter mixtures, better handling, and greater brilliance when they are diluted.
Microscopic photography by Florida State University

Lapis lazuli, magnified x 150
Lapis lazuli, the semi-precious stone from the hills of Afghanistan, is the secret of the blue used by the old masters. Modern pigments used for Ultramarine Blue are chemically indistinguishable from lapis lazuli, resulting in a beautiful blue with the characteristics of lapis lazuli at an affordable price.
Microscopic photography by
The Natural History Museum, London

Cochineal beetle shell, magnified x 150
The rich pigment of Carmine is created from the cochineal beetle, yielding a unique crimson that is beautiful, but not lightfast. In 1996 Winsor & Newton scientists finally succeeded in formulating Permanent Carmine, a new pigment that enables artists to enjoy this unique colour with superior permanence.
Microscopic photography by Florida State University

Madder root, magnified x 240
The unique pigment of Genuine Rose Madder is impossible to match precisely in hue, strength and texture with modern pigments. Winsor & Newton's formula for Genuine Rose Madder pigment, developed by George Field in 1806, still yields the most permanent Genuine Rose Madder colour available today.
Microscopic photography by Florida State University

Indian Yellow, magnified x 240
Used in India from the fifteenth century, this warm transparent yellow of great depth and beauty was said to be made from the urine of cows fed solely on a diet of mango leaves. Production of the colour halted in the 1920s due to concern over the religious status of the cows and the rise of improved, more easily manufactured colours.
Microscopic photography by Florida State University

Alizarin Crimson, magnified x 150
Alizarin Crimson has been one of the most popular colours down through the ages. However, it can fade in thin layers or washes. In recent years, Winsor & Newton, in the pursuit of improved lightfastness, developed and introduced Permanent Alizarin Crimson into its ranges wherever possible.
Microscopic photography by Florida State University

There are a number of universal systems and standards that help artists to identify and build knowledge in key areas of concern. Most importantly artists are interested in the specific characteristics of pigments so that they may use them to achieve their own creative ends.

Next, they need information regarding the permanence of pigments. The characteristics of a colour – such as granulation, staining, bleeding, transparency or opacity, colour bias, drying rate etc. – are to be found in both reference books and manufacturers' colour charts. Permanence ratings are also provided by manufacturers.

There are no set standards for pigment characteristics. After all it is the diversity and individuality of each material that painters want to exploit. Generally, good quality products are offered by the whole art materials industry and for most artists the literature and information supplied is sufficient for their needs. However, you may want to know more about the media you are using and to do this pigments need to be clearly identified.

The Colour Index International
Since the development of modern organic pigments, pigment names are no longer sufficient to identify the actual pigment being used. For instance, there are dozens of naphthol reds with varying characteristics and different levels of lightfastness. The Colour Index International identifies each pigment (see pages 18–19), ensuring artists know what they are using. Most artists' materials manufacturers publish the pigment content of their colours.

Colours are not the same
Just as loaves of white bread from different bakers will differ, so will artists' colours from different manufacturers. The formulation or recipe of the colour in conjunction with the manufacturing method and choice of raw materials produces variations between colours with the same name from different suppliers.

ASTM

The ASTM abbreviation stands for the American Society for Testing and Materials. (The UK equivalent is the British Standards Institute.) The ASTM has set standards for the performance of art materials and this includes lightfastness. It is the lightfastness ratings with which artists are most familiar. Pigments are tested in reduction with white in both artificially accelerated conditions and desert sunshine. Ratings I and II are recommended as 'Permanent for artists' use'. Art materials manufacturers rate their colours in a similar way and where no ASTM rating is given this usually means that the pigment is new and has not yet been tested by ASTM. In these cases the manufacturer's rating will be available.

Do not take colour for granted!

With just one colour there are many factors that affect what you see on the paper or canvas; these include thickness of colour, medium used, surface used, strength of pigment, use in mixtures, juxtaposition, transparency, colour bias and more. This variation is multiplied by the number of colours available. In a well-spaced artists' range there may be as many as 80 single pigment colours. Combine this with individual artists and an infinite array of results is an understatement!

Painting is a joy and there are certainly more colours available than any one artist can use in a lifetime. Of course, it is important to remember that each artist is aiming for self-expression and this means that what is right for one painter is not suitable for another. Some may never need opaque colours; some will never use more than six hues, for example. The important point is that the widest variety of characteristics is available to all artists.

☛See also

CI International 18–19
Colours of the spectrum 24–25
The basic colour wheel 26–27
Creative directions 96–153
Colour Index 156–179

The Colour Index International is the standard compiled and published by both The Society of Dyers and Colourists and the American Association of Textile Chemists and Colorists. The Colour Index classifies pigments by their chemical composition. This is an excellent identification method for lightfastness as the Index separates variations of pigment types like Naphthol so that you can see if the permanent versions are being used. However, the physical characteristics as well as the chemical ones affect the actual colour of the pigment. For example, all Cadmium Reds are PR108, yet hues exist from scarlet to maroon. Most art materials manufacturers print the abbreviations and often the chemical description on the tube label and in their literature.

☞See opposite page for explanation of tables and pigment identification systems.

PY: PIGMENT YELLOW

CI Name	Colour/Pigment Name	Chemical Description
NY24	Gamboge (Natural Yellow)	Garcinia gum resin
PY1	Hansa: Arylamide	Arylide
PY3	Hansa: Arylamide	Arylide
PY4	Hansa: Arylamide	Arylide
PY5	Hansa: Arylamide	Arylide
PY10	Hansa: Arylamide	Arylide
PY12	Diarylide Yellow	Diarylide yellow
PY13	Diarylide Yellow	Diarylide yellow
PY14	Diarylide Yellow	Diarylide yellow
PY16	Diarylide Yellow	Diarylide yellow
PY17	Diarylide Yellow	Diarylide yellow
PY30	Benzimidazolone Yellow	Benzimidazolone
PY32	Strontium Yellow	Barium chromate
PY34	Chrome Yellow	Lead chromate
PY35	Cadmium Yellow	Cadmium zinc sulphide
PY37	Cadmium Yellow	Cadmium sulphide
PY40	Aureolin	Potassium cobaltinitrite
PY41	Naples Yellow	Lead antimoniate
PY42	Yellow Oxide	Synthetic yellow iron oxide
PY43	Yellow Ochre	Natural yellow iron oxide
PY53	Nickel Titanate Yellow	Nickel titanium oxide
PY65	Hansa: Arylamide	Arylide
PY73	Hansa: Arylamide	Arylide
PY74	Hansa: Arylamide	Arylide
PY83	Diarylide Yellow	Diarylide yellow
PY97	Hansa Yellow	Diarylide yellow
PY98	Hansa Yellow	Diarylide yellow
PY100	Tartrazine Yellow	Tartrazine lake
PY108	Indian: Gamboge Modern	Anthrapyrimidine
PY109	Isoindolinone Yellow	Isoindolinone
PY110	Isoindolinone Yellow	Tetrachloroisoindolinone
PY112	Flavanthrone Yellow	Naphthol
PY119	Mars Yellow	Zinc iron oxide
PY120	Benzimidazolone Yellow	Benzimidazolone
PY128	Azo Condensation Yellow	Azo condensation
PY129	Green Gold	Azomethine copper complex
PY137	Isoindolinone Yellow	Isoindoline
PY138	Isoindolinone Yellow	Isoindoline
PY139	Isoindolinone Yellow	Isoindoline
PY150	Nickel Azo Yellow	Nickel azomethine
PY151	Benzimidazolone Yellow	Benzimidazolone
PY153	Nickel Dioxine Yellow	Nickel dioxine
PY154	Benzimidazolone Yellow	Benzimidazolone
PY155	Benzimidazolone Yellow	Benzimidazolone
PY156	Benzimidazolone Yellow	Benzimidazolone
PY175	Benzimidazolone Yellow	Benzimidazolone
PY184	Bismuth Vanadium	Bismuth vanadate

PO: PIGMENT ORANGE

CI Name	Colour/Pigment Name	Chemical Description
PO13	Pyrazolone Orange	Pyrazolone
PO20	Cadmium Orange	Cadmium selenosulphide
PO34	Pyrazolone Orange	Pyrazolone
PO36	Benzimidazolone Orange	Benzimidazolone
PO43	Perinone Orange	Perinone orange
PO48	Quinacridone Gold	Quinacridone gold
PO49	Quinacridone Gold	Quinacridone deep gold
PO62	Benzimidazolone Orange	Benzimidazolone
PO65	Golden Barok Red	Methine nickel complex
PO67	Coral Orange	Pyrazoloquinazolone
PO69	Isoindoline Orange	Isoindoline
PO71	Translucent Orange	Diketo-pyrrolo pyrrole orange
PO73	Pyrrole Orange	Diketo-pyrrolo pyrrole orange

PR: PIGMENT RED

CI Name	Colour/Pigment Name	Chemical Description
NR4	Carmine	Cochineal lake
NR9	Rose Madder	Lake of natural madder
PR3	Toluidine Red	Toluidine
PR4	Chlorinated Para Red	Chloriated para red
PR5	Naphthol Red	Naphthol
PR8	Naphthol Red	Naphthol
PR9	Naphthol Red	Naphthol
PR12	Naphthol Red	Naphthol
PR23	Naphthol Red	Naphthol
PR48	Scarlet Lake	Beta oxynaphtholic acid
PR48:3	Geranium	Strontium salt
PR49	Lithol Red	Lithol
PR81	Basic Dye Toner (Red)	Rhodamine
PR83	Alizarin Crimson	Dihydroxyanthraquinone lake
PR88	Thioindigo Violet	Thioindigo
PR101	Venetian/Indian/English/Light Red	Calcined synthetic red iron oxide
PR102	Red/Burnt Ochre/Mars	Calcined natural red iron oxide
PR104	Molybdate Orange	Lead molibdate
PR106	Vermilion (genuine)	Mercuric sulphide
PR108	Cadmium Red	Cadmium selenosulphide
PR112	Naphthol Red	Naphthol AS-D red
PR122	Quinacridone Red/Magenta	Quinacridone
PR146	Naphthol Red	Naphthol
PR149	Perylene Red	Perylene
PR166	Azo Condensation Red	Azo condensation red
PR168	Dibromanthone	Anthraquinone scarlet
PR170	Naphthol Red	Naphthol AS carbamide
PR171	Benzimidazolone Maroon	Benzimidazolone
PR173	Basic Dye Toner (Red)	Rhodamine/Aluminium lake
PR175	Deep Scarlet	Benzimidazolone
PR176	Benzimidazolone Red	Benzimidazolone
PR177	Permanent Alizarin Crimson	Anthraquinonoid red
PR178	Perylene Red	Perylene
PR179	Perylene Maroon	Perylene
PR188	Scarlet/Naphthol	Naphthol/Arylamide
PR190	Perylene Red	Perylene
PR202	Quinacridone Crimson	Quinacridone
PR206	Quinacridone Burnt Orange	Quinacridone burnt orange
PR207	Quinacridone Red	Quinacridone
PR209	Quinacridone Red	Quinacridone
PR214	Deep Red	Disazo condensation red
PR224	Perylene Red	Perylene
PR251	Permanent Red	Pyrazoloquinazolone scarlet
PR254	Pyrrole Red	Diketo-pyrrolo pyrrole red
PR255	Pyrrole Scarlet	Diketo-pyrrolo pyrrole scarlet
PR260	Vermilion Extra	Isoindoline scarlet
PR264	Pyrrole Red	Diketo-pyrrolo pyrrole red
PR270	Pyrrole Red	Diketo-pyrrolo pyrrole red

☛**Identification system** Pigments are identified in two ways:

1. CI Name – Colour Index Generic Name

Pigments are placed within their part of the spectrum and then given a number. For example: Cadmium Red is Pigment Red 108, abbreviated to PR108; PG is Pigment Green; PB is Pigment Blue, and so forth. PBr is Pigment Brown and PBk is Pigment Black.

2. CI Number – Colour Index Number

Pigments can also be identified by their number. For example: Cadmium Red is 77202.

Of the two methods the Colour Index Generic Name is the most common and is used in these tables.

PV: PIGMENT VIOLET

CI Name	Colour/Pigment Name	Chemical Description
PV1	Basic Dye Toner (Violet)	Rhodamine violet
PV2	Basic Dye Toner (Violet)	PTMA toner
PV3	Basic Dye Toner (Violet)	PTMA toner
PV4	PTMA Violet	PTMA toner
PV14	Cobalt Violet	Cobalt phosphate
PV15	Ultramarine Violet	Sodium aluminium sulphosilicate
PV16	Manganese Violet	Manganese ammonium pyrophosphate
PV19	Quinacridone	Quinacridone
PV23	Dioxazine Violet/Purple	Dioxazine violet
PV31	Isoviolanthrone Violet	Isoviolanthrone
PV42	Quinacridone	Quinacridone
PV49	Cobalt Violet	Cobalt aluminium phosphate

PB: PIGMENT BLUE

CI Name	Colour/Pigment Name	Chemical Description
PB15	Phthalo Blue	Copper phthalocyanine
PB15:1	Phthalo Blue	Alpha copper phthalocyanine
PB15:3	Phthalo Blue	Beta copper phthalocyanine
PB15:4	Phthalo Blue	Beta copper phthalocyanine
PB15:6	Phthalo/Blue	Epsilon copper phthalocyanine
PB16	Phthalo Blue/Turquoise Green	Metal-free phthalocyanine
PB27	Prussian Blue	Hydrous ferriammonium ferrocyanide
PB28	Cobalt Blue	Cobalt aluminium oxide
PB29	Ultramarine Blue	Sodium aluminium sulphosilicate
PB33	Manganese Blue	Barium manganate
PB35	Cerulean Blue	Cobalt tin oxide
PB36	Cobalt Turquoise	Cobalt chromium oxide
PB60	Indanthrene Blue	Indanthrone
PB72	Cobalt Deep	Cobalt zinc aluminate
PB73	Cobalt Deep	Cobalt silicate
PB74	Cobalt Deep	Cobalt zinc silicate

PG: PIGMENT GREEN

CI Name	Colour/Pigment Name	Chemical Description
PG7	Phthalo Green	Chlorinated copper phthalocyanine
PG8	Naphthol Green	Nitroso iron complex
PG10	Green Gold/Nickel Azo Yellow	Azomethine nickel complex
PG12	Naphthol Green	Ferrous nitroso-beta naphthol lake
PG17	Chromium Oxide Green	Anhydrous chromium sesquioxide
PG18	Viridian	Hydrous chromium sesquioxide
PG19	Cobalt Green	Cobalt zinc oxide
PG23	Terre Verte	Green earth
PG24	Ultramarine Green	Polysulphide of sodium alumino-silicate
PG26	Cobalt Green Deep	Cobalt chrome oxide
PG36	Phthalo Green	Brominated copper phthalocyanine
PG50	Cobalt/Teal/Light/Oxide Green	Cobalt titanium oxide

PBr: PIGMENT BROWN

CI Name	Colour/Pigment Name	Chemical Description
NBr8	Vandyke Brown	Bituminous earth
PBr6	Mars Brown	Calcinated synthetic iron oxide
PBr7	Raw & Burnt Sienna/Umber	Natural iron oxide
PBr23	Azo Condensation Brown	Azo condensation brown
PBr24	Naples Yellow Deep	Chrome titanium oxide
PBr25	Benzimidazolone Brown	Benzimidazolone brown
PBr33	Mineral Brown	Zinc iron chromite

PBk: PIGMENT BLACK

CI Name	Colour/Pigment Name	Chemical Description
NBk6	Bitumen	Gilsonite
PBk1	Aniline/Jet Black	Aniline black
PBk6	Lamp/Blue Black	Carbon black
PBk7	Lamp Black	Carbon black
PBk8	Vine Black	Wood charcoal
PBk9	Ivory Black	Bone black
PBk10	Graphite	Powdered graphite
PBk11	Mars Black	Ferrite black iron oxide
PBk19	Davy's Grey	Powdered slate/Hydrated aluminium silicate
PBk28	Mineral Black	Copper chromate
PBk31	Perylene	Perylene

PW: PIGMENT WHITE

CI Name	Colour/Pigment Name	Chemical Description
PW1	Flake White	Basic lead carbonate
PW4	Zinc White	Zinc oxide
PW5	Lithophone	Coprecipitated zinc sulphide/Barium sulphate
PW6	Titanium White	Titanium dioxide
PW18	Whiting	Calcium carbonate
PW19	China Clay	Hydrated aluminium silicate
PW20	Mica	Aluminium potassium silicate
PW21	Blanc Fixe	Barium sulphate
PW22	Barium Sulphate	Natural barium sulphate
PW24	Aluminium Hydrate	Aluminium hydrate
PW25	Gypsum	Calcium sulphate
PW26	Talc	Magnesium aluminium silicate
PW27	Silica	Silica

☛**See also**

Blue 50–53

Violet 55

Red 56–59

Orange 60–61

Yellow 62–65

Ochres/Earth colours 66–67

Green 68–71

Brown/Earth colours 72–75

Black 76–83

White 86–87

Colour Index 156–179

'… it is no more possible to learn to paint from books than it is to learn to swim on a sofa.'

MAX DOERNER (1870–1939)

The subject of colour is so vast and the ranges of pigments and materials available to the artist so wide, variable and subtle, it is inevitable that the best means of finding out how particular colours really look and handle is by actually using them. In this book there is a great deal of information about colour and its value to the artist. Hundreds of colours are mentioned and shown in the various media in numerous combinations, mixtures and applications. To a certain extent Doerner's comment holds true and most artists will admit that the only effective way to knowledge and confidence is to experiment with the actual colours and different media yourself.

Four colours make all colours

It is hoped that this book can provide a springboard into the world of colour for the artist. Unfortunately, there is one obvious drawback to it. This is that when it comes to the subtlety of reproducing colour all of the colours shown in this book are printed, not painted. They are not the actual colours at all, but are reproduced by the four-colour printing process using only four ink colours.

Modern printing technology and the skills of graphic reproduction have brought us very close to the reality of seeing real, pure pigment colour on the printed page. Although colour printing has been around for a long time, fifty years or so ago, or even twenty-five years ago, it would not have been easily possible to mass produce a colour-printed book to this standard, and the expense of doing so would have been immense. Colour printing is among those technologies that, in the right hands, improves in quality year on year.

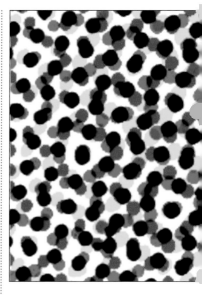

Four-colour enlargement
White is crucial to the four-colour printing process. Without a white background the full-colour illusion does not work properly.

Billboard detail, actual size
The four-colour dots that create a full-colour image can be clearly seen on outdoor advertisements that are designed to be viewed from a distance.

Process colours
Artists' paint colours that resemble the process ink colours used by printers are available. Some manufacturers, particularly in acrylic ranges, offer colours that are specifically identified as process colours and these too are very versatile for mixing and for colour experimentation.

PROCESS CYAN
120

PROCESS MAGENTA
412

PROCESS YELLOW
675

PROCESS BLACK
040

CMYK ('smike')

Every colour you see in this book is printed by using the four-colour process. Every hue, tint and shade is made up of a combination of only four colours. These are: cyan – a bright, greenish blue; magenta – a bluish-shade red; yellow – a middle yellow, neither reddish nor greenish; and black. White is provided by the white of the paper on which these four colours are printed.

In printing terms these colours are known as the process colours and are designated as CMYK – C for cyan, M for magenta, Y for yellow and K for black. The last letter K is used for black because if the initial B were used this might lead to B being misinterpreted as meaning blue. The acronym for the four process colours is 'smike'. This was previously only a term that was heard within the confines of the printing industry, but, with the advent of PCs, scanners, desktop publishing and digital photography, it is becoming more familiar to the general public.

Colour control
At the foot of every page proofed a control strip is printed. This enables the printer to judge the weight, density and accuracy of the four colours used to create a full-colour image.

CMYK
Cyan, magenta, yellow and black are the four process colours from which all mass-produced, full-colour images are derived.

PROCESS CYAN		
BLEU CYAN	10%	30%
NORMAL BLAU		
AZUL CYAN	50%	70%
CYAAN BLAUW		

C/100%

PROCESS MAGENTA		
MAGENTA	10%	30%
NORMAL MAGENTA		
MAGENTA	50%	70%
MAGENTA		

M/100%

PROCESS YELLOW		
JAUNE	10%	30%
NORMAL GELB		
AMARILLO	50%	70%
GEEL		

Y/100%

PROCESS BLACK		
NOIR	10%	30%
NORMAL SCHWARZ		
NEGRO	50%	70%
NERO		

k/100%

Druckkontrollstreifen © 1981 system Brunner CH-6600 Lo

B
C+M+Y C+Y
C
C+M
M
M+Y
Y
25%
75%
B
50% Super Balance Kreuzmiren
C
50% Super
M
50% Super
50%

Roy Lichtenstein (1923–97)
Masterpiece, 1962
Oil on canvas
137.2 x 137.2cm (54 x 54in)
Hirsch Collection, Los Angeles
© DACS

Lichtenstein exploited the dot screen seen in crude comic-strip printing, using what was cheap and popular as the inspiration for his imagery. He did not, in fact, use the process colours to achieve his colour effect, but a kind of purplish blue, a lemon yellow, a green that was between the red and blue in value, a medium-standard red, and black and white.

Georges-Pierre Seurat (1859–91)
Le Chahut, 1889–90
Oil on canvas
169cm x 139cm (66½ x 54¾in)
*Kröller-Müller State Museum,
Otterlo, Netherlands*

Seurat juxtaposed dots and dashes
of colour to produce brilliant,
luminous effects in his paintings.
The detail below is actual size.

Dot screens

The infinite range of printed colours is formed out of dots of only the four process colours. These dots conform to a regular pattern or screen for each of the four colours, though they are printed in various combinations and proportions to achieve a multi-coloured effect. Along with the white of the paper these minute dots form the printed image. This process is known as optical mixing since it is the eye of the viewer that translates the dots into recognizable pictures or shapes with continuous tone and colour.

As well as being a technical process, optical mixing is a device that has been employed by artists in their quest for colour originality. In the late nineteenth century Georges Seurat (1859–91) and Camille Pissarro (1831–1903) were two painters who experimented with dots of colour to great effect, a technique that became known as pointillism. This approach to colour mixing in painting was happening at the same time as, but independently of, late-nineteenth-century developments in printing. Later, in the twentieth century, artists such as Sigmar Polke (b. 1941) and Roy Lichtenstein (1923–97) exploited optical colour mixing and dot screen effects in their work, consciously celebrating the effects to be derived from four-colour printing methods.

Sigmar Polke (b. 1941)
Girlfriends, 1965–66
Oil on canvas
150 x 190cm (59 x 75in)
Froehlich Collection, Stuttgart

Polke based his paintings on magazine photographs. By emphasizing the printed dot patterns he could transport a low-quality, mass-culture snapshot to the high-culture realm of painting.

☛**See also**

CI International 18–19

Optical illusions 20–21

Choosing media 30–35

Colour by colour 50–93

Creative directions 96–153

Colour Index 156–179

Sir Isaac Newton (1642–1727)
English mathematician, physicist, astronomer and philosopher, known particularly for his law of gravitation and for his work on the physics of colour. In this engraving made after a painting by George Romney, Newton demonstrates the formation of the spectrum through a prism.

After George Romney
Newton and the Prism
From *The Life of George Romney* by William Hayley, 1809

The prism and the spectrum
It was Newton who discovered that sunlight (white light) is separated into coloured components when passed through a prism. He observed a sequence of colours ranging from violet through indigo, blue, green, yellow and orange to red. This range of colours is called the visible spectrum.

White light can also be separated into colours when it is reflected from very thin films and layers. Many transparent natural objects form colours in this way. Soap bubbles, sea spume, oil on water, and some birds' plumage are prime examples of colours produced by interference through thin layers.

A similar phenomenon of segmented coloured light known as 'Newton's Rings' can also be seen in light reflected through a curved glass lens laid on a mirror.

☞ See also

Optical illusions 20–21
The basic colour wheel 26–27
Colour by colour 50–93
Creative directions 96–153
Colour Index 156–179

In physics colour is defined as an attribute of an object or entity that results from the light that is reflected, transmitted or emitted by that object or entity. This light is transmitted in different wavelengths, which are perceived by the viewer as different colours – thus, for example, butter is yellow, the sky is blue, a rose is red.

The spectrum
The simplest demonstration of colour physics is to transmit a beam of white light (sunlight) through a prism and see how the white light is refracted and separated into different wavelengths. The wavelengths are transmitted through the other side of the prism as a spectrum or band of colours, from red, the longest wavelength, to violet, the shortest. Seven colours are usually distinguished in a spectrum and these are red, orange, yellow, green, blue, indigo and violet.

John Everett Millais (1829–96)
The Blind Girl, 1856
Oil on canvas (whole image, unframed) 82.6 x 62.3cm (32½ x 24½in)
Birmingham Museums and Art Gallery

George Hardie
The Dark Side of the Moon, 1973
Album cover 30 x 30cm (12 x 12in)

On this well-known Pink Floyd album cover the artist employs a graphic illustration of the prism and the spectrum as a powerful visual metaphor for expectation, anticipation, and uncertainty.

Colours of the rainbow
A rainbow is a prime example of sunlight passing through millions of prisms – raindrops – to create a spectrum. In this sentimental painting the sighted girl is awe-struck by the rainbow, but, sadly, her companion can never experience its beauty.

Iridescence

The photograph of the insect displays a spectrum of colours that shimmer and change due to interference and the scattering of light as the observer's position changes. This phenomenon is known as iridescence.

Additive colour mixing

The term additive colour mixing refers to the mixing of light. When you mix coloured light it behaves quite differently from when you mix paints. Coloured light is essential for film, theatre, television and video, and photography to a certain extent, so a knowlege of additive colour mixing is important for those working in these media.

The additive primary colours are red, green and blue, and are often referred to as RGB. When white light is projected through filters of these colours and two of the beams are mixed they produce the secondary colours yellow, cyan and magenta. When you combine the three primaries, RGB, the result is white light.

Subtractive colour mixing

The term subtractive colour mixing refers to the mixing of pigments, and this is where some knowledge of the colour wheel helps (see page 26). Pigments approximate the appearance of reflected and projected light, but when mixed together they produce very different results from those achieved by mixing coloured light. Subtractive colour mixing is the concern of the painter and in subtractive mixing the primaries are red, yellow and blue. When two of these primaries are mixed they produce the secondary colours orange, green and violet. When the three primaries are combined the result is black.

Additive primary colours
The additive primary colours are red, green and blue, and are often referred to as RGB.

Additive secondary colours
When white light is projected through filters of these colours and two of the beams are mixed they produce the secondary colours yellow, cyan and magenta.

Mix red, green and blue
When you combine the three primaries, RGB, the result is white light.

Subtractive colour
Red, yellow and blue make black.

Patrick Gries
The Hand of Nature
Photograph
Fondation Cartier pour l'art contemporain, Paris
Nature démiurge, insectes
Collection Anne et Jacques Kerchache, Paris

Spectrum colours
The seven distinguishable colours of the spectrum are all available in the various artists' media. These colours are red, orange, yellow, green, blue, indigo and violet.

The spectrum is the foundation for understanding the physics of colour. From this a useful system for classifying pigment colour for artists, known as the colour wheel, has been developed.

This circular diagram helps to explain subtractive colour mixing and provides a theoretical basis for using colours. The colour wheel acts as common reference for the terminology and language of colour for artists and shows how colours relate and interact with one another. An understanding of the colour wheel helps with colour mixing and colour identification.

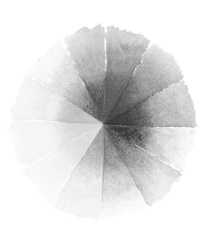

Diagrammatic colour

The colour wheel, also known as the colour circle, may be described as the spectrum turned into a circle, reflecting the natural order of colours. The primary colours are red, blue and yellow and are unmixable. Secondary colours are mixtures of any two primaries. Complementary colours – for example, yellow and violet, or red and green – are colours that are directly opposite one another on the diagrammatic colour wheel.

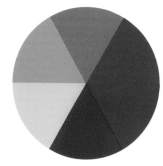

Six-colour division

A basic six-colour division of the wheel shows the primaries – red yellow and blue; and the secondaries – orange, green and violet.

Twelve-colour division

By increasing the number of divisions the intermediate colours linking the basic primary and secondary colours become apparent. These colours are often described as having a bias – bluish reds or reddish yellows, for example.

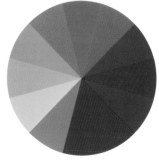

Ad infinitum

It is theoretically possible to continue subdividing the colour wheel until the appearance of a continuous merge is achieved.

Primary red

Secondary orange

Primary yellow

Primary colours

Primary colours are those that cannot be mixed from others. These are red, yellow and blue. Since pigment colours are not as pure as those of the spectrum, when all three are mixed together they produce 'black' or grey-brown. Varying proportions of the primaries mixed together will produce all other colours, and different sets of primaries will produce different mixes.

Primary blue

Secondary green

Primary yellow

Colour experimentation

Many manufacturers recommend primary colours within their ranges that are suitable for clean mixing. Follow the concept of the colour wheel to experiment with colours and mixing combinations.

Cadmium Red is a yellowish red.

Top tone and undertone

The particular hue or top tone of a primary colour may have an undertone that veers towards one of the other primaries – for instance, a red may be a yellowish red, such as Cadmium Red, or a bluish red, such as Alizarin Crimson – and this will affect the resulting mixes.

Basic primaries

Three primaries that can produce a practical range of mixed colours are those used in photography and printing – magenta, yellow and cyan. These colours, or close approximations to them, are available in many ranges of artists' colours.

Naturally occurring colour inspiration

Secondary colours

A colour produced by mixing two primaries is termed a secondary colour. Red and yellow produce orange as a secondary colour; yellow and blue give green; and blue and red make violet. The secondary colours are situated between the primary colours on the colour wheel.

When mixing secondary colours cleaner and brighter hues may be obtained by mixing primaries that have related undertones and veer towards each other. A yellowish red mixed with a reddish yellow, for instance, will result in a clean, bright orange.

Tertiary colours

A further set of colours, termed tertiaries, are produced by mixing a primary with one of its secondaries – for instance, blue mixed with violet gives blue-violet and red mixed with orange gives red-orange. An infinite number of colours can be mixed by combining tertiaries with secondaries, and so on with neighbouring pairs, enlarging the colour wheel into a gradated progression of colours.

Orange jug with complementary accent

Complementary colours

Colours that are immediately opposite each other on the colour wheel are termed complementary. A primary colour is complemented by the secondary colour mixed from the other pair of primaries. So green is the complement of red, violet of yellow and orange of blue. This process continues around the colour wheel, with red-orange the complementary of green-blue, and so on.

Using complementary colours

Artists can use pairs of complementary colours to good effect, since visually one enhances the other when they are juxtaposed. For instance, an orange placed next to a blue will make it look much brighter, and vice versa. Conversely, adding a small amount of the complementary to a colour can help to grey it slightly, toning down its brightness.

Darks or 'palette mud'

When two complementaries are mixed they produce a grey or brown because the resulting colour contains all three primaries. These mixes may be planned, but it is all too easy to make mixes that lack subtlety. Artists term these 'mud'.

Harmonious colours

Colours from the same section of the colour wheel share common colour roots and are termed harmonious. They involve the use of only two primaries and the colours in between. When combinations of harmonious colours are used together they create no visual discord.

Warm and cool colours

An important aspect of a colour for use is its temperature. Colours are considered to be warm or cool. Generally, warm colours are those that are in the red/orange/yellow sector of the colour wheel, while cool ones are in the green/blue/violet sector. The undertone of a colour can make it appear cool or warm when compared to other colours of the same hue. Warm colours appear to advance towards the viewer, while cool colours recede towards the background. Assessing the temperature of a colour can help the artist create space and depth in a painting.

Tints and shades

Adding white to a colour lightens it and creates a tint. Similarly, a colour darkened with black is called a shade. Tints and shades may be further classified by their tone – that is, how dark or light they are compared with other colours. Tone can be altered by adding varying amounts of grey, not necessarily mixed from black and white, but also from combinations of colours that contain the three primaries.

☛**See also**

CI International 18–19

Optical illusions 20–21

Colour by colour 50–93

Colour Index 156–179

Theory into practice

Peter Graham is an artist who uses a radiant palette, and is anything but faint-hearted when it comes to colour use and interpretation. Employing a bold and robust brushwork technique, he achieves an unexpected visual harmony with the use of seemingly opposite colours. His vibrant oil and watercolour paintings show hot red, pink and orange hues forming exotic relationships with blues, turquoise, violet and accents of yellow.

Manhattan (detail)

Peter Graham
Manhattan
Watercolour
43.4 x 61cm (17 x 24in)

'Through colour I strive to bring the canvas to life. Looking into the evening sun presented me with a chance to evoke the sounds and flavours of the scene, and interpret what I saw into how I felt.'

Peter Graham
Southern Sun
Oil on canvas
30.5 x 40.5 cm (12 x 16in)

Manhattan (full image)

'The layers of watercolour tell my story of New York. Here colour conveys my experience of a great city that's full of sensation and power – a city glowing with confidence.'

This section is included to give those who may be uncertain as to what to buy an idea of the media available. Nearly all the major manufacturers provide informative leaflets and brochures on their products and publish comprehensive catalogues.

Many independent suppliers, too, have detailed catalogues of materials that are available by mail order. Most towns have an art supplies store, ranging from a corner display in the stationery department of a book shop to large retail outlets dedicated solely to art materials. Here you can look at the stock and pick up useful product information, so a visit to one of these is well worth it in order to inform your choice.

A huge amount of different media is available to artists who wish to express themselves in colour. Oil paint is probably the accepted traditional medium, while the most popular option favoured by amateur artists, and widely respected by professionals, too, is watercolour.

In comparison to these two traditional media, acrylics are a relatively modern invention and provide a medium that combines the versatility of both watercolours and oil paints. More specialized media are also available and these include egg tempera and gouache or body colours, which have their own unique characteristics.

Some colouring materials cross the divide between drawing and painting – pastels, water-soluble coloured pencils and oilbars are among the numerous products in this category that you can use for creative expression. Many manufacturers and suppliers also list products with applications in craft and hobby areas for painting on textiles, ceramics and glass.

Art materials can be expensive, particularly if you consider products labelled 'artists' quality', which indicates that they contain the finest pigments. This is not to say that students' quality and less expensive products are not good, for there are continuing significant advances in pigment manufacture. In some cases the less expensive brands from the major manufacturers may have particular desired characteristics.

In the upper price ranges you will find more choice of colours and stronger pigments, but when it comes to making a personal selection, particularly if you have not picked up a paintbrush for a number of years and you are in the experimental stage, it may be worth considering buying a starter set or a limited selection of mixable primaries in your chosen medium before making a greater investment.

In addition to cost, other important considerations when choosing your media are space and facilities for cleaning up. Do you have a studio or dedicated working area? Is there a sink and water supply close? Are you affected by chemicals and solvents? The style of your work may inform your first choice of medium, too. Will you need volume and texture? Is your approach precise and graphic? Think about the support or surface on which you will be applying your chosen colour. Will it be board, canvas, paper, textile or some other material? These factors all have price and practicality considerations.

Oil colours

Traditional Oils
When they were first developed during the fifteenth century oils were described as 'a most beautiful invention'.

Many leisure painters think they are too difficult, or too smelly, to tackle at home – and even if they did want to have a go, they do not know where to begin, or what exactly they need to get started.

Oil colours have a mild odour, but it is not strong or unpleasant. The powerful smell associated with them is produced by the turpentine or white spirit used to thin colour and to clean brushes. You can reduce the smell considerably by keeping a lid on your jars and using low-odour thinners.

Drying times
Oils take longer to dry than watercolours or acrylics because they dry by absorbing oxygen from the air, rather than by the more speedy evaporation of water. But it is still possible to complete a painting in one session or, as it is sometimes known, 'alla prima'. The Impressionists worked in this way, capturing the transient mood of a subject and completing a finished painting in a matter of hours. Different colours dry at different rates, so drying agents are usually added to the slower drying colours, like Alizarin Crimson and Ivory Black, to help equalize them.

Correcting mistakes
An advantage of this slow-drying medium is that you can simply wipe mistakes away or paint over them.

Quality and price
Artists' quality oil colours are the most expensive and are usually priced in series, according to the cost of the pigment. Students' quality oil colours are more affordable and, with the increasingly sophisticated synthetic pigments that are now available, they are even better value for the newcomer to painting.

Most colours are made by dispersing pigment in linseed oil, which is generally considered to be the best oil for a flexible paint film. However, linseed has a natural tendency to yellow, so it is often replaced with sunflower oil or similar in the manufacturing process for making whites.

A basic starter palette
Six to eight colours are all you need to begin with – three primaries, an additional green, an earth colour and white. A good starter palette might be Cobalt Blue, Alizarin Crimson, Cadmium Yellow (Hue), Yellow Ochre, Raw Umber, Viridian (Hue), Cadmium Red (Hue) and Titanium White. This is the sort of selection you often find in small sets, or you can buy them individually.

As you progress you will want to broaden your palette of colours and there is no shortage of good ready-mixed tube colour from which to select.

White

White is probably the most important colour on an oil painter's palette. Titanium White is the whitest and the most opaque, with the best covering power, and is the best to use for highlighting. It is also a useful white for mixing paler tints. Although the most versatile all-purpose white, because of its strength the beginner may find it overpowering for mixing precise tints.

Zinc White is a less powerful, semi-opaque white, so it is good for tinting and translucent glazing. (See White on pages 86–87, 179.)

Solvents and diluents

Turpentine is the most commonly used diluent for thinning oil colour and cleaning up, but low-odour thinners are more pleasant to use since they give off less harmful fumes and irritate the skin less. They are also less flammable, so safer, too – and they keep better.

Household turpentine is not recommended for art use. It contains impurities that can leave a sticky residue, cause yellowing and stop the colour drying.

Oils and mediums

The more oil or painting medium you add to colour, the 'fatter' it becomes (see Mediums on page 36). 'Fat' paint is more prone to movement as it dries, so it prevents cracking. It is usual to thin early layers of paint with diluent and increase medium as you go.

In the early stages of drying, oil colour increases in weight and it expands. As it continues to dry, it loses weight and starts to shrink and harden. So, if you apply less flexible 'lean' paint over more oil-rich, flexible paint there will be more movement in the lower layers than the top ones. This may result in wrinkling and cracking.

Water-mixable Oils

There is a saying that 'oil and water will not mix', but the introduction of water-mixable oils has proved that it can be done. If you hate the smell of turpentine, white spirit or even low-odour thinners, but you want to paint in oils, these could be the materials for you.

The linseed and safflower oils used to make water-mixable oils are modified so that they mix with water rather than repelling it. For best results you are advised to use compatible water-mixable mediums to improve paint flow, to build heavy impasto and to alter drying times. During drying the water evaporates quickly, but the oil component takes the usual two to twelve days to become touch dry.

Alkyd Oils

Alkyd oils are a fast-drying alternative to conventional oils. They are ideal for single-session 'alla prima' painting, as an underpainting medium for oil painting, for quick design work and decorative painting on a range of surfaces from glass to ceramics.

They are made from pigment mixed with oil and a synthetic resin, originally developed for use in industrial coatings and house paints, which accelerates drying and creates a durable water-resistant finish. In use they are very similar to traditional oils. Thin them with a diluent such as turpentine or low-odour thinners and enrich them with linseed oil or Liquin.

Resin Oil Colours

Natural resins, extracted from living and fossilized trees, have been used by artists for almost 2000 years. Byzantine painters added natural resins to enhance colour brilliance and the impression of depth – and in the early days of oil painting artists are known to have added resins such as mastic and copal.

The practice died out when it was found that resin colours did not take kindly to transportation in leather or hide pouches, which was the traditional packaging for oil colour before the invention of the metal tube.

In 1881 a collection of old masters' formulations was acquired from a Professor Cesare Mussini, who lent his name to today's Mussini resin oils.

The paints are made from artists' quality pigments, mixed with artists' oils and natural dammar resins that allow light to penetrate further into the paint layers. It is this enhanced reflectivity that makes colours look more brilliant. The addition of resin also promotes more even drying times, giving a more stable paint film.

Resin oils come in over 100 ready-mixed tube colours. You will not find them in every art shop, but they are available from larger specialist art stores and mail-order suppliers.

Oilbars

Drawing and painting come together in one fluid movement with oilbars, also known as oil-painting sticks. Not to be confused with oil pastels, oilbars are made from artists' quality pigments mixed with drying oils and waxes.

Oilbar enthusiasts love their immediacy and the direct link they forge between artist and canvas, without the intervention of a brush.

Colours can be blended and spread directly on the surface with a knife or brush and traditional diluents, or you can buy special colour-less bars, designed to blend colours and increase their transparency. Dipping the tip of the stick in turpentine will improve the flow of colour. Applied in thick layers, then modelled with a knife or brush, creates heavy impasto effects. You can use oilbars on their own, or as a painterly drawing tool in combination with traditional tube oil colours.

Oils

Oils are the traditional artist's medium. Renowned in modern times for their opacity and robustness, they can equally be used thinly to create delicate glazes, depth and luminosity.

☛**See also**
Mediums 36–37
Choosing palettes 40–41
Colour by colour 50–93
Creative directions 96–153
Colour Index 156–179

All artists have an urge to communicate their own unique view of the world, and one of the beauties of watercolour is its immediacy. It invites a direct and spontaneous response to a subject – whether you are painting a landscape, a portrait, a figure study, still life or an expressive abstract.

No other medium has the capacity to capture a subject with such speed and economy of brushstroke. Far and away the most popular painting medium, watercolour is also probably the most challenging for the artist. Used well, it can make a clear statement in pure colour.

The clarity and freshness of a good watercolour painting depends on skilled glazing with dilute washes of richly pigmented paint. For best results lightly mix the colour in a clean palette with clear water and apply with single, confident strokes.

☛See also

Mediums 36–37

Choosing palettes 40–41

Colour by colour 50–93

Creative directions 96–153

Colour Index 156–179

Availability, price and quality

In recent years advances in pigment technology have extended the choice of colours available, improved tinting strength and enhanced permanence.

Watercolour can be bought in tubes and moist cakes, also known as pans. As with oils and acrylics, major manufacturers produce both artists' and students' quality colours.

Professionals and serious amateurs working indoors usually choose tube colour, squeezing out small blobs of paint, then picking up the colour they need with a brush. Beginners and artists working outdoors often find dipping into pans easier and more immediate.

Buying watercolours

You can buy both tubes and pans as individual colours or in sets. Starter sets and field boxes offer a limited selection of colours, which you can mix to give all the colours you will need. The larger the set you choose, the bigger selection of ready-mixed colour you will have to work with – but that is not always an advantage.

A basic starter palette

Traditional pigments still form the basis of many colours, but newer pigments such as quinacridones have opened the way to brilliant new transparent colours.

Newcomers tend to use too many colours and the finished work lacks harmony across the whole surface. If you opt to buy colours separately, a basic palette might include Alizarin Crimson, Yellow Ochre, Cadmium Yellow Pale, Cadmium Red, Hooker's Green and French Ultramarine. Useful additional colours would be Cerulean Blue, Raw Umber and Burnt Sienna. (See also page 41.)

Black and white

Watercolour sets usually contain Chinese White and Ivory Black. Nothing causes more heated debate among watercolour painters than the rights and wrongs of using black and white. Most watercolour artists consider tube black to be too flat and lifeless, preferring to mix their own darks. For paler tints the traditional technique is to add more water, but Chinese White is useful for highlighting and adding opaque body to pastel tints. For even more covering power try Titanium White, which is useful for highlighting in cases where the white of the paper has been lost.

Bright white highlights can add sparkle to a watercolour painting. The traditional method of portraying white is to leave the area unpainted and rely on the reflected white of the paper, but this is not always as easy as it sounds, especially for less experienced painters.

Art masking fluid can be applied to keep white areas white as the painting progresses. Once it is dry it creates a waterproof rubbery film that can be painted over with complete confidence. When the paint is dry

remove the masking fluid by simply rubbing it away to reveal the white of the paper beneath.

Watercolour boxes and mixing palettes

Until a few years ago, watercolour boxes were either made of wood or tin and you can still buy these today. More recently, tubes and pans have been packaged in lighter-weight plastic boxes. These in turn have seen some innovative changes with additional features such as extra slide-out palettes added.

You can even buy cylindrical field sets now that flip open to reveal mixing areas. The wells within a watercolour box set probably offer enough mixing area for small outdoor sketches, but they have to be cleaned regularly as you paint or colours will lose their clarity and become muddy and confused.

More serious watercolourists tend to choose large flat-sectioned plastic palettes or bun-tin style mixing wells. Choice of mixing surface is largely a matter of personal preference, but because of the transparency of watercolour, it must always be white.

Transparency and opacity

The formulations used by leading makers vary according to the nature and behaviour of the individual pigment, which is suspended in a solution of gum arabic dissolved in water. The mix is then passed repeatedly through a triple roll mill to grind it to super micron fineness and release the full intensity of the colour.

By their nature, pigments vary in their transparency and opacity. Highly transparent colours allow the reflective white of the paper to shine through, imparting an airy luminosity that captures light, space and atmosphere. As you would expect, more opaque colours have more covering power. Check artists' quality colour charts for details of transparency and opacity.

Staining and granulation

Artists' quality colour charts will also give you information on properties such as staining and granulation. Powerful colours such as Prussian Blue and Alizarin Crimson tend to penetrate the fibres of the paper, leaving traces of colour behind when you try to lift them off – whether to correct a mistake or when creating a special effect.

Some pigments, particularly the traditional earth colours, have a natural tendency to separate out when you mix them with water. As the wash dries, particles of pigment float to the surface and tiny granules may sink and settle into the hollows of the paper surface, causing an effect known as granulation. This is a useful phenomenon when you want to add character and texture, but where a smoother, more uniform wash is required, choose a colour that will not granulate as it dries.

Acrylic resin was first developed in the early nineteenth century for industrial use. Its potential for development into artists' colours was quickly spotted by art materials companies and the first acrylics were available by 1947. Today they are used around the world by leisure painters and professionals, working in both watercolour and oil painting styles.

When acrylic colours were first developed many purists discounted them as 'plastic paints', since they lacked the subtlety of colour and tone associated with oils. They have improved considerably since then and their position as the second most popular painting medium speaks for itself. Acrylics are particularly popular among illustrators, floral artists and silk painters who move from fabric to paper as a painting surface (see Colour on cloth on page 148).

Versatility
You can use acrylic colours in a variety of techniques for fine-art painting, murals, mixed media, airbrushing, screen printing and decorative crafts. No other painting medium matches acrylic colour for versatility.

Thinned with plenty of clean water, acrylics create transparent washes of colour. Used straight from the tube, they retain the mark of the brush to add character to artwork – and you can create highly textured impasto surfaces by applying with a knife.

Quality and price
The major manufacturers produce a choice of students' and artists' qualities, sold in standard size tubes and larger pots for high-volume users. As with other painting media, the quality of the pigment used in artists' quality brands is reflected in the price, but it is worth noting that with advances in colour technology, some of the student-quality brands now on the market perform exceptionally well and offer high levels of permanence.

An acrylic starter palette
Being a heavy-bodied medium, a basic acrylic starter palette can follow closely that recommended for oil paints and might comprise Cadmium Red, French Ultramarine, Cadmium Yellow, Burnt Umber, Raw Umber, Yellow Ochre and Titanium White – but you will probably want to include a few more useful colours such as Permanent Rose, Phthalo Blue, Cerulean Blue and Cobalt Blue.

Diluents and mediums
Since acrylics are water based you do not need to use solvents during the painting process. You can add a variety of mediums to alter the consistency, texture, handling properties and drying times (see Mediums on page 36).

Acrylic whites do not yellow with age and the painting surface does not become brittle over time, so paintings on canvas can be safely rolled and stored without danger of cracking.

Drying times
Acrylic colours dry more quickly than oils through uniform evaporation of the water in the binder. As the colour dries, the acrylic resin around each tiny particle of pigment fuses to create a flexible water-resistant film with an eggshell-satin finish.

The rapid drying time of acrylic colours enables the artist to apply layers of colour in quick succession, and finish a painting in a fraction of the time it would take in oils.

The down side is that because acrylic colour dries so quickly, the paint cannot be manipulated for long periods on the surface. Also it soon tends to dry out on the palette. To overcome this problem you can use special palettes that keep the colour moist for weeks.

It is also important to wash the colour thoroughly out of brushes because once it has dried into the head it sets like concrete.

While it is still wet acrylic paint looks slightly milky, but that disappears as it dries and the colour deepens. Neat acrylic paint applied thinly takes about a

quarter of an hour to dry, but allow a day or more for thick layers of impasto.

Some oil painters use thin layers of acrylic colour as a quick-drying underpainting to speed up the painting process.

Correcting mistakes
As each glaze dries it becomes insoluble, so you can safely paint over it without fear of lifting the layer beneath and losing the clarity of the colour. The water resistance of acrylics makes them an ideal choice for outdoor work.

Good quality acrylics have great covering power, and it is easy to paint over mistakes, so they are a boon for beginners.

Liquid acrylics
Liquid acrylics can be used like watercolours, applied with a traditional brush or an airbrush. They are sold in small bottles and, like their thicker, creamy counterparts, are also available in tubs. With liquid acrylics you can create transparent layers of brilliant permanent colour that can be repeatedly glazed over without disturbing the colour beneath.

Acrylics
Acrylics have become a popular medium since their invention in the 1960s. They can be diluted for use like watercolour or with added mediums for impasto effects similar to oil paints.

Gouache

Before the advent of computer-generated design, gouache was the most popular painting medium in professional design studios, where it was widely used to create crisp visuals and illustrations in solid colour that reproduced well in print.

Gouache is, in fact, a refinement of the more familiar poster paints, but the quality and permanence of pigments used in good makes are far superior.

Also known as body colour, gouache is a water-based paint with chalk or *blanc fixe* added to create opaque colour with good covering power, which can be further enhanced with the addition of Permanent White. It dries to a matt, chalky finish and can be used on its own or with transparent watercolour.

Considering its versatility, gouache is an underrated medium. Use it in dilute washes to achieve attractive misty effects. Thicker gouache creates a more rugged finish, ideal for bold, energetic paintings. A starter palette might include Cadmium Yellow, Cadmium Red, French Ultramarine, Viridian, Raw Umber and Yellow Ochre – plus the essential Permanent White.

Egg tempera

Egg tempera is one of the oldest painting media, used by the Ancient Egyptians and later by the legendary master artists of the Renaissance before it was overtaken by oil colour in popularity.

Egg tempera is not a mainstream painting medium. In fact, it is probably the least used of all the wet colour media on the market, but it offers an exciting challenge to the more experienced artist who is prepared to experiment.

As its name suggests, this paint is made by dispersing pigment in egg yolk to produce a long-lasting, highly adhesive painting medium. Some dedicated tempera artists make their own paint, but it is a tricky process that takes time and experience to perfect. Newcomers to egg tempera are more likely to buy colour ready-mixed in tubes, which often contain a little added linseed oil to make the paint easier to work and increase its flexibility.

The painting techniques associated with egg tempera have much in common with watercolour, but glazing with transparent washes of tempera gives a denser, more painterly quality to a painting.

Egg tempera paintings are characterized by their pure, translucent colour, and their luminosity and sheen. As a fine-art medium tempera is particularly suited to painters who like to pre-plan, make detailed preliminary drawings and paint with precision.

Qualities essential for successful tempera painting are patience and sureness of touch. The medium works best when thin veils of colour, diluted with clean water, are carefully applied in one-stroke washes. The brightness and translucence of a tempera painting relies on gradual and controlled build-up of these layers of dilute colour.

While it is still wet, ready-mixed egg tempera is quite easy to lift and rework. It takes about a week or two to 'cure', then it is fixed in place for good. To maintain the purity of the colour, each layer must be left to dry completely before adding the next.

Egg tempera is best suited to smooth, rigid board or canvas panels, often primed with layers of white gesso to increase the surface reflection and intensify the luminosity of the colour. Paper is not recommended unless it is soaked in gesso, stretched and backed with cardboard or metal. Hardboard is a good support for tempera painting, but it must first be sealed back, front and sides with rabbit-skin size.

Gouache and Egg tempera
Gouache or body colour is an opaque watercolour paint favoured by illustrators for artwork for reproduction. High pigment quality ensures brilliant colours that dry to a slightly chalky appearance.

Egg tempera consists of pigment bound with egg yolk and vegetable oils. Applied in thin layers, its pure colour has a luminous sheen.

Pastels

Pastels, sold in sticks or larger chunks, and also in pencil form, are probably the most popular of the so-called dry painting media. Unlike wet colour, where the pigment bonds with the painting surface, pastel marks are held by the 'tooth' or interweave of the paper fibres.

Pastel sticks

Pastel sticks are made from a mix of unground pigment, chalk, china clay and small amounts of binder and preservative. The mixed 'dough' is passed through an extruder to produce long strips of colour, which are cut to size and dried.

Choosing

Soft pastels have a deep velvety texture, best suited for broad sweeps of rich colour and painterly effects. Hard pastels, pastel pencils and conté sticks contain more binder and give a harder, more defined mark; they are ideal for drawing and illustration work.

Chalk-based pastels of all kinds can generally be used together for a variety of effects – but they are not compatible with oil pastels (see opposite).

Hard pastels and pastel pencils

Hard pastels, usually square in shape, come in fewer colours, and because they are more robust, they tend to be sold unwrapped. In use, they do not release their colour so immediately as soft pastels, so you need to exert firmer pressure. The same goes for pastel pencils, which are cleaner to hold and easier to carry for sketching outdoors.

Buying pastels

Artists' quality pastels are sold in sets and as individual sticks of colour. A starter set will probably contain about a dozen colours and you can add to these as you discover which colours you find most useful. In addition to basic assorted sets, there are also boxes of colours specially selected for use in landscape and portraiture.

Colour choice

The major manufacturers of soft pastel offer a vast choice of up to 200 colours, subdivided into tints ranging from the palest to the deepest shade based on the same pigment. Better quality soft pastel sticks come handwrapped in paper to protect them from crumbling and contamination.

A basic palette

You can start with as few as six colours in cool and warm tints of red, yellow and blue, which can be used to mix a wider range of colours on the paper surface. If you are not confident of your mixing skills it is wise to choose a larger starter set.

Papers for pastels

Pastels need a paper with enough 'tooth' to catch the fragile colour and hold it. Watercolour papers work well, but most pastel artists prefer to use tinted paper, which gives greater harmony and depth. You can choose from a range of subtle tones according to your subject and key colour theme. Darker colours add dramatic effect.

Ingres, named after the master pastellist who devised its characteristic chain-and-laid surface, is the most popular pastel paper. It comes in a wide range of tints in single sheets and books, or bonded to board for a more rigid working surface.

Fixing pastel work

It is worth noting that work in soft pastel must be fixed to stop it smudging. Aerosols give a fine, even spray, but they should be used outside if possible, or at least in a well-ventilated room. Bottled fixative delivered through a diffuser may be less harmful, but more tricky to apply evenly.

Oil Pastels

Oil pastels are one of the least understood of painting mediums, yet they are also one of the cheapest and most convenient.

Not to be confused with soft and hard pastels, oil pastel sticks are made from pigment bound in oil, and sometimes animal fat. Applied directly onto paper they make marks similar to wax crayon. Brush over with turpentine and the result is brilliant fluid colour. Oil pastels are sold in sets, which are inexpensive and handy to carry for on-the-spot sketching and colour notes.

Coloured Pencils

Coloured pencils are an essential part of just about everyone's childhood, so they are not always granted the recognition they deserve as a more serious art medium.

Choice

Recent years have seen a rapid expansion of different types of pencils for both drawing and fine art, with significant improvements in permanence at the top end of the market.

Alongside traditional graphite pencils, there are now water-soluble versions that are ideal for preparatory tonal sketches, or for pieces of artwork in their own right. They are graded from hard to soft, giving powerful blacks to gentler tones of grey.

Coloured pencils, with a waxy colour core, come in a huge range of colours. Major manufacturers offer up to 120 colours, which may be bought individually and in a wide choice of sets in tins and boxes.

Colour mixing

Colour mixing in pencil can be achieved with a variety of mark-making techniques, but you still need a wider range of colours than you do with wet media. Early attempts at coloured pencil drawing usually have a childlike quality, but with some experience you can achieve a high quality fine-art finish.

Watercolour and aquarelle pencils

Watercolour and aquarelle pencils are increasingly popular, especially for outdoor sketching. You can use them dry like conventional coloured pencils, or add water to the colour on the paper for an instant wash of colour.

Pastel pencils

Pastel pencils give a harder mark than soft pastels, but they do not create the same clouds of dust, so they are cleaner to use, and easier to carry. Charcoal pencils have similar advantages over sticks or pieces.

Other media

In addition to the most popular drawing and painting media covered here, you will find a host of other options in any good art store. For decorative art, there are specialist colours for painting on glass and ceramics, as well as silk paints and fabric colours.

You can draw and paint using felt tips, watercolour sticks, wax crayons and chalks. By their nature, artists love to experiment, and it is not unknown for the Royal Watercolour Society to hang a work painted in mud! The only limitation to creativity is lack of imagination – but, before you get too carried away, make sure your chosen colour medium is lightfast so that your work will not fade when it sees the light of day.

Dry colour media
Among the dry media (right) are traditional soft pastels with a chalky, friable texture (top), and pastel pencils, which are normally harder in texture and easier to control (centre). There are many varieties of coloured pencil including the water-soluble types (below).

☞See also

Colour by colour 50–93
Creative directions 96–153
Colour Index 156–179

Oil painting mediums

In art materials' terminology the word 'medium' can sometimes be confusing. The type of paint you choose – for example, oil, acrylic or watercolour – is known as a medium (plural 'media'). If you use two or more materials in a painting it is termed a 'mixed-media painting'. However, the term 'medium' (plural 'mediums') is also used to refer to the various liquids, gels and pastes that may be added to paint when you use it. These mediums can be added to colour to alter paint's handling properties or its surface appearance.

Mediums can be used to change paint characteristics of flow, transparency and drying rate. They include a wide variety of additives such as gloss mediums, matt mediums and various oils and drying agents. Pastes and gels can be added to build textures that the paint alone, if used neat from the tube, cannot provide, and certain other mediums may be used to create special effects.

The addition of mediums can also affect the colour of the paint. Exactly how the addition of a medium will finally alter paint and colour depends to a certain extent on the quality of the paint and the type and amount of medium added to it. Experimentation and trial and error are the best methods of learning and mastering the use of mediums.

The list on this page and opposite outlines the commonly available painting mediums and gives a brief description of what they can do to bring an extra dimension to the colour and texture of your painting.

The 'fat over lean' rule

Thinners are used for the initial coats of paint and for washes. If you are intending to apply several layers of paint, however, you will need to add oil to the paint to prevent the possibility of the surface cracking at a later stage when dry. This 'fat over lean' rule involves adding progressively more oil or medium ('fat') as you paint further layers.

Turpentine

As water is to watercolour, so turpentine is to oil painting. It is the classic, traditional solvent-thinner used in oil painting. Used as a solvent it thins paint to provide tints and washes of colour. It is fairly slow in evaporation and when mixed with colours tends to give a matt finish. There are various types of turpentine available – you may come across 'rectified turpentine essence' or 'distilled turpentine', for example. Products such as these enjoy the same features as turpentine, but have been further processed and distilled to improve strength and purity.

White spirit

Artists' quality white spirit, a purified form, provides an alternative diluent to turpentine and, while it has a characteristic smell, its odour is less pronounced. A completely odourless formulation is also available that evaporates more slowly. White spirit dissolves the paint a little less than turpentine, however, and like turpentine it should only be used for the first layers of painting. Oily thinners, which are a mixture of solvent and linseed oil, are used to reduce the consistency of oil paint in later layers without affecting its richness; they may yellow though.

Low-odour thinners

Since turpentine is high in odour and flammable, in many studio situations it has been superseded by less hazardous, commercially formulated low-odour or odourless products that perform a similar function. Another liquid thinner that avoids the smell of turpentine is oil of spike lavender, but this dries more slowly than turpentine or white spirit.

Alkyd mediums

These mediums are based on alkyd resin. Depending on their formulation, they can be used not only to thin oil paint, increasing its flow and transparency, but can considerably accelerate its drying time. They provide durable glazing and can be thinned with white spirit. To avoid the risk of cracking, care should be taken not to use alkyd mediums over slow drying underlayers. Alkyd mediums are available in the form of liquid or gel.

Artists' painting mediums

A huge range of proprietary liquid thinners and gels have been developed to minimize yellowing of colours and to dry to a durable, flexible film. Generally, these products improve transparency and the flow of paint, so are particularly useful for fine detail work. They also tend to enhance the gloss effect and some are formulated for glazing. However, specific products are also available that ensure a matt surface when dry.

Linseed oil

The traditional oil used as an additive for later layers of paint is linseed, available in many different forms. It may be described as 'purified', 'cold-pressed', 'bleached', 'boiled', 'thickened', 'refined', 'stand' or 'drying' linseed oil. Each has its own characteristics and you should read the manufacturers' labels to check which type is suitable for your purpose. Generally, linseed oil increases the flow, transparency and gloss of the paint. The various types tend to have different drying rates, though most increase it. One disadvantage of linseed is that it tends to yellow the colours. Linseed oil can be thinned with white spirit or turpentine.

Poppy oil
Variously described as 'purified' or 'bleached', this oil extracted from poppy seeds has less tendency to turn colours yellow and is more suitable for use with light colours and white than linseed. It also enhances the gloss effect, though the surface when dry is slightly less durable. Poppy oil generally takes longer to dry than linseed oil, but a 'drying' version is also available. Thin with white spirit or turpentine.

Walnut oil
Walnut oil, extracted from walnut kernels, is similar in use to linseed oil, but it does not store as well. It enhances colour brightness and dries well.

Safflower/Sunflower oil
These oils have properties that are similar to those of poppy seed oil, and are used by some manufacturers. Since they do not have a yellowing effect they are especially useful for light colours and white. They tend to soften the paint and increase fluidity.

Drying mediums
These proprietary liquids and gels may be added to speed the slow drying times associated with oil painting. Sometimes, however, you may wish to increase the drying time and retarding mediums are available for that purpose.

Impasto mediums
Special gels and pastes provide the means of adding bulk and texture without using greatly increased amounts of oil paint. They are ideal for impasto work and for more expressive painting where you wish to retain the brush and knife marks on the surface.

Gloss mediums
Liquid gloss mediums impart a gloss finish to acrylic paint, forming a flexible film in the painting when dry. They maintain the colour, sometimes making it look brighter, and also improve the flow and fluidity of the paint, so that it is easier to work with as well as more translucent. Gel gloss mediums thicken the paint slightly so that brushmarks are retained, while dense or heavy gel mediums are available for even thicker paint and particularly for painting with a knife.

Matt mediums
These mediums decrease the gloss effect of acrylic paint and produce a matt or eggshell finish. They can also be mixed with gloss mediums to control the degree of shine required. In liquid form they improve the flow of colour, while gel formulations are more useful for thick painting.

Retarding mediums
Since acrylic paint dries relatively quickly, you may find it helpful to use an additive that changes the drying rate. Translucent gels are available that do not affect the consistency of the paint, though they may slightly increase brightness of colour. These mediums are useful if you wish to work 'wet-in-wet', and they also slow down the rate of drying on the palette. They should generally be used sparingly. Larger amounts may increase the transparency of the colour.

Flow improvers
Various commercially formulated products are designed to increase the flow of acrylic paint, so that large flat areas can be applied evenly and still retain richness of colour. The addition of a flow enhancer is particularly useful for painting where hard edges are required.

Texture gels and pastes
There are many texture gels and pastes on the market that will make it easier for you to achieve textured, impasto and moulding effects with acrylics. These are available in a variety of thicknesses, such as light, medium and hard, or fine, medium and coarse, so choose depending on exactly what is required for your painting. The thicker formulations are more suited to knife painting. Some pastes contain texture materials such as sand, pumice, marble dust or flint and you will need to experiment to discover any small changes in colour when they are used.

Special-effects mediums
For more unusual colour changes you could try some of the additives that alter the effect of the colour in a specific way. Pearlescent or iridescent mediums produce a shimmering metallic or pearlized surface, particularly when used with transparent colours. Interference mediums are available in colours and using one of these with your chosen colour will result in a surface that appears to change according to the direction of light and the angle from which the painting is viewed.

Gum arabic
Gum arabic is the traditional binder for watercolour paint, and it can also be used as a medium. It is available as a pale solution in water. When added to colour it increases its gloss and transparency. Gum arabic may also be used with gouache paint to make it more flexible and less prone to cracking when dry.

Ox gall
This is another traditional additive for watercolour. Only a few drops are needed to improve the wetting and increase the flow of colour. Ox gall also helps the adhesion of the paint on the ground and helps to prevent change in colour. It is available in synthetic form.

Watercolour medium
These specially formulated mediums consist of formulations of gum arabic and glycerine in water. This combination helps to enhance the brightness of the colour and increases the transparency of the paint. Glycerine extends the drying time a little and improves the solubility of the paint.

Gouache medium
Special mediums for gouache or designers' colours help adhesion of the paint and prevent it from peeling when dry. By thinning the paint they reduce its coverage and it also dries with a slightly glossy sheen.

Impasto gel
Impasto techniques are not usually associated with watercolour, but the addition of this gel enables washes to stay put and not flow into each other. They give watercolour the effect of impasto.

☞**See also**

Choosing media 30–35
Colour by colour 50–93
Creative directions 96–153
Colour Index 156–179

Oils, robustly applied for bold colour and texture

Oils for glazing and delicate transparency

Watercolour, a classic medium for a classic subject

Paper pulp, an alternative medium for painterly effects

(Left, clockwise from the top)

George Rowlett
Sudden storm over Thames, Rotherhithe Pier, 1996
Oil on board
61 x 101.5cm (24 x 40in)

Ray Balkwill
Morning mist
Watercolour
12.5 x 17.5cm (5 x 7in)

Judith Chestnutt
Shoreline, 2001
Paper pulp
30 x 30cm (12 x 12in)

Marina Yedigaroff
Red Tulips
Oil on board
51 x 91.5cm (20 x 30in)

(Right, clockwise from the top)

Jackie Simmonds
Carnevale di Venezia (detail)
Pastel on paper
43 x 46cm (17 x 18in)

Douglas Wilson
Lemon (detail)
Acrylic on board
20.3 x 15.3cm (8 x 6in)

Tim Riddihough
Check headband
Reed pen and ink,
and mixed media on tinted paper
50 x 35cm (19¾ x 13½in)

☛**See also**

Choosing media 30–35

Mediums 36–37

Choosing palettes 40–41

☛*Creative directions 96–153*

Watercolour: straight and mixed 98

Fast colour for flesh 106

Massive colour in oils 114

Transparency and luminosity 124

Colours from the mail 140

Dry colour and line 152

Pastels,
a versatile dry medium for painting

Pure acrylic,
water-soluble opacity for depth of colour

The visual qualities of materials

There are many aspects to consider when choosing media and many of the practical options are discussed on the previous pages. Oil paint is the traditional choice for professional artists, and the most popular choice among amateur painters tends to be watercolours. The versatility and high quality of today's acrylic colours are increasingly recognized, and there is a wealth of dry colour and stick media available too. Various types of pastels, coloured pencils and oilbars provide fabulous colour and handling abilities, and expressive possibilities in their own right, as well as contributing to the success of many mixed-media works. In Chapter Three 'Creative directions' you can learn first hand how the works shown on these two pages came about, plus many more, and this information on the creative process combined with the practical may help you make a more informed and personal choice when it comes to media.

Mixed media, pen and ink combined with pastel

The traditional wooden kidney-shaped thumbhole palette has become an emblem of fine art, but it is only one of many options you can choose.

Before you rush out and buy an expensive mahogany palette, it is worth considering the variety of shapes, sizes and types of palette now available, and what is best suited to your media.

When it comes to your choice of palette, size matters. Bigger is better because it gives a greater mixing area, which helps keep colours clean and pure. It is possible to work with a small palette, but you have to be an assiduous housekeeper. Once you are carried away with your painting it is a chore to have to keep a tiny mixing area clean.

Palettes for oils
Wooden thumbhole palettes are available in oblong and traditional kidney shapes. They are designed for oil painters who like to hold their palette as they stand at the easel. A well-designed thumbhole is contoured to relieve stress on the hand during long periods of painting. Try it before you buy it.

Traditional palettes
Mahogany looks sumptuous, and is ideal if you are painting on a dark, preferably reddish brown, background. When painting on white and more neutral grounds a paler shade of wood is preferable so that you can gauge tonal relationships as you mix colour on the palette.

Before using a new wooden palette, prime it with linseed oil to seal the surface and prevent the oil colour seeping into the grain and drying out. Cover both sides, and leave the palette for a few days to allow the oil to penetrate the grain of the wood and harden.

Once you have prepared your palette, blobs of unused oil colour need not be wasted. Simply break the surface film with a painting knife when you come back to it and use as normal.

Tear-off paper palettes
For a convenient disposable alternative, try tear-off paper palettes. You may waste some unused paint, but you will save yourself the task of cleaning up.

Palettes for acrylics
Wooden palettes are not very suitable for water-based colours, and this includes acrylics. A non-porous material such as metal, white plastic or melamine is a more practical option.

One of the benefits of acrylic colour is its speed of drying, but this is also one of its disadvantages when it comes to colour on the palette. Like mustard on the plate, you can waste as much as you actually use.

Stay-Wet Palette
The Stay-Wet Palette is designed to keep colour workable for longer. The colour is held on a semi-permeable membrane that draws water up from a reservoir sheet below. The paint will stay moist for

days, as long as you keep topping up the reservoir and keep the lid on between painting sessions. It also helps to store it in the fridge.

Palettes for watercolour
Fluid colour calls for a palette with mixing wells. Metal and plastic paintboxes have mixing areas incorporated in the lid, and some have additional fold-out and slider palettes. They are useful for quick colour sketches outdoors, but the mixing area is limited. Unless you keep cleaning them, you will end up with muddy colour mixes.

Plastic palettes
Plastic palettes are sold in the traditional kidney shape with thumbhole, and as oblong, square and round table palettes, with deep and shallow mixing wells. Artists working with broad sweeps of colour need large deep wells so they can mix enough paint to complete a wash. Bun-tin style palettes provide plenty of separate deep mixing areas and they help keep colour mixes clean and contained. A big table palette with a variety of shallower mixing areas in a range of sizes is also useful.

White porcelain
As an alternative to white plastic you could go for a versatile china palette, made from hard white porcelain, which resists staining and can also be used with solvents for oil painting.

Home-made palettes
Many artists working in a studio devise their own table-top palettes from a sheet of non-porous material such as white laminate or a sheet of glass. Others use a glass-topped table with a neutral backing underneath or a piece of hardboard sealed with white or neutral-coloured paint. You can also mix water-based colours on an old white plate and in cups, cans and jars, which can be sealed with clingfilm and stored. Whatever type of palette you use, the same rule applies – keep it clean and it will last for years.

Palette management
It pays to get into the habit of laying your colours out in a systematic order. You will soon get to know where each colour is and find yourself picking them up automatically. A systematic layout allows you to concentrate fully on mixing and painting.

There are no hard and fast rules for the order in which you place colours on a palette, but many painters follow one of the following well-known layouts.

Warm to cool
Keep the warm colours and cool colours separate, with the white and the earth colours in between.

Light to dark
Precisely as it says, an anticlockwise layout ranging from white through to the darkest hue selected.

Spectrum order
A classic layout, which follows the colours of the visible spectrum as seen on the colour wheel – from red through to violet, with the earths and darks separated by white.

☛**See also**
Colours of the spectrum 24
The basic colour wheel 26
Choosing media 30–35
Colour by colour 50–93
Colour Index 156–179

Choosing colours
As well as meaning a transportable surface, usually oblong or oval, on which a painter arranges and mixes colour, 'palette' also refers to the selection of colours the artist has chosen to work with or has selected to use in a particular picture. You will come across descriptions such as 'limited', 'restricted', 'hot' or 'cool' palettes and these terms refer to the colour range being used by the artist.

When buying colours for the first time, or if returning to painting after a number of years, it may be difficult to decide which colours to buy. Most manufacturers publish helpful leaflets on colour choice for the beginner, with recommendations on the most useful reds, yellows and blues to choose from their ranges – the primary colours that give the widest and cleanest variety of mixing combinations.

Some manufacturers prefer buyers to make the decision on individual colour purchases themselves, saying they believe colour choice is a personal matter. However, all the major manufacturers offer sets of colours and these can represent good value for the beginner who is uncertain of which direction to go in.

This is especially the case with watercolours. You can buy empty watercolour boxes and fill them with pans and tubes yourself, but more often than not people will start with a box selection that the manufacturer has put together. These boxes cover a wide range of painting situations and are a good initial investment; in addition to the colours they provide a mixing area and, of course, a

means of storage. By the time the colours are finished you may be more certain of your own creative direction and you can replace them with colours of your own choice.

Sets vary in size. The more colours they contain and the quality of the paint – whether artists' or the less expensive student ranges – dictates the price, as does the box design – the number of mixing wells, brush storage areas, integral palettes and so on.

Similarly, starter sets are available in other media, particularly oils and acrylics. Some manufacturers even go so far as to market sets with colour selections that are identified as appropriate for specific subjects – portraits or landscapes, for example.

From these fairly limited starter selection boxes the choice proceeds upwards to lavish, wooden presentation cases and chests, which, in addition to colours, contain brushes, and mostly everything else you may need. These selections can be hugely expensive and even look a little intimidating, but they are usually wonderful productions and the boxes alone will probably increase in value as the years go by.

Starting points
There are many practical considerations to take into account when shopping for individual colours, such as budget, subject and media, and there is a temptation to buy more colours than you need at first. It is better to begin with a restricted range, adding to these gradually as you gain more experience.

A typical, small pre-packaged box of starter watercolours contains about twelve colours: for example, Cadmium Yellow and Red, Alizarin Crimson, Burnt Umber, Raw Sienna, Yellow Ochre, Light Red, French Ultramarine, Prussian Blue and Ivory Black. (See also page 32.)

Palette choice is a subjective and individual area, too, but the colours listed above are good all-rounders from which it is possible to mix many hues. You could extend your range further with the addition of a green hue – Viridian, for example. A lighter blue and a greenish blue are useful – perhaps Cerulean and Phthalo Blue – and you will have to include a white. Titanium White is usually the popular choice.for the opaque media, and Chinese White for watercolours.

Colour is a language and it has a vocabulary of its own. Just as spoken or written words have shades of meaning, so too do individual colours. Pink may convey soft, feminine; blue – brittle, cool; red – hot, dangerous; yellow – optimistic, sunny. An artist can record a scene much as a camera does, but you also have complete freedom of choice to call upon any colour to communicate atmosphere or to emphasize a feeling or state of mind. You have full control over the palette to manipulate mood in your art.

Colour as function
The camera body is black plastic, which is cheap, seviceable, functional, and honest. Green and gold are used for circuits and contacts; red, yellow, orange, grey and blue for the wiring loom. The person who assembles the camera knows what goes where every time, as does the engineer who services or repairs the camera. Both recognize the function of each coloured wire.

Manipulating mood and atmosphere
A simple palette of colours was used to make both these colour sketches. Naples Yellow, Cobalt Blue, Raw Umber, Permanent Green and Titanium White, and a touch of Cadmium Red, form the basis of two quite different atmospheres.

The subject matter greatly influences the different moods, too – moods that are again reinforced by the proportions of the colours and the way they are mixed and blended.

In the top study simple uncomplicated colour application conveys brightness and warmth. The bottom sketch is more sombre in tone and darkened with mixes and washes of Raw Umber.

Practical colour
As well as being an emotional communicator colour is important for practical purposes. It is used to tell people what to do and what not to do: red – stop, green – go, yellow – caution; red again – danger, and so on. Colour can tell you what does what, and what goes where: green wire to earth, red wire to live. Colour is widely used as a code to impart and order information and to give instructions.

Change of use
Surplus telephone cable has been used to create this woven-wire basket.

Anon., South Africa
Woven Basket
Plastic-coated wire
15.2cm (6in) diameter

Colour as communicator
Colour has the power to instil images; it is a great communicator. When we look at a map we can interpret the printed colours to imagine the busy main road and the country lane. We build a picture in our mind's eye of roads, lakes and mountains and visualize what to expect on our journey.

Polychrome sculpture

Much sculpture from the ancient world, particularly from the civilizations of Greece and Rome, was originally highly coloured. Vestiges of pigment have been found on many examples that indicate sculpted figures may have been given blue hair and beards, and blue eyes, in addition to coloured flesh and clothing.

The idea of sculpture remaining in the uncoloured state of its natural material seems to have taken hold during the Renaissance period of the fourteenth to sixteenth centuries; artists were influenced by surviving sculptures and monuments from the classical period of Greece and Rome, most of which then survived only in their natural state, time having stripped them of their pigments.

British artist Damien Hirst was attracted by the colour and form of an educational toy (shown right) and reinterpreted it on a massive scale in painted bronze. His sculpture, entitled *Hymn*, stands some 6.10m (20ft) tall and weighs six tonnes in contrast to the few ounces and 26cm (10½in) height of the original toy. On its unveiling in April 2000 Richard Cork, art critic of *The Times* in London, described Hirst's interpretation as the best sculpture of the twenty-first century. It cannot be denied that it is ambitious in size and colour.

Joustra/Humbrol Ltd
Young Scientist Anatomy Toy
Plastic
Height 26cm (10½in)

Artists use colour to convey atmosphere and emotion. Designers, scientists and engineers similarly use colour as a language to convey information.

Three-dimensional colour

The anatomical model (left) is a child's educational toy made of coloured plastic. The colours of the components are chosen to make them distinguishable from one another. To a certain extent they follow the natural colours of the body parts – the bones are white, the liver is dark in colour and the lungs are lighter – but they are loose and symbolic representations to give an organic and anatomical feel to the model while maintaining a clear visual separation between the various organs.

Left
Damien Hirst (b.1965)
Hymn
Painted bronze
Height 6.10m (20ft)

In this ten-minute sketch the colours in nature are described as orange and yellow fruits on a white plate, on a black table. The setting is a neutral-beige room, and the back of a red chair breaks the line of the table.

These basic colours and simple shapes are influenced by the lighting conditions and the chosen media, as well as the artist's mood and technique. Chance and accident play a large part, too, in this quick study. Acrylics, gouache and ink are freely applied over a simple outline sketch, then vigorously worked and intermixed to build up a rapid interpretation of the natural colours of a classic still-life subject.

☞**See also**

Colours of the spectrum 24–25
The basic colour wheel 26–27
Choosing media 30–35
Colour by colour 50–93
Creative directions 96–153
Colour Index 156–179

Plate of Fruit
Mixed media on paper
25.5 x 20cm (10 x 8in)

Robust solid colours and thinner washes show a versatile approach to mixing acrylic and gouache. Thinned with water and speedily applied, accidental blots occur and the pure colours bespatter one another. Outlines made with water-soluble crayon and ink bleed and merge, tinting adjacent areas.

Mixing media
Do not be afraid to mix media. Lay down colours using coloured pencils, pastels, acrylics and gouache for lively colour experimentation.

Experimenting with colour
Experiment with how you look at colours in nature; the colours are rarely like you think they are. Use any materials to hand, and ignore correct usage – lay gouache over acrylic, mix it with ink, and scribble over it with coloured pencils and pastels.

Rub, scratch and scrub into the surface, using a simple limited palette of two or three colours to avoid the results looking too muddy. Use thick and thin paint, draw lines and apply washes.

Forget about making an accurate drawing or a photographic likeness of the objects – just apply the paint as fast as you can. All you are trying to do is capture a vibrant impression of the simple still life in front of you, so concentrate on the colours. See what turns out. If you like what you have done, keep it. If not, discard it and have another go.

Neutral-beige
White provides a neutral colour to indicate the back wall. Scrubbed with watery red and a touch of black, it creates a warm interior.

Red against black
The back of the chair behind the edge of the table is a basic red. Behind that, a dark patch of a thin wash of black indicates a doorway.

Black
Black is used for the solid table top and shadows, with a touch of white and copious amounts of water. The green tint is created by the coloured pencil outline used for the drawing.

Orange
Cadmium Yellow Deep combined with pure red and a medium yellow makes a vibrant mix. White provides highlights and surface reflection.

White
Here a detail of the plate shows white used at its purest. Other colours break into its purity, giving a sense of light and shadow.

Yellow
Cadmium Yellow Light forms the skin of the fruit, which is freckled with typical ripe markings indicated by random black and a touch of red.

Playing with colour
An orange is orange and a banana is yellow – but in art you can paint an orange or a banana any colour you like. There are no rules about having to stick to nature's colours. So try painting the orange blue and the banana red.

COLOUR
BY COLOUR

CHAPTER 2

Blue 50 51 52 53

Blue **Turquoise** 54

Blue **Violet** 55

Red 56 57 58 59

Brown/Red Earth 72 73

Brown/Red Earth 74 75

Black 76 77 78 79
Darks 80, 81, 82, 83

Grey 84 85

On the following pages we explore many of the most popular 'core' colours that are currently available to artists. We learn about the history, composition and attributes of these colours, and how they have been developed and refined into the artists' pigments we are familiar with today.

▬Red▬ **Orange** ▬60▬61▬

Yellow▬ 62▬63▬64▬65▬66▬
Yellow Ochre 66

▬67 **Green** ▬68▬69▬70▬
Green Earth 67

NB
Metallic colours,
Iridescent colours,
Fluorescent colours,
Interference colours, and
Mica formulations.
Due to limitations of the four-colour printing process it is not possible to reproduce these special-effect colours with any degree of accuracy. See page 88 for further details and refer to manufacturers' colour charts.

▬**White**▬86▬87▬

▬**Metallic**▬88▬89▬
and special-effect colours

▬**Flesh**▬90▬91▬92▬93▬
and reddish yellow tints

☞**See also**
Optical illusions 20–21
Colours of the spectrum 24–25
The basic colour wheel 26–27
Choosing media 30–35
Colour by colour 50–93
Creative directions 96–153
Colour Index 156–179

'In music a light blue is like a flute, a darker blue a 'cello; a still darker a thunderous double bass; and the darkest blue of all – an organ.'

WASSILY KANDINSKY (1866–1944)

Blue is overwhelmingly present in our lives for it is the colour of the sky, providing an ever-changing backdrop that is echoed and reflected in the sea, rivers and lakes. In relation to the spectrum and the colour wheel, the term 'blue' applies to all those colours that are between violet and turquoise. Blue retains its distinct character more clearly than the two other primary colours, red and yellow, when white or black is added.

From space our planet looks blue. Described by Kandinsky as the 'typical heavenly colour', blue carries a sense of the spiritual. It suggests calmness and serenity in its lighter tones and mystery as it approaches black. In some situations it may convey sadness and melancholy, hence to have 'the blues'. Used in mid-bright clarity it is an ethereal, expansive colour, while deeper, richer blues have velvety depths that evoke opulence and mystique.

Early blues

Though blue was known and used by the ancient civilizations, it was considered a lesser colour. The Greeks had no separate word for blue, instead classifying individual blue colours with terms such as *kuanos*, from which we derive the word 'cyan'. Blue as an overall term was categorized as a black or dark.

Frit

The Ancient Egyptians used several shades of blue, among them a colour that was synthesized from copper silicates and calcium oxide. These ingredients were fired with sand to produce a ceramic glaze and a glass-like substance known as 'frit'.

When ground this produced a soft blue pigment powder, a colour later referred to by the Romans as Egyptian Blue or Alexandrian Blue.

Azurite

Another colour found in Egyptian wall paintings was derived from azurite, a copper carbonate mineral related to malachite. This gave a deep blue that veered towards green. Azurite was also used by the Greeks, who obtained its source mineral from Armenia, referring to it as 'Armenian stone'. It was still in use in the fifteenth century by Renaissance artists who tended to use azurite as an underpainting for the more costly Ultramarine. The colour was also known as *azzurro della magna* or sometimes as Mountain Blue.

Woad

Woad had been used in northern Europe since the time of the Ancient Britons, who dyed their faces blue in an effort to strike fear into the invading army of Julius Caesar in 55BC. It was obtained from the leaves of the *Isatis tinctoria* shrub and was a colour similar to indigo. Artist monks used woad for blue to illuminate the *Book of Kells* in the eighth century.

What is blue?

'Of the colour between green and violet in the spectrum, coloured like the sky or deep sea (also of things much paler, darker, etc., as smoke, distant hills, moonlight, bruise; and qualified by or qualifying other colours ...).'

OXFORD ENGLISH DICTIONARY

The growth of blue

Respect for blue increased with the discovery of the extraction of Ultramarine from lapis lazuli during the Middle Ages. It was not until the sixteenth century, however, that blue was properly recognized as an essential basic colour.

Naming blues

Many old names have been superseded, but you may see historical references to the following:

Alexandrian Blue
Antwerp Blue
Berlin Blue
Blue Ashes
Blue Bice
Blue Verditer
Bremen Blue
Delft Blue
Egyptian Blue
Indian Blue
Leyden Blue
Mountain Blue
Paris Blue
Pozzuoli Blue
Sky Blue
Smalt
Smalt Blue
Thénard's Blue
Vestorian Blue

☛See also
CI International 18–19
The four-colour process 21
Turquoise 54
Violet 55
Colour Index/Blues 165–169

Oriental blues

While the Greeks and, particularly, the Romans had brought colours and dyes from the East, the Middle Ages saw flourishing trade routes re-established. Two colours were especially important – Ultramarine and Indigo.

Ultramarine

The name Ultramarine – meaning 'from beyond the sea' – gives some indication of the colour's exotic standing. This pigment, rich royal-to-purple blue in colour and more expensive than gold, was obtained from a semi-precious gemstone called lapis lazuli ('blue stone'). Still rare, lapis lazuli is chiefly found in Afghanistan.

The cost of Ultramarine was reflected in its use, and master painters of the Renaissance were instructed to use the colour to denote their patron's status and wealth. These artists were even contractually required not to economize on Ultramarine by substituting a cheaper blue such as azurite. Artists tended to use the colour symbolically for the most important areas in a painting, such as the Virgin Mary's robe. With the advent of oil paint Ultramarine appeared less saturated unless lead white was added, and the colour lost favour a little.

The stone's main colouring component is the mineral lazurite, but other components cause the pigment to take on a greyish tinge if it is ground, so another method is required to extract the brilliant blue. The process involves mixing the stone into a kind of dough that is washed to leave a sediment. Further washes give varying intensities.

Indigo

Indigo, as its name implies, was imported from India. Fermented from the leaves of the *Indigofera tinctorum* plant, it produced a deep purple-blue dye that was thirty times stronger than woad.

For painters it was available in the form of a lake pigment produced by dyeing. Indigo was sometimes used by Renaissance artists as an underpainting to azurite to give depth and to warm its effect.

Indigo dye

In the nineteenth century under the Raj the British turned Indigo production in India into a major industry. As a textile dye the colour was used all over the world for uniforms. Though all blues are fugitive, Indigo is particularly prone to fading. It is still used on a large commercial scale for work clothes such as overalls, but the colour has been synthesized since the early twentieth century. Perhaps its most popular and obvious use is for the colouring of denim blue jeans.

Blue Bice

Light blue could be obtained from combining copper carbonates with the precious metal found in silver mines in India. Used in the seventeenth century, these colours were descriptively referred to as 'ashes'.

Smalt

Smalt was one of the first useful blues that had cobalt as an ingredient. A deep blue colour, Smalt was used widely from the sixteenth to the eighteenth century and superseded azurite. It was ground from a glass frit produced from cobalt oxide and J. M. W. Turner (1775–1850) is said to have used great quantities of 'smalts of various intensities'.

Iznik tiles
During the sixteenth century the potters of Iznik in Turkey created beautiful glazed tiles based on geometric and floral motifs. Cobalt blue was used first as a single colour, but later colours such as turquoise, copper greens and a manganese red-purple were incorporated.

Leyden Blue
A type of cobalt blue called Leyden Blue was used as the glaze for the Dutch seventeenth-century earthenware that became known as Delftware. In their turn the Dutch were imitating the Ming Blue (also cobalt oxide) and white porcelain from China.

The quest for blue

Chemical experiments and advances in industrial technology in the nineteenth century saw the discovery of new ways of synthesizing blues that were the forerunners of colours used by artists today.

How to make an excellent Ultramarine Blue

'Take lapis lazuli and grind it fine on a porphyry stone. Then make a mass or paste of the following ingredients: for a pound of lapis, 6 ounces of Greek pitch, two of mastic, one of spike or linseed oil, and half an ounce of turpentine; bring it all to boil in a pot until almost melted, then filter and gather the product in cold water. Stir and mix it well with the powdered lapis lazuli and let sit for a week or so. The longer it rests, the better and finer the blue will be. Next, knead the paste with the hands, sprinkling it with warm water; the blue will come out with the water. The first, second and third rinsing should be done separately. When you see the blue fall to the bottom of the container, throw out the water and keep the blue.'

LIBRI COLORUM
(THE BOOK OF COLOURS)
COMPILED BY JEAN LEBEGUE
(FIFTEENTH CENTURY)

Prussian Blue

The first colour to be made artificially was produced by accident. In 1704 a paint maker called Diesbach, working in the Prussian city of Berlin, added some impure potash containing animal oil into a cochineal lake he was making. The result was a chemical mix of ferric ferrocyanide and its colour was a deep, slightly greenish blue.

A powerful, staining colour, Prussian Blue was fairly inexpensive to produce for use in dyeing textiles and as artists' colour. Other chemists in Europe were soon making their own versions. Prussian Blue is also known as Berlin Blue or Paris Blue. Antwerp Blue is a lighter version.

Cobalt Blue

The first synthesized Cobalt Blue was created in 1802 by a French scientist called Thénard; thus the colour was also known as Thénard's Blue. Its chemical composition was cobalt aluminate and it took over from Smalt. Cobalt Blue is a clean-looking blue that is neither warm nor cool and is available in shades from light to deep. Cobalt is also used to describe other colours derived from the metal, including violet and green.

Cerulean Blue

Named from *caeruleus* (Latin for 'blue'), this colour was discovered in 1802 by Höpfner, a German scientist, who produced it through heating cobalt and tin oxides. In 1870 it became an artists' colour when the English paint maker George Rowney marketed it as Coeruleum. It is a bright, greenish blue, particularly suited to painting watercolour skies.

French Ultramarine

Since Ultramarine was sourced from the rare lapis lazuli, it was prohibitively expensive. In 1824 the French Société d'Encouragement pour l'Industrie Nationale offered a prize of 6000 francs to any chemist who could discover how to manufacture an artificial Ultramarine. Four years later the French colour maker J.-B. Guimet came up with a winning recipe that included aluminosilicate, sodium carbonate, silica and sulphur. Heating and washing processes resulted in an ultramarine colour that could be changed slightly by simply adapting the ingredient amounts. The colour became known as French Ultramarine, reflecting its provenance. Its cheapness ensured that it became a core colour for all artists.

Modern blues

Many of the core modern blues that artists use have familar names – such as Prussian Blue, Cobalt Blue, French Ultramarine and Cerulean Blue. In addition there are several new blues such as Phthalo, Monastral and Indanthrene Blue. Manufacturers have developed their own colours and variations of them. With no historical tradition to these colours, they sometimes bear the maker's name or a descriptive name. Check on the manufacturers' charts for accurate chemical descriptions.

Pigment use

The blue pigments most frequently seen and widely used by modern manufacturers are PB15 Copper phthalocyanine, PB73 Cobalt silicate and PB27 Ferric ferrocyanide. PB15 is an ingredient in Indigo, Manganese Blue (Hue), Neutral Tint, Payne's Grey and Mauve, as well as the colours named Phthalo. PB73 is used as a single pigment in Cobalt Blue Deep.

Blue pigments

PB15 Copper phthalocyanine
PB27 Ferric ferrocyanide
PB28 Cobalt aluminium oxide
PB29 Complex sodium aluminium silicate
PB35 Cobalt tin oxide
PB36 Cobalt chromium oxide
PB60 Indanthrone
PB73 Cobalt silicate

Chemical blues

The twentieth century saw new synthetic chemical pigments and dyes that mimicked natural colours. These colours have considerably expanded the choice available to artists.

Phthalo Blue

This powerful colour is made from copper phthalocyanine, first synthesized in the early 1930s. As a deep, intense blue (it is sometimes named Intense Blue), it has replaced Prussian Blue to a great extent. Phthalocyanine provides a variety of blue shades that are mostly slightly greenish, but sometimes have a reddish tinge – for instance, Winsor Blue (Green Shade) and Winsor Blue (Red Shade). Other blues with phthalocyanine as their base are Hortensia Blue, Monastral Blue, Monestial Blue, Old Holland Blue, Rembrandt Blue and Thalo Blue.

Manganese Blue

This colour, developed in the early twentieth century, was made from barium manganate. Described as having 'an ice-blue undertone' it was a bright greenish blue, similar to Cerulean, but weaker in tinting power. Unfortunately, the pigment is now unavailable.

Indanthrene Blue

This violet blue, similar to Indigo, was developed in 1901. Some manufacturers market this colour instead of Prussian Blue and it creates good dark colours when mixed with umbers. It is more lightfast than the phthalocyanine blues, especially when used in tints. It is also called Indanthrone Blue.

Core blues

The most common blues are Phthalocyanine, Cyan or Primary, Cerulean, Ultramarine and Cobalt. The pigment contents are usually the same, but hues vary from one maker to another depending on the formulation and the medium.

Phthalocyanine Blue

Cyan and Primary Blue

Cerulean Blue

Basic blues

Many manufacturers offer basic mixing blues – ones that are recommended as good mixers for creating secondary colours. Among these you will often see Cyan Blue and/or Primary Blue. Cyan is traditionally a highly saturated green-blue that is the complementary of magenta. Cyan Blue and magenta, along with yellow, form a set of primary colours that are well known within the printing industry (see page 21). The word 'cyan' is from the Greek *kuanos*, meaning 'dark blue'.

Cobalt Blue

Ultramarine Blue

Blue obsessions

One of the most well-known examples of a blue obsession is probably Picasso's blue period (1901–04). Many other artists and movements in art have also become known for their association with blue.

Homage to blue

French artist Yves Klein (1928–62) produced vivid single-hue paintings in the 1950s. In his desire to celebrate the full intensity of pigment he developed a new Ultramarine, patenting it as International Klein Blue (IKB). Suspending pure pigment in clear resin allowed the particles of colour to be displayed with startling vibrancy. IKB became Klein's trademark colour.

International Klein Blue

Franz Marc, Blue Horse 1, 1911 (detail)

The Blue Rider

Known in German as *der Blaue Reiter*, this group of Expressionist artists were associated with an art almanac founded by Kandinsky and Franz Marc (1880–1916). The name was chosen because Kandinsky and Marc both liked the colour blue, and were interested in painting horses and their riders.

The colour turquoise replicates the hue of the same-named semi-precious stone. Europeans gave the mineral its name in the thirteenth century because they imported turquoise through Turkey, though its source was probably Persia. Turquoise was also found in the American continent, where the Navajo, Zuni and Hopi Indians crafted artefacts and jewellery, working turquoise with silver.

Prepared turquoise colours
Manufacturers offer several colours named turquoise, but you can mix these hues.

(From left to right, top to bottom)
Phthalo Turquoise Light, Phthalo Turquoise, Turquoise Blue, Turquoise Deep, Turquoise Blue Deep, Phthalo Turquoise, Cobalt Teal, Cobalt Turquoise, Phthalo Turquoise, Cobalt Green Turquoise, Cobalt Blue Turquoise Light, Cobalt Turquoise (Hue).

Blue or green
In ancient Mexico the Aztecs used turquoise mosaics to decorate sculptures and precious objects, combining the stone with jade. This juxtaposition of the two minerals perhaps led naturally to the use of one word to mean both blue and green. From the artist's point of view this is apt, for turquoise sits between these two colours in the spectrum, though it is not named as a separate hue.

Turquoise pigments
Natural turquoise varies in colour from a bright greenish blue to a pale bluish green. Its components are hydrated aluminium and copper phosphate. A pale turquoise green ceramic glaze can be produced from roasting aluminium, chromium and cobalt oxides.

There is no single synthetic organic turquoise. Artists can simply mix turquoise from blue and green pigments, thus controlling the precise colour of the turquoise required. There are also many prepared artists' colours that now bear the name turquoise. Manufacturers create turquoise by combining blue (PB) and green (PG) pigment ingredients. These are mainly based on phthalocyanines; these synthesized substances produce a range of blues that can veer towards red at one end, but generally tend to be greenish. Single pigment cobalt turquoises are also available. They give clear, bright colours in watercolour, and both bright and duller colours in oils and acrylics that are said to more closely resemble the opaque, matt appearance of the natural stone.

Experiment with turquoise
It is easy to mix numerous varieties of turquoise using chosen blue and green pigments, which allows precise control of the required bias of the colour.

☞See also
Blue 50–53
Green 68–71
Colour Index/Turquoise 168–169
Colour Index/Violet 165–166

Violet is a secondary colour and is the complementary of yellow. The term violet is derived from the Old French 'violete' or 'violette', a plant or flower of the genus *Viola*, whose flower is of this colour. Violet lies at one end of the visible spectrum, next to blue. Together with mauve and purple, violet describes colours ranging from reddish blues to bluish reds and also violet-tinged reddish browns (Mars violets).

'I have finally discovered the colour of the atmosphere. It is violet.'
CLAUDE MONET (1840–1926)

Prepared violet colours
There are numerous manufactured violet hues available.
(From left to right, top to bottom)
Brilliant Violet, Light Violet, Quinacridone Violet, Deep Violet, Ultramarine Violet, Light Blue Violet, Medium Violet, Violet, Dioxazine Violet, Violet Bluish, Caput Mortuum, Permanent Violet Dark.

Violet pigments
A number of violets exist as pure synthetic pigments. For example, PV15 (Ultramarine Violet), PV19 (Quinacridone) and PV23 (Dioxazine Violet) are frequently seen in product declarations on paint tubes. However, many manufactured colours that bear the name violet, including similar hues, such as the mauves, magentas and purples, are often combinations of red and blue pigments, sometimes with added white (see Light Blue Violet, above left). Many of the prepared violet hues can be obtained by mixing.

Caput Mortuum
This is a subdued violet-brown colour seen in artists' oil colours and sometimes in watercolours. Its strange name, 'death's head', which originated in the eighteenth century, is said to be derived from the colour of skulls piled in the catacombs in Rome. As none of the constituents of the pigment are obtained from bone a more feasible explanation is that the colour was obtained from iron salts that were baked down to their 'dying' embers. Caput Mortuum or Mars Violet has a subtle violet character that some artists find useful in their repertoire of earth colours. It makes good flesh tones when mixed with white. Mars Violet is an artificial pigment (red iron oxide PR101). It is a colour which can be easily mixed on the palette.

Caput Mortuum is a maroon Mars violet.

'If one says "Red" (the name of a color) and there are 50 people listening, it can be expected that there will be 50 reds in their minds ...'
JOSEF ALBERS
(1888–1976)

What is red?
'Of or approaching the colour seen at least-refracted end of spectrum, of shades varying from crimson to bright brown and orange, esp. those seen in blood, rubies, glowing coals, human lips, and fox's hair ... .'
OXFORD ENGLISH DICTIONARY

Red is the most dynamic and vibrant colour in the artist's palette. In its purest, saturated form it is the hottest of the warm colours. It is a colour that needs to be used judiciously, since overuse may reduce its vibrancy. Set against its complementary, green, even a small amount will sing and sparkle. It is one of the oldest colour names – the first colour word we speak after black and white.

Red is a colour with countless symbolic and contradictory associations in different cultures. It can signify danger, or life; good luck, as well as evil. In India red is the sacred colour of Lakshmi, the goddess of wealth and beauty, and in China a ruby represents longevity. The red planet Mars is named after the Roman god of war. Early physicians wore red robes to signify their healing profession, and doors were painted with a red cross to signify the presence of the bubonic plague.

The first red palettes
Red was a difficult colour to make successfully and early pigments were often fugitive, turned black when mixed with others and were sometimes extremely toxic. Early red pigments were mostly made from earth colours, berries, roots, insects and resins, and many of the red paints were originally obtained from dyes.

The Egyptians found a way of fixing dyes onto a transparent white powder (probably gypsum or even chalk); paint pigments made by this process are termed 'lakes'. Much later, Renaissance artists also used red lake pigments from resinous sources such as brazil wood, and the Indian lac and kermes insects.

Red lead
Once a highly prized colour, first manufactured by the Greeks, this pigment is not used by artists today since it is composed of lead monoxide and lead peroxide and therefore highly toxic. It is also known as Minium or Saturn Red. It was used for many years to protect steel from rusting.

Earth reds
Red iron-oxide pigments produce many reddish hues with similar properties, but slightly different variations, such as Mars Red and Venetian Red with light, warm tones and Indian Red, Mars Violet and Caput Mortuum, which are darker, cooler versions. Earth reds are permanent, lightfast colours with good covering power. Other colour names within this category are known as English Red, Pompeiian Red, Persian Red, Sinopia and Terra Rosa (see Brown and Red Earth, pages 72–75). These colours can be either natural or synthetic.

Realgar
Realgar was made from red arsenic sulphide. It was a natural pigment found in volcanic areas and hot springs, and was used in ancient Mesopotamia. The word realgar stems from 'rahj al-ghar' (Arabic for 'powder of the mine'). Now an obsolete pigment, its use continued until the nineteenth century when it was no longer used because of its extreme toxicity.

☛See also
CI International	18–19
Violet	55
Orange	60–61
Brown and Red Earth	72–75
Colour Index/Reds	161–165
Colour Index/Earths	174

Cardinal Red
In the Middle Ages bright colours were rare since they were tedious and difficult to produce. Hence red (along with purple) became the exclusive preserve for kings, judges, the nobility, and the pope and his cardinals. In 1464 Pope Paul II introduced 'Cardinals' Purple', which was not purple at all, but a red dye made from the kermes insect.

Redrot

Red-letter day
The early Christian church used red for directions in prayer books as to the conduct of church services and to show feast days on the ecclesiastical calendar, and so a red-letter day became a lucky day.

Scarlet women
Red is associated with lust, and a woman suspected of committing adultery in Puritan times was branded with a scarlet letter. Even before Christianity linked red with the devil, the colour had negative connotations. An ancient Egyptian incantation, praying for salvation from evil, was 'Oh, Isis deliver me from the hands of all bad, evil, red things.'

Using red to attract attention

Red attracts the attention of the viewer because the colour appears to advance, making red objects seem closer than they actually are. This visual phenomenon occurs because red has the longest wavelength of all visible light. Artists can use this property of red to their advantage for added dimension. Making some colours warmer will make them stand proud of a picture's surface, while cooler colours will appear to recede.

Cinnabar

Cinnabar, the precursor to Vermilion, was made from a dense hard rock. According to Theophrastus (c. 300BC) in *The History of Stones* cinnabar ore was dislodged from inaccessible cliffs by shooting arrows to loosen it. The chief mining area for cinnabar was Almaden in Spain. The Romans made paint from cinnabar and it was their only source of a bright orange-red colour. It was not as bright as Vermilion, though both are forms of mercuric sulphide.

'Judas hair'

A term used to denote bright-coloured hair in paintings, particularly red hair. The expression originated because artists traditionally gave Judas distinctive red hair in paintings.
Giotto di Bondone (1267–1337)
The Kiss of Judas, *c.* **1305–06**
(detail)

Dragon's Blood

Also called Indian cinnabar by the Greeks. Pliny maintained that the colour came from a mixture of an elephant's and a dragon's blood, following a fierce battle between the two beasts. In fact, it is a red-brown resin produced by the sap of an Asian shrub known as *Calamus draco*. The leaves have prickly stalks that grow to resemble long tails and the bark is covered with spines.

Vermilion

The Greeks made an artificial form of cinnabar, called Vermilion, which was an orange-red pigment. The recipe was not known until the twelfth century in the West and it took another 300 years for the pigment to be in common use. Again it was the best bright red available. The colour was often used in manuscript painting where it was glazed with either egg yolk or 'glair' (egg white). Similarly in painting Vermilion was often glazed with madder or cochineal lakes in order to increase the purity of the colour.

Vermilion is made by heating mercury and sulphur together in a flask. The combined substances vaporize and recondense at the top of the flask in the form of a black mixture. A red colour develops as the mixture is cleaned. The longer it is ground, the brighter the colour becomes. Cennini claimed that 'if you ground it every day for 20 years, the colour would still become finer and more handsome'. Vermilion continued to be used until the mid to late twentieth century.

Naming reds

A wide variety of reds is available in any of the media. Many of the colours are also known under secondary names – Alizarin Crimson is also referred to as Rose Madder or Permanent Madder, for instance. Some manufacturers attach their own names to colours they have developed, such as Winsor Red. There are individual inconsistencies that only become apparent to the artist after time and familiarity with a medium or particular paint manufacturer. Generally speaking, oil colours tend to have old names, while new media such as gouache or acrylic are often given more descriptive colour names. Flame Red, for example, is a gouache name that is very close in terms of handling and range of colour mixing abilities to the oil paint called Cadmium Red. Often an old name may be attached to a paint colour, but it is now made synthetically and the problems of permanence or toxicity that were associated with it in the past are no longer relevant. These are some of the names you may come across to describe various hues of red pigments:

Alizarin Crimson
Bright Red
Brilliant Red
Burgundy
Cadmium Red
Carmine
Chinese Vermilion
Crimson
Florentine Red
French Vermilion
Genuine Red
Geranium
Helios Red
Intense Red
Magenta
Munich Lake
Nacarat Carmine
Naphthol Red
Pyrrole Red
Rose
Rowney Red
Ruby
Scarlet
Transparent Red
Vermilion
Winsor Red

Alizarin Crimson
Generally speaking Alizarin Crimson mixes well with blues to obtain violet. Purples and violets mixed with Cadmium Red tend to be brownish in colour.

Cadmium Red
Cadmium Red, however, is good for mixing with yellows to produce a clean bright orange.

Complementary colour
As the complementary of green, red is a useful colour for toning down bright saturated greens. Eventually the two mixed together with the addition of white will produce either a greenish grey or a warm pinkish grey.

Reds in the artist's palette

As one of the primary colours red is one of the most important elements in the artist's paintbox. Different artists choose different colours for their palette according to individual preferences, but a minimum palette will invariably include Alizarin Crimson, a coolish blue-red, and Cadmium Red, a warm orange-red. Alizarin Crimson is a transparent colour and good for glazing, especially in oils and acrylics – for adding a blush to a cheek, for example – while Cadmium Red is opaque and has an excellent and greater covering power. From these two reds it is possible to mix a wide spectrum of colours.

Preparing natural madder
Alun Foster, chief chemist at Winsor & Newton

Madders

Madder Lake and Rose Madder are now produced synthetically, but the colour was originally made from the root of the madder plant *Rubia tinctorum*. Native to Greece, it was introduced into France and Italy in the twelfth century. George Field, a great colourman of the nineteenth century, who supplied John Constable (1776–1837) and William Holman Hunt (1827–1910), invented a press in order to extract the dye from the madder root.

Dried madder root

Genuine madders
Winsor & Newton are the only remaining large commercial company to produce a natural madder in artists' colours, one that has a pinkish rose hue. The pigment declaration NR9 shows the product contains genuine madder. However, many modern colours (see left) bear the name madder, and these vary in hue from a medium rose colour to a darkish violet-brown and contain various synthetic organic pigment combinations.

Synthetic madders range in hue from light, pinkish rose to deep reddish browns.

Madder plant
Rubia tinctorum

Red legs
Natural madder produced the deepest and most permanent reds until the invention of Alizarin Crimson in the 1860s. The French government attempted to protect its traditional madder-growing industry by making it the compulsory red dye for army-uniform trousers.

Alizarin Crimson
Alizarin Crimson is a synthetic substitute for madder and was first introduced by two German chemists, Graebe and Liebermann, in 1868. It was the first natural dye to be manufactured artificially. By 1920 it had replaced most of the old lakes and madders, which were often weak colours that discoloured rapidly and were not lightfast. Alizarin Crimson is a colour with a strong staining power – a little goes a long way. It is also transparent and is therefore used a lot with glazes.

Crimson and Carmine
The original paint colours known as crimson or carmine were precursors of Alizarin Crimson. The names come from the kermes insect, from which this colour dye was first extracted. The sixteenth century saw the introduction of the same colour derived from the cochineal beetle *Dactylopius coccus*. This tiny Mexican *Coccus cacti*-eating insect produces a transparent and highly fugitive colour when ground and precipitated on clay. There are approximately 70,000 insects per pound of cochineal. The colour was held in high regard by the Aztecs, and was brought to Europe shortly after the discovery of Central and South America. It is more commonly used as a food colouring now since as a paint it proved to be extremely fugitive. Paints using the word carmine or crimson are now synthetically produced.

Scarlet Lake
Scarlet Lake is made from various pigments, but was originally a mixture of Vermilion and Cochineal Lake. The colour is also known as Scarlet Vermilion.

Chrome Red
Orange-red was derived from chromium, discovered in the early nineteenth century. Although brilliant in hue, the colour is toxic and unstable, and is no longer used. It is also called Chinese Red.

Aniline reds
A number of aniline pigments were developed in the 1850s and 60s (see page 81). Among these were a cherry red that was named fuchsin and a violet-red that was named Magenta after the battle of 1859.

Cadmium colours

In 1817 the heavy metal cadmium was discovered by the German scientist Friedrich Stromeyer. By the mid nineteenth century various cadmium colours were being developed. Brilliant in hue, they were opaque and also reliable to use. These colours all veer towards the hotter part of the spectrum through the red/orange/yellow range.

Cadmium Red

Cadmium Red was not introduced until the early 1900s, since when it has become a core red. Developed from Cadmium Yellow, Cadmium Red is made from cadmium sulphide and cadmium selenide. Top quality ranges are composed of pure cadmium, while cheaper makes are a cadmium-barium mix, which has less tinting strength and may produce a less vibrant colour.

Cadmium Red is one of the most important colours in the artist's palette and is the best substitute for Vermilion. It is a very bright, hot red. Very often paint manufacturers will have a variety of Cadmium Reds in their chart designated as light, medium and dark.

In a limited palette Cadmium Red is often balanced by the inclusion of Alizarin Crimson, which acts as a cooler red. It makes an opaque permanent colour, but there are some concerns with toxicity, particularly if neat pigment is used rather than ready-made paint.

New reds

The twentieth century has seen the advent of new chemical pigments that have considerably augmented the artist's choice of reds. Many of these provide reliable versions of natural colours that are unstable.

Sample selection of cadmiums

Sample selection of quinacridones

Sample selection of magentas

Quinacridones

The first quinacridone colours were brought onto the market in the 1950s. These are a wide and vibrant range of reds that range through oranges, pinks and purples. They have gradually replaced most of the lake colours and provide new colours, particularly increasing the choice of bright magentas. They are lightfast and resistant and even in their oil versions have a luminous quality. In acrylic and watercolour they provide transparent luminosity and clean mixes. A particularly deep dark or coloured black may be obtained from mixing Quinacridone Crimson with Phthalo Green.

Perylene Red

Developed in the 1980s, these are strong deep brown-red and maroon pigments. In mixes they produce warm darks.

Pyrrole Red

As their name implies, this is a group of bright, fiery orange-red colours. Introduced only in the 1990s, they are lightfast, have reasonable opacity and produce clean mixes that may have the advantage over cadmium colours.

Naphthol Red

Naphthol reds are a large group of organic pigments, first introduced in the 1920s. They range from yellow-shade reds right through to deep crimsons, and they belong to one of the most complex chemical families. The main factor that is of concern to artists is the variable lightfastness of the category, with some Naphthols being unsuitable for artists' colours. The more commonly used high-lightfast pigments are PR112, PR170 and PR188, which appear as Naphthol Red Light, Naphthol Red Medium and Scarlet Lake.

Inspired by red

The Fauves

The Fauves (French for 'wild beasts') were the first artists to break away from using descriptive colour and to use it as an emotive vehicle. Prime among them was Henri Matisse (1869–1954), one of the great colourists of the twentieth century. His influence can be seen in the early works of André Derain (1880–1954), who chose a bright, emotional palette before reverting to more subtle, traditional colours.

Colour field painting

The American painters of the 1950s and 60s developed a style of abstract painting that became known as Abstract Expressionism. The work of the artist Mark Rothko (1903–70) emerged from this movement. Rothko's work was reliant on the pure sensation of colour. He painted huge canvases, overlaying large areas of colour so that the field of colour seemed to go beyond the picture plane to allow the viewer to become totally absorbed by the emotional impact of colour.

> *'Orange is like a man, convinced of his own powers. Its note is that of the angelus, or of an old violin.'*
>
> WASSILY KANDINSKY (1866–1944)

The colour orange is named after the Sanskrit word 'narangah' for the fruit. Orange conjures up warmth and vibrancy and the colour appears in the hot part of the spectrum between red and yellow. In pigment form orange may often have a slight bias towards either red or yellow. Although it may be mixed from these two primaries, the clearest and brightest oranges are single-pigment hues.

Antonio Mensaque
Oranges, 1863
Anglesey Abbey, Cambridgeshire
Collection of The National Trust

Orange has traditionally been sourced from earth colours ranging from golds to browns. The toxic Realgar, derived from volcanic minerals, which was used from ancient times and through the Renaissance period right up until the nineteenth century, could be classified as a red-orange. New mid oranges were developed from chromium and cadmium in the early 1800s, and recent improvements in synthetic colour manufacture have ensured reliable, lightfast versions of these.

Chrome Orange
This bright reddish orange was developed from chromium in 1809. It was produced by the reaction of lead nitrate with potassium chromate and sodium hydroxide, and the resulting mix was filtered and dried to produce the pigment.

Different proportions of ingredients gave deeper shades. The chrome colours were not lightfast and most were later replaced by cadmiums. Chrome Orange was also known by several other names, including Persian Red and Derby Red.

Cadmium Orange
There is a huge number of cadmium colours that range from pale yellow to deep red. Cadmium was first discovered as a by-product of zinc production in the early part of the nineteenth century, but cadmium colours were not widely used until much later when cadmium was more generally available. Cadmium Orange is a bright warm colour that is composed of cadmium sulphide and cadmium selenide. It is a reliable, permanent colour and has good covering power. Some makers add Cadmium Red to Cadmium Orange to increase its reddish tone and the range of colours on offer.

Some modern oranges
Advances in chemical synthesis in the twentieth century have given the artist new orange pigments that are bright, clear and lightfast. Among these are the perinone, benzimidazolone and pyrrole oranges.

Perinone Orange
An intense orange with a red bias, this colour was first used as a dye in the 1920s. Eventually produced as a lake pigment, it is available in light or dark shades. In watercolour it may appear to be a granular and semi-opaque pigment. It is lightfast and is sometimes combined with aluminium flakes to produce a copper-looking metallic paint.

Benzimidazolone Orange
This mid orange has a slight yellow bias. It is a reliable, staining colour and is often used now instead of Cadmium Orange. These 'azo' colours are often given manufacturers' names; an example is Winsor Orange. They may not be quite as strong as cadmium colours when mixed, but they have good lightfast properties.

Pyrrole Orange
The pyrrole pigments were discovered in the early 1980s and give colours in the orange to red sector. Pyrrole Orange is a bright mid orange that is transparent and lightfast. This is another colour that may be used as a substitute for Cadmium Orange and it produces a broad range of colours when mixed.

☛**See also**

CI International 18–19

Red 56–59

Yellow 62–65

Colour Index/Orange 161

Experimenting with orange

Orange exists as a single pigment (see page 18), but it is one of the easiest and most satisfying secondary colours to mix from reds and yellows.

'Warm red, intensified by a suitable yellow, is orange.'
Wassily Kandinsky

Prepared orange hues

Manufacturers offer several prepared orange hues. Many are single pigment oranges and will carry the declaration PO, followed by the appropriate reference number. Others are mixed pigments containing red PR and yellow PY ingredients.

(From top to bottom, left to right)

Cadmium Yellow Orange (Old Holland)
Scheveningen Orange (Old Holland)
Perinone Orange (Winsor & Newton)
Chrome Orange Hue (Rowney)
Brilliant Orange (Liquitex)
Cadmium Orange Azo (Talens)
Transparent Pyrrole Orange (Golden)
Cadmium Orange (Lukas)
Indo Orange Red (Liquitex)
Cadmium Orange (Tri-Art)
Cadmium Orange (Rowney)
Cadmium Orange (Maimeri)

Naming orange

Orange used as a name to describe a colour was unknown until the importation of the fruit into Europe in the Middle Ages. Even in the fifteenth century Cennini describes Realgar, which is an obvious orange hue, as a yellow.

Burnt Orange

There are various hues carrying the descriptive name orange that veer towards transparent reddish browns. Among them are Chinese Orange and Quinacridone Burnt Orange.

Yellow is a versatile primary colour and an indispensable mixing ingredient in the artist's palette. The yellow family ranges in hue from acid cool green-yellows, through clean crisp lemons, by the way of pure unbiased primary yellows, rich warm cadmiums and chromes, and neutral creamy, fleshy Naples, to earthy ochres.

Yellow is perhaps the most schizophrenic of colours in terms of the associations it holds and the uses to which it is put. Yellow may suggest sunshine and cheerfulness, or sickness and cowardice. While yellow primroses and daffodils herald the spring, yellow and black stripes signal the warning of a wasp's sting, or the danger of heavy machinery. Yellow has highly emotive connections. Yellow ribbons tied on trees signify hope and optimism for returning loved ones.

'There are painters who transform the sun into a yellow spot, but there are others who, thanks to their art and their intelligence, transform a yellow spot into the sun.'

PABLO PICASSO (1881–1973)

What is yellow?
'Of the colour between green and orange in the spectrum, coloured like buttercup or primrose or lemon or sulphur or gold … .'
OXFORD ENGLISH DICTIONARY

Origins of yellow
Yellows are derived from the earth, from arsenic, plants and even cow's urine. The word 'yellow' comes from the Old English 'geolu'; and similar names for yellow are found in Old Saxon and Old High German ('gelo'), and in Old Norse ('gulr'). The Latin for yellow is *helvus* and a similar word Helios is the name of the Greek sun god, a name that has been appropriated to identify certain modern brands of yellow.

Prehistoric yellow
Yellow was one of the four colours used by the cave painters of the Stone Age; yellow and red earth, white chalk, and black carbon have been dubbed the 'prehistoric primaries'. The iron content in the earth gives the yellow and red hues a full, soft quality, evident in the cave paintings of Lascaux and Altamira. Yellow earths and ochres are still used to this day.

Massicot
A lead-monoxide earthy yellow pigment, massicot was a by-product of the production of red lead, made by the Greeks.

Yellow Ochre
Yellow ochres, or earths, have continued to be used throughout history and provide strong, economical, opaque colour. Yellow Ochre consists of a mixture of clay, siliceous matter and hydrated iron oxide (limonite). It is known by many names, including Earth Yellow, Mars Yellow and Mineral Yellow (see page 66).

G. ROWNEY & Co.'s
MOIST COLOR.
YELLOW OCHRE.

Orpiment
The Egyptians developed a brighter, more acidic yellow mineral pigment, a sulphide of arsenic, known as orpiment. It came from Smyrna and has been identified in Egyptian, Persian, Syrian and Chinese painting. It is mentioned in the writings of Pliny and, later, by Cennini. This highly poisonous and unpleasant-smelling colour was also used in medieval and Renaissance manuscript illumination, from Europe and Ireland to Persia and Byzantium. Much later it was made chemically and known as King's Yellow. Other names for it are Arsenic Yellow and Chinese Yellow.

Naming yellows
These are some of the names for yellows that you may see:

Aureolin	Indian Yellow
Azo Yellow	Lead-tin Yellow
Barium Yellow	Lemon Yellow
Brilliant Yellow	Massicot
Cadmium Lemon	Naples Yellow
Cadmium Yellow	Orpiment
Chrome Yellow	Paris Yellow
Cobalt Yellow	Vanadium Yellow
Gamboge	Winsor Yellow
Golden Ochre	Yellow Ochre
Hansa Yellow	Zinc Yellow

Plant yellows
Turmeric and saffron have been used as colours. Saffron is a bright yellow colour obtained from *Crocus sativus*, but is said to fade badly in daylight.

☛ See also
CI International 18-19

Orange 60–61

Yellow Ochre 66

Brown and Red Earth 72–75

Colour Index/Yellows 157–159

Colour Index/Yellow Ochres 172

Pigment formulations

Most yellows are made from a single pigment formulation and employ chemicals such as cadmium zinc sulphide, arylamide, nickel titanate, potassium cobaltrinitrate and natural iron oxides. A few members of the yellow family are combination pigments, which can be approximated in mixes. Cadmium Yellow Deep is a good example where the yellow element has been warmed up with orange to give deeper hues. Naples Yellows have been softened and neutralized with additional white and ochres, and are closely related to earth and oxide colours in hue.

Lemon Yellow

Lemon Yellow may now be made from one of the arylamide synthetic organic pigments or nickel titanate. The colour is a cool, clear acidic yellow that is considered useful for mixing powerful greens and oranges. It is transparent, with a rather weak tinting power.

'… it would be easy to define by association the physical effects of colour, not only upon the eye but the other senses. One might say that bright yellow looks sour, because it recalls the taste of a lemon.'
WASSILY KANDINSKY
(1866–1944)

Indian Yellow, Gamboge and Golden Yellows

Nearly all of the older pigment yellows are now synthesized from combinations of red and yellow pigments. Indian Yellow is formulated from diarylide yellow pigment PY83 and synthetic iron oxide PR101. Many of the closer hues, often named Golden Yellows in catalogues, share similar ingredients. The exception is Gamboge Genuine, which is still available made from naturally occurring Gum resin NY24.

Van Gogh and yellow

Vincent van Gogh (1853–90) often used yellow in his vibrant paintings. Setting up studio in Arles, the south of France, in the Yellow House, he painted his surroundings of cornfields, sunflowers and yellow rooms.

Yellow Ochre

Yellow Ochre is an important natural mineral yellow and has been used since prehistoric times. It is still made from natural iron oxide PY43 (see page 66). Many other ochre colours, such as Gold Ochre, may now be replicated by synthetic iron oxide ingredients (see Brown and Red Earth pages 72–75).

Unfortunately, many of Vincent's vivid yellows have not aged well. In the nineteenth century many artists adopted chrome yellows to replace earlier yellow pigments that were unreliable or susceptible to fading, such as Gamboge and original Indian Yellow. But, Chrome Yellow, too, brought problems and in many paintings the colour has turned green and in some cases nearly black. Even van Gogh's famous sunflowers have darkened and the rather sickly yellows that appear in many of his pictures are signs that the Chrome Yellow is deteriorating.

66 Yellow Ochre

Ochres
A selection of colours whose ingredient is PY42, synthetic yellow iron oxide. Ochre hues can vary from light brownish yellows to darker reddish yellows.

Yellow Ochre is a dull yellow earth pigment. It is one of the oldest natural minerals and has been in use since prehistoric times. Like all earth pigments, it is mined from surface deposits and is therefore easily accessible and fairly cheap to obtain. The natural yellow iron-oxide pigment is PY43. Yellow Ochre is usually listed among the yellows in art materials manufacturers' literature and its hue can vary from a reddish brown to an earthy, golden yellow. It is said that the higher the iron content the darker the hue becomes.

Since the 1920s manufacturers have also used synthetic yellow iron oxide PY42, which replicates the permanent and lightfast qualities of mined Yellow Ochre. However, it can sometimes be more transparent because of the absence of clay. Natural Yellow Ochre PY43 is found in many places including India, South Africa, Italy and the USA. France also has good deposits of high grade ochre. Past names such as Oxford Ochre from the Shotover Hills, Oxford, England, relate to other sources of the colour.

Other ochres to be found are:
Attish Light Ochre
Bronze Yellow
Burnt Yellow Ochre
Deep Ochre
Flesh Ochre
Gold/Golden Ochre
Mars Yellow
Nickel Azo Yellow
Orange Ochre
Roman Ochre
Yellow Oxide

Modern pigment production at the Maimeri plant in Italy

Palaeolithic cave paintings, c. 15,000BC
As far as we can tell, the Palaeolithic artists used a limited palette of three colourfast pigments: yellow, red and black. All the colours are based on iron-oxide deposits from the earth, and carbon, thought to be from fire ashes.

See also

Pigments in history	12–15
CI International	18–19
Brown and Red Earth	72–75
Colours for free	144
Colour Index/Yellow Ochres	172
Colour Index/Siennas	172

Green Earth straight from the tube and in tint with Titanium White

(From left to right, top to bottom)

Green Earth (Old Holland)
Terre Verte (Talens)
Terre Verte (Sennelier)
Verona Green Earth (Lukas)

Natural and synthetic sources

Green Earth sources are not as widespread as iron oxides and the natural deposits of the pigment, mainly from Cyprus and central Europe, are almost exhausted. A famous source of the mineral was near Verona in Italy; hence its name Terra verde di Verona, dating to the Middle Ages. Current manufacturers may replace the natural earth with Phthalo (PG7) or Viridian (PG18) plus yellow or brown oxide.

Creta viridis

Records of Green Earth date back to Roman times, when it was used as a base for frescos and called *Creta viridis*. It has also been discovered in wall paintings in Pompeii, Asia Minor and India. In medieval and Renaissance painting, Green Earth was incorporated as an underpainting for flesh tones (see pages 112–113). Natural Green Earth is translucent and has a high oil absorption, and is well suited to water-based media. In the past the pigment was mixed with various plants, such as parsley, rue and columbine to enhance its greenness. When heated, Green Earth turns brown and is sometimes known as Green Umber.

☛ See also

CI International 18–19
Green 68–71
Brown and Red Earth 72–75
Renaissance skin tones 112–113
Colour Index/Greens 171
Colour Index/Ochres 172

Green Earth colours

A variety of Green Earths and hues are similar to traditional Terre Verte. Green Earth colours are available from most manufacturers in nearly all the popular media.

(From left to right, top to bottom)

Green Earth (Talens)
Green Earth (Sennelier)
Green Umber (Lukas Studio)
Olive Green (Talens)
Green Umber (Lukas Sorte 1)
Rowney Olive (Designers' Gouache)
Bohemian Green Earth (Lukas Studio Oil)
Rowney Olive (Artists' Oil)
Bohemian Green Earth (Lukas Gouache)
Green Earth (Old Holland)
Olive Green (Winsor & Newton)
Greenish Umber (Talens)

Other trade names you may see are:

Belgian Green	**Holly Green**
Celadon Green	**Rhenish Earth**
Cyprus Green	**Saxon Earth**
Green Bice	**Tyrol Green**
Green Stone	**Venice Green**
Hessian	**Verona Green**

Green Earth is a natural pigment (PG23), ranging in colour from yellow-olive green to a grey-blue green. It is one of the earliest known pigments and is commonly known as Terre Verte or Terra Verde. Its origins, unlike other earth pigments, which are iron oxides, are commonly from marine clays containing iron silicate. The mineral contents are mainly celadonite (bluish grey) or glauconite (dark brownish olive).

Chlorophyll is the source of green in the earth's vegetation. It traps the sunlight and retains the red and blue-violet parts of the visible spectrum, allowing the green portion to be reflected. Green lies between yellow and blue in the colour spectrum and is readily mixable on the palette from blue and yellow.

Green in history

Most descriptions of early green pigments refer to copper and arsenic ingredients, which were common until the invention of synthetic pigments in the nineteenth century.

Copper green and malachite

The history of malachite runs closely parallel to that of azurite (see Blue page 50). Malachite is a naturally occurring copper green derived from a basic carbonate of copper. It is found in many parts of the world, usually in association with azurite. Among the obsolete names for this bright green pigment are Mineral Green, Mountain Green and Hungarian Green.

Cennini writes of the virtues of malachite in the fifteenth century:

'A half natural colour is green; and this is produced artificially, for it is formed out of azurite; and it is called malachite .... This colour is good in secco, with a tempera of yolk of egg, for making trees and foliage, and for laying in.'

Chrysocolla

In classical and medieval writing there are references to a blue-green mineral known as chrysocolla, found in combination with malachite. The name is derived from the Greek words for 'gold' and 'glue', since it was used by the ancients for soldering gold. Chrysocolla has been identified in wall paintings in China and Central Asia and in Egyptian tombs dating to 2000BC.

☛**See also**

CI International 18–19
Blue 52–53
Turquoise 54
Yellow 62–66
Green Earth 67
Colour Index/Green 169–171

Carl Wilhelm Scheele (1742–86)

Scheele's Green

In 1775, while experimenting with arsenic, Swedish chemist Carl Wilhelm Scheele discovered an acid, copper arsenite. Scheele did not immediately publish details for the manufacture of this copper green pigment because he felt that potential users should be first aware of its poisonous nature. The colour was later named after him, but there is some doubt about the extent to which Scheele's Green was used by artists. It is not mentioned in literary sources of the period except for the following account in George Field's *Chromatography* (1869):

' ... To make the green, some potash and pulverised "white arsenic" (that is arsenious oxide) were dissolved in water and then heated, and the alkaline solution was added, a little at a time because of effervescence, to a warm solution of copper sulphate. The mixture was allowed to stand so that the green precipitate could settle, the liquid was poured off, and the pigment was then dried under a gentle heat .... '

Pigment green (PG)

In art materials terms green exists as a pigment in its own right, identified on products as PG (pigment green). For example, you will come across PG7 Phthalo Green, PG8 Naphthol Green, and PG18 Viridian as single pigments. Conversely, several greens on offer are made of combinations of pigments and contain yellow, blue and white (see page 70).

Naming greens

Green is the largest colour family discernible to the human eye. Prior to the standardization of pigment nomenclature many names were used to describe hues of green. Some of the following names are still in current use, while many have now disappeared:

Almond Green	Leaf Green
Apple Green	Leek Green
Arnaudon's Green	Lily Green
Avocado Green	Mineral Green
Bottle Green	Mittler's Green
Brunswick Green	Moss Green
Casali's Green	Mountain Green
Celadon Green	Munich Green
Chartreuse	Myrtle Green
Chlorophyll	Nitrate Green
Chrome Green	Pansy Green
Cinnabar	Paris Green
Cobalt Green	Plessy's Green
Copper Green	Prussian Green
Dingler's Green	Scheele's Green
Emerald Green	Schnitzer's Green
Evergreen	Schweinfurt Green
Hungarian Green	Verdigris
Jade Green	Vienna Green
Kelly Green	Woodland Green

Verdigris

Verdigris (from the French meaning 'green of Greece') is a blue-green pigment made by scraping the patina from copper that has been exposed to vinegar or wine. It is the most well known of the early artificially prepared green copper pigments. Its production originated in wine-growing areas and it was made by alternately stacking copper sheets and grape husks. A crust would form on the surface of the copper sheets and, when scraped off, the scrapings were pulverized to produce a light blue powder sold as verdigris. Verdigris is not seen nowadays as an artists' pigment, but *Vert antique* is a decorative finish used for bronzing plaster casts and other surfaces to simulate the natural green patina of old bronze or copper.

Vegetable greens

Green pigments were extracted from flower petals in the seventeenth century and lake colours with names such as Pansy Green, Lily Green, Iris and Honeysuckle were created. Sap Green, a name still in use to describe a bright leafy colour, was made from ripe buckthorn *(Rhamnus)* berries and is mentioned frequently from the twelfth century. In the eighteenth century Sap Green became popular for use in watercolour. It was also termed Bladder Green because it was often stored in bladders.

Sap Green
Today the vegetable ingredient of Sap Green is replaced by modern arylide, phthalocyanine or naphthol pigments.

Chromium Green

This is a dull greyish green derived from chromates or chromium, which was discovered by Nicolas Vauquelin in 1797 in a mineral known as Siberian red lead, later known as chrocoite. Many coloured compounds including Chrome Red and Chrome Yellow were derived from chromium (see Chrome Yellow page 64). Of chromium oxide greens, Vauquelin wrote:

'On account of the beautiful emerald colour it communicates, ... will furnish painters ... with the means of enriching their pictures, and of improving their art.'

Chromium oxide green
Green pigments that owe their colour to chromium have been used widely since the nineteenth century. Chromium oxide green was listed by Winsor & Newton in the 1840s, and the pigment is widely available today. Identified as PG17, the chromium oxide greens are well known for their opacity or 'hiding power', and their great tinting strength. In mixtures with white, yellow or blue, brilliance can be substantially increased.

Cinnabar

Cinnabar is a shade of green or yellow, widely available in makers' catalogues. It is made of a combination of modern green and yellow pigments. In the nineteenth century a variety of chrome green, also called Zinnober Green, or Royal Green, was made by mixing Prussian Blue and Chrome Yellow.

Emerald Green

Emerald Green generally has a bright, bluish green colour and was one of the most brilliant of the inorganic colours. Popular among the French Impressionist and Post-Impressionist painters, it has been identified in many of their works. Original Emerald Green contains both copper and arsenic, and is also known as Paris, Munich or Vienna Green, and Schweinfurt Green. The improved pigment was brighter, more durable and had a more intense colour than other copper greens. Winsor & Newton introduced Emerald Green in their watercolours and oil colours in their first catalogue in 1832. Paul Gauguin, writing in February 1897 to George Daniel de Monfreid, requested 20 tubes of Emerald Green along with other colours.

The colour was used in the decorative arts for colouring wallpapers, cloth lampshades and linoleum, for decorating domestic furniture and fabrics, and as a component of paint for toys. It was also used as an exterior and interior house paint. One of Emerald Green's main applications was as an insecticide and fungicide and it was still being marketed in the 1950s, despite its toxicity, because of its bright tone and lightfastness.

Winsor & Newton discontinued the original copper-arsenic Emerald Green in the 1960s, replacing it with Winsor Emerald, a mixture of azo yellow and phthalocyanine green. Most manufacturers have followed this initiative.

Hooker's Green

William Hooker painted pottery and may be the source of this name. Hooker's Green is a mid green with a blackish undertone. Originally a mixture of Gamboge and Prussian Blue and considered an unreliable pigment, it is now based on more modern pigments such as Phthalo Green and Cadmium Yellow.

Olive Green

This is a dull brownish yellow-green, often derived from Raw Sienna, offered by several manufacturers. A similar colour may be mixed by the artist by toning down a bright leaf green with a little orange.

Modern greens

A vast number of green hues are available in manufacturers' catalogues and one of the main ingredients used is Phthalo Green, even though some original pigment names are still incorporated as a description on the tube. This modern organic pigment, introduced in 1938, was a product of artificial dyestuffs. The pigment is from brominated or chlorinated copper phthalocyanine. Its colour is similar to the bright, traditional Emerald Greens, which contained copper and arsenic.

Phthalo-based greens

Phthalo Green (PG7 and PG36) has excellent lightfast qualities and high permanence in all media and is produced by most manufacturers under the name Phthalo Green and a variety of trade name variations.

Other very widely used greens, all of which rely on Phthalo but have a modern yellow pigment added, are the bright mid greens named Permanent, Cadmium, Emerald, Yellowish, Chrome, Cinnabar, and the blackish blue-green, Hooker's.

Sap Green, a bright leafy colour produced since the Middle Ages, originally from unripe buckthorn berries, is now synthesized from Phthalo or Naphthol Green.

Even the popular Viridian Green is today often made from Phthalo. Olive Green, originally made from fugitive lakes, uses Phthalo Green pigment as a base, mixed with a variety of red, yellow, orange, blue or violet.

Exceptions

Exceptions to the extensive Phthalo usage is the greyish green Chromium Oxide, consistently made from its oxide of chromium pigment, compared to Chrome Green made from Prussian Blue and Chrome Yellow. Cobalt Green, a bluish version of Emerald, is made from a cobalt oxide and Green Earth (Terre Verte or Green Umber), a blue-grey green, which usually consists of the natural inorganic pigment (see Green Earth page 67).

Prepared greens

You will see various names in colour charts. Some of them are single pigments and others are combinations of pigments. The list (right) gives an average guide to formulations, which will vary from manufacturer to manufacturer.

(From top to bottom, left to right)

Cadmium Green	(PG18 or PG7 + PY35/PY37)
Chromium Oxide Green	(PG17)
Cinnabar	(PG7 or PG36 or PG18 + PY1/3/35/42)
Cobalt Green	(PG19 sometimes PG26 or PG50)
Emerald Green	(PG7 or PG36 + PY1/3/97/154)
Hooker's Green	(PG7 or PG36 + PY3 or PY42)
Olive Green	(PG7 + PY42/PR101/PBr7)
Permanent Green	(PG7 +PY1/3/35/128)
Phthalo Green	(PG7 or PG36)
Sap Green	(PG7 or PG8 or PG36 + PY1/42/73/83)
Viridian Green	(PG18 or PG7)
Yellowish Green	(PG7 or PG36 + PY3/74/154)

Viridian

A transparent variety of chromium oxide, now known as Viridian, was created in Paris in 1838. Viridian is a stable, very dark, deep pure green. As a glaze or wash this pigment appears as a vivid emerald colour with a slight blue undertone. When applied thickly it takes on a duller blackish green appearance. The pigment is popular with artists because of its excellent tinting strength and stability in all mediums. It is invaluable not only for use as a green, but also for cooling reds, pinks and browns. Portrait and life painters find Viridian a useful colour in flesh tints. When mixed with Mars or Cadmium Yellow this colour produces a rich scale of brilliant greens.

Experiment with green

The little canvas example below shows how the range of ready-made greens is increased by simply adding white to create a tint.

(From top to bottom, left to right)

Cobalt Green Deep (Winsor & Newton)
Phthalo Green Yellow Shade (Golden)
Phthalo Green Blue Shade (Golden)
Viridian (Lukas)
Emerald Green (Winsor & Newton)
Hooker's Green Hue (Liquitex)
Bohemian Green Earth (Lukas)
Permanent Green Light (Tri-Art)
Chrome Oxide Green (Golden)
Sap Green (Lukas)
Olive Green (Rowney)
Permanent Green (Winsor & Newton)

'Why do two colours, put one next to the other, sing? Can one really explain this? No. Just as one can never learn how to paint.'

Pablo Picasso (1881–1973)

Green sketch

Ready-made acrylics were used to create this green sketch – light leaf green for the hills, pale olive for the mid ground, opaque oxide of chrome for the foreground, and finally a light green again. The details are Viridian.

Complementary opposites

Green is a secondary colour, and the opposite to red. This complementary colour combination has contributed to the vibrant energy in the design of many paintings.

'I tried to express through red and green the terrible passions of humanity.'
Van Gogh on his painting *The Night Café*

Vincent van Gogh (1853–90)
The Night Café, 1888
Oil on canvas (detail)
70 x 89cm (27½ x 35in)
Yale University Art Gallery

Mixing greens

Many ready-made greens are very clean and bright and are difficult to replicate. However, at its simplest, green is a combination of blue and yellow, and many manufacturers recommend the best blues and yellows to buy for the purest mixtures. Experimentation with different types and proportions of blue and yellow can lead to interesting results.

> *'Give me mud and I will paint you the skin of Venus.'*
> EUGENE DELACROIX (1798–1863)

☛ See also

Pigments in history 12–15

CI International 18–19

Yellow Ochre 66

Green Earth 67

Colours for free 144–145

☛ *Colour Index* 172–175

Yellow Ochres–Raw Siennas 172

Brown Ochres–Red Oxides 173

English Reds–Burnt Siennas 174

Brown Madder–Neutral 175

Raw and Burnt Sienna, Raw and Burnt Umber, the red-brown oxide colours such as Venetian and Indian Red, and Yellow Ochre, Red Ochre and Terre Verte (Green Earth) are all earth colours. They are some of the oldest pigments known to man. Burnt Sienna is produced by roasting the raw pigment, named after the Italian city near which it was first found, and Burnt Umber is made in a similar way. Earth pigments come from clay and other substances in the ground. Cennino Cennini described the wonder of seeing these colours of the earth:

'And upon reaching a little valley, a very wild steep place, scraping the steep with a spade, I beheld seams of many kinds of colour: ochre, dark and light sinoper, blue, and white; and this I held the greatest wonder in the world – that white could exist in a seam of earth … And these colours showed up in this earth just the way a wrinkle shows in the face of a man or woman.'

Earth pigments

These very ancient rich mineral sources produce yellow, red, brown and green pigments, depending on the natural iron-oxide colouring agent in the deposits. They were used in prehistoric cave paintings and are probably the most permanent colours available as they are little affected by atmospheric conditions. The minerals are dug from the earth, washed and then ground to produce the pigments.

Ancient earth pigments
It is thought that oxides of iron were dug right out of the ground in the form of lumps that were rich in clay, and that the blacks were derived from manganese ores, charcoal and ashes. The raw pigments were then ground with various fluids such as blood, urine, animal fat, saliva and bone marrow to make a paintlike paste.

Red Ochre and iron oxides

These natural pigments range in colour from dull yellow (see page 66) to red and brown. Ochres and oxides in art have a long history.

Red Ochre is a warm red-brown earth colour and is based on deposits of hematite (see opposite). Traditonally, Spain and the Persian Gulf were excellent sources of this iron oxide and the large variety of names used for the colour relate to its original source locations. Red Ochre can also be produced from calcined (roasted) Yellow Ochre. The colour was used in medieval times for fresco and oil-painting grounds because of its quick drying time and low oil-absorption qualities.

Some other reddish ochre hues are:

English Red	Pozzuoli Red
Indian Red	Red Oxide
Light Red	Sinopia
Mars Orange	Spanish Red
Mars Red	Terra Rosa
Persian Red	Turkey Red
Pompeiian Red	Venetian Red

Brown Ochre

Brown Ochre is another reddish brown, but the name is not used as much as the other ochres. The natural iron-oxide pigment is PBr7 and it is widely used today in the manufacture of siennas and umbers. In seventeenth-century England this colour was sometimes described as Spanish Brown. It was prepared by heating Red Ochre, the name relating to its similarity to the natural Red Ochre from Spain. However, there are references to Spanish Brown as a synonym for Vandyke Brown. Mars Brown (PBr6) is the modern synthetic version.

Spanish Brown

In the frequent mentions of Brown Ochre under this name is the charge that it was coarse and gritty. The best ochres traditionally come from France, and range from light yellow to deep red.

Iron Ores
and reddish browns

Iron oxide is a principal colouring agent derived from four main types of iron ore: hematite, limonite, magnetite, and siderite.

Hematite

Most iron oxides come from hematite and limonite ores. Hematite is a name derived from the Greek *hema* (meaning 'blood'). Hematite means 'bloodlike' and refers to natural red earth. A hard, compact and pure natural variety of anhydrous ferric oxide is used in the production of dark red pigments.

Sinopia

This is the old Latin name for natural red earth pigment. More particularly, it is an obsolete name for the red iron-oxide pigment derived from Sinope, the Turkish town on the Black Sea, where it is mined. This was an important classical source of red oxide (see also Renaissance skin tones page 112). In the fifteenth century Cennini recorded 'a natural colour known as sinoper', which when mixed with lime white was 'very perfect for doing flesh, or making flesh colours of figures on a wall.' The colour was often used for the underdrawing on plaster in mural painting and the drawing itself was called the 'sinopia'.

Browns are generally considered to be drab colours, but this is clearly untrue when viewing the variety of brownish hues and earth pigments on offer. Their documented usage from prehistoric times to the present day indicates the reliability and popularity of these easily obtainable and permanent colours.

'I cannot pretend to feel impartial about colours. I rejoice with the brilliant ones, and am genuinely sorry for the poor browns.'

WINSTON S. CHURCHILL
THOUGHTS AND ADVENTURES (1932)

Sir Anthony van Dyck (1599–1641)

Mars colours

Mars colours are artificial iron oxides. Used as substitutes for natural earth pigments, they are often more brilliant and opaque with higher tinting strengths. Like the natural oxides they are highly permanent. Mars Brown is a mid-chocolate shade, generally made from pigments PR101 and black. Mars Violet contains synthetic red oxide (PR101) and is a chocolate purple-brown, also known as Caput Mortuum and Violet Oxide (see page 55). Mars Black is a dense neutral black (see pages 77–78).

The descriptive 'Mars' may have originated from the name given by alchemists for iron or to the yellow ochre-coloured pigment formed through oxidization of iron in air, *crocus martis*, of which the literal translation is simply Mars Yellow.

Other frequently seen colours bearing the prefix are: Mars Yellow, similar to Yellow Ochre; Mars Orange, a cross between Red and Yellow Ochre; and Mars Red, similar to the red ochres, which can range from scarlet to maroon.

Synthetic oxides

Natural iron-oxide pigments are still in use today and are considered among the most permanent colours available. Most are not affected by atmospheric conditions and most of the pigments are non-hazardous. Iron-oxide paints resist corrosion and the distinctive red-brown hue is commonly seen as a basecoat protection on raw steel. Since the eighteenth century a synthetic product, Mars Red (PR101), has been used as a substitute for the natural red earth pigments as it has similar properties of durability and permanence. Most red oxides today are made from the synthetic pigment.

☛ **See also**

Colour Index 172–175	
Yellow Ochres–Raw Siennas	172
Brown Ochres–Red Oxides	173
English Reds–Burnt Siennas	174
Brown Madder–Neutral	175

Vandyke Brown

This brown ranges from pale to black in colour. Its original composition was of humus or vegetable earth ingredients in the form of peat or lignite, plus iron. The colour was popular with Flemish painters such as Rubens, Rembrandt and van Dyck, after whom it is named. It is also known as Kassel Earth, from the place in Germany where the natural ingredients were found. In its original formulation the pigment is not permanent and it fades. Owing to its transparency artists found it useful for shading and wood staining. Vandyke Brown is often substituted by Umber. The natural pigment bituminous earth (NBr8) is still available and used. However, most modern ingredients for this colour consist of synthetic red oxide (PR101) or natural iron oxide (PBr7) plus black. Other names are Cassel Earth, Cologne Earth, and sometimes Ruben's Brown, although this name is seen in association with Brown Madder too.

Sepia

This organic pigment originates from the ink-sacs of cuttlefish *(Sepia officinalis)*, found in the Adriatic Sea. It is reputed to have been used by the Romans as an ink, but its popularity was marked after 1780 by its introduction by Prof. Jacob C. Seydelmann in Dresden. It was used mainly as a watercolour or ink. Today's colours named Sepia are synthesized using black, brown or red oxide pigments.

Brown Madder
A brownish orange colour, originally derived from madder (see page 58), this was also known as Ruben's Madder. Now based on Alizarin Crimson (PR83), it is a transparent permanent lake, and current formulations may contain red, brown, yellow and green pigments.

Raw Sienna
An orange-brown colour, produced from a natural yellow-brown earth oxide. The natural clays contain iron and manganese, the finest variety of earth, and were originally mined near Siena in Tuscany, Italy. The deposits are now depleted and the source of the pigment has been superseded by other regions in Italy, particularly Sardinia and Sicily. Raw Sienna is one of the most permanent pigments. Current manufacturers of the colour often use synthetic yellow (PY42) or red oxides (PR101). Some producers still employ natural oxides, also known as Italian Earth and Terra di Siena.

Burnt Sienna
A warm red-brown, produced by calcining (roasting) Raw Sienna, this is an extremely permanent pigment, clean and transparent. Because of its lack of chalkiness, it is perfect for mixtures of dark colours. Like Raw Sienna, modern production uses either synthetic red oxide (PR101) or the natural iron oxide (PBr7).

Raw Umber
A greenish brown earth colour, Raw Umber is obtained from oxides containing iron and manganese. The name is thought to originate from the Latin *umbra* (meaning 'shadow'), as the pigment was often used for shadows and shading other colours. It is a highly permanent, transparent and lightfast pigment. Records indicate its use since the 1600s. Most modern umbers consist of natural oxide (PBr7), but some use a mix of synthetic oxides (PY42 and PR101). Also known as Cyprus Umber, Turkey Brown and Sicilian Brown.

Burnt Umber
Produced by calcining Raw Umber, this is a darker reddish brown with similar properties to Raw Umber, but more transparent. Current pigments mainly use natural iron oxide (PBr7), although combinations of synthetic oxides (PY42 and PR101) and black are also manufactured. Old names for Burnt Umber include Chestnut Brown, Euchrome and Jacaranta Brown.

Mummy Brown
A brown pigment made from asphaltum used for embalming, this was originally obtained from Egyptian tombs. Its recorded usage as an art colour was from the 1800s until the 1920s.

Asphaltum
Also called Bitumen (see page 83), this ancient blackish brown colour, composed of modified organic matter, is not a true pigment. It is made from asphalt, a natural resin often sourced from Trinidad or the Dead Sea, which is dissolved in oil or turpentine. It was popular with van Dyck, and because of its instability it was used thinly. It dries badly, cracks and wrinkles. Since the nineteenth century it has been replaced with synthetic coal-tar dyestuffs, and today's asphaltum uses combinations of modern yellow, red, green, violet and black. However, a natural black exists, NBk6 (trade name Gilsonite), and is still available as an oil paint.

Bistre
This is a yellowish brown pigment made from boiling the soot produced through burning beechwood. It was used from the fourteenth to the nineteenth centuries in watercolour or in tonal wash drawings. It is now replaced with Burnt or Raw Umber.

Pozzuoli Earth
A native red earth pigment from Pozzuoli near Naples, this is the traditional brown-red used in the frescos of the Italian Renaissance. The colour produces a clean, bright reddish hue and it is renowned for its unique property of setting as hard as cement. Some makers still offer a synthetic red oxide pigment that bears the name Pozzuoli Earth or Pozzuoli Red, and there are many similar hues available too, such as Terra Rosa and Venetian Red.

'White may be said to represent light, Without which no colour can be seen; yellow the earth; green, water; blue, air; red, fire; and black, – black is for total darkness.'

LEONARDO DA VINCI
(1452–1519)

It is often said that black is unnecessary in an artist's palette as it hardly ever appears at its purest in nature – perhaps black velvet seen on a dull day is the nearest there is. So, is black a colour that could easily be disposed of and omitted from the artist's palette? It is common knowledge that you can readily mix successful deep, solid blacks from the primary colours, and from many of the secondaries too. You can also use these mixtures to darken other colours and tint whites as required.

☛ **See also**

CI International 18–19	
Experimenting with blacks 78	
Variations in blacks 80	
Tinting and shading 81	
Mixing blacks 82	
Working without black 104	
Colour Index/Black 176	

Technically speaking, neither black nor white has any colour. However, for the purposes of this book we shall describe black and white as colours.

Defining black
'Of the colour of jet or carbon, having no hue due to the absorption of nearly all the incident light. Without light, completely dark.'
COLLINS ENGLISH DICTIONARY

Black as a tinting colour
Creates a multitude of grey tints.

Making black
It is easy to mix black in all media, particularly from the primaries.

Dominator
Black can easily overpower and deaden colours.

Respect black
Black in its own right, however, is a useful and convenient colour, ideal for fluid, spontaneous brush drawing and for attaining a tremendous range of grey tints when mixed with white. It is a colour worth getting to know and has a rightful place in every studio, but its strength and power should never be underestimated. Respect black and handle it with caution.

Black as a darkener
Creates a multitude of shades.

Naming blacks
You will come across many descriptive names for types of black in books on art and in makers' catalogues and colour charts. Several of the names are old fashioned and may refer to obsolete brands or original, naturally occurring pigment sources that are now manufactured synthetically. Other names are manufacturers' descriptive brand names, often giving different names to what is essentially the same product. Some of the names you may see are:

Animal Black
Black Lake
Blue Black
Bone Black
Carbon Black
Coke Black
Deep Black
Drop Black
Elephant Black
Flame Black
Grape Black
Iron-oxide Black
Ivory Black
Jet Black
Kernel Black
Lamp Black
Magnetic Black
Marc Black
Mars Black
Mineral Black
Mummy Black
Oil Black
Oxide Black
Paris Black
Process Black
Velvet Black
Vine Black

Black pigment disclosure
These are the references for black pigments, the colouring ingredient of black paint. You will see these in small print on tubes and packaging. Note that the product name, more often than not, is different from the name of the pigment that constitutes the product.

Aniline Black, **PBk1** (50440)	
Bone Black, **PBk9** (77267)	
*Carbon Black, **PBk6/PBk7** (77266)	
Synthetic Iron Oxide, **PBk11** (77499)	

*Note: some listings show Carbon Black as either PBk6 or PBk7

Taken at face value black is black, and all blacks look the same. Once you are familiar with the different blacks, however, their subtle and individual characters become evident.

A variety of blacks is offered across the media ranges in oil, watercolour, gouache, acrylic, pastel, etc. When you look in manufacturers' catalogues and at their colour charts you will

see many of the descriptive names seen opposite, particularly in cheaper student and craft colour ranges.

Among the quality blacks are Ivory, Lamp, Vine and Mars Black, and Payne's Grey, or very close relatives to them. These five are generally the most popular. They are offered by most of the major art materials' manufacturers and are widely available in most painting media.

Ivory Black
This is Bone Black sold under the name Ivory Black. As its name suggests, Ivory Black was originally obtained by roasting elephant tusks, a process that produced a pure and intense pigment. Happily, this practice no longer exists, but that is why Ivory Black is also sometimes known as Elephant Black. At its simplest, Ivory Black is a pigment derived from charred bones. Its predecessors were known as Bone Black and Animal Black and were often impure and unreliable in paint. A finer grade of Bone Black was later developed and manufactured under the name of Ivory Black. It is an intense black pigment, being permanent and stable. Ivory Black has a brown undertone compared to the bluish Lamp Black. In tints with white it tends to produce warmish greys.

Mars Black
Mars is originally a trade name that has been adopted to prefix earth-colour pigments derived from the mineral iron oxide; Mars was the alchemical name for iron. Among these colours is Mars Black, which is dense and heavy, a pigment that behaves well in oils, but is often recommended as being most desirable for use in watercolour and other water-based media.

Vine Black
Originally made by roasting vine stalks and other vegetable matter at high temperatures (calcining), Vine Black was considered a lower quality pigment to Lamp Black due to its inferior intensity. It was also found to be unreliable for fresco painting where the vegetable content of the pigment would react badly with the minerals of the plaster. Vine Blacks have a bluish undertone and when mixed with whites produce cool-grey tints. Vine Blacks offered today are composites of black and blue pigments. Grape Black and Kernel Black are among the old-fashioned names for this type of black pigment.

Payne's Grey
Among the blacks in artists' colour charts you will nearly always see this colour listed. Payne's Grey is not a pure black but a composite pigment containing more than one basic ingredient, commonly Ultramarine Blue (sodium polysulphide aluminosilicate) and Mars Black (synthetic iron oxide), and sometimes crimson pigments are included too. It is considered useful by watercolourists as it thins well and is good for glazes. In the opaque media – oil and acrylic – it mixes well with white to produce a range of cool, blue-shade greys. Many purists find such a composite unnecessary. However, it is popular in most media and is offered for sale in nearly all of the manufacturers' catalogues. Payne's Grey is named after William Payne (1760–1830), a British watercolourist, active in Devon and the Lake District.

How to make lamp black

'... there is a perfect black which is made in this manner: take a lamp full of linseed oil ... and light the lamp. Then put it, so lighted, under a clean baking dish ... and the smoke which comes out of the flame will strike the bottom of the dish and condense. Sweep this colour that is the soot into some dish for it is a very fine colour, and make as much of it in this way as you need.'

'Grind this black for half an hour or an hour, or as much as you please; but know that if you were to grind it for a year it would be blacker and better ...'

CENNINO CENNINI
THE CRAFTSMAN'S HANDBOOK
(FIFTEENTH CENTURY)

Lamp Black
This carbon pigment is made from burning oils and collecting the residual soot. Lamp Black is one of the oldest manufactured pigments. It is not quite a pure black, having a slightly bluish colour that is more evident when seen in tints. Lamp Black produces good neutral greys veering slightly to the cool, blue side. Oil Black and Flame Black are old-fashioned names for earlier and often impure varieties of Lamp Black.

There are subtle differences between the various blacks when spread thinly as undertone. You can begin to discern greater differences when the colours are diluted with medium. The differences become even more apparent when mixed with white in tints. The blacks begin to behave differently again when mixed with other colours to produce tints and shades.

Top tone

Undertone

+ Medium

+ Titanium White

Colour observations

Tests were made using random blacks taken from the paint-storage box. The medium used for these illustrations was oil paint. You will find that the properties of the various blacks will vary from maker to maker and behave differently, depending on whether the vehicle is oil, water or acrylic.

☛**See also**

CI International 18–19

Variations in blacks 80

Mixing blacks 82

Shop-bought darks 83

Working without black 104

Colour Index/Black 176

Ivory Black
A dense black, slightly brown in undertone, produced warm glazes and tints. Widely available in oil paint, composed of PBk9. *(Sample: Winsor & Newton, Artists' Oil, PBk9)*

Vine Black
Traditionaly considered inferior in intensity to Lamp Blacks. Vine Blacks have a bluish undertone and when mixed with whites produce cool, bluish grey tints. Vine Black is often a composite of Ivory Black PBk9, Carbon Black PBk7 and Ultramarine PB29 and is commonly available in oil paint. *(Sample: Lukas, Series 1, Artists' Oil, PBk9)*

Lamp Black
A very dense opaque black that produces neutral greys in tint. *(Sample: Daler-Rowney, Artists' Oil, PBk7)*

Mars Black
Dense, neutral, veering towards cool grey in tints. Widely available in acrylic and composed of PBk11. *(Sample: Old Holland, Classic Artists' Oil, PBk9)*

Payne's Grey
A composite colour commonly made of Lamp Black PBk6, Ultramarine PB29 and powdered slate PBk19. A cool-shade black, producing cool, blue-greys. Ingredients of Payne's Grey vary from manufacturer to manufacturer. (See also Blue Black in some ranges.) *(Sample: Schmincke, Mussini, Resin Oil, PBk7, PB29, PR101)*

Pure black

The most famous black in the history of modern art is *Black Suprematist Square* (1914–15) by the Russian artist Kasimir Malevich (1878–1935). This is among the first absolutely abstract paintings, as it seems to refer to nothing but itself. Histories of twentieth-century art attach much importance to this work. *Black Suprematist Square* is a painting that works on the imagination of the viewer, prompting reflection, and is wide open to interpretation. It is a simple black square painted on a white ground. The irony is that over the years this all-black canvas has become cracked and crazed and this seemingly blank image continues to change before our eyes.

Kasimir Malevich (1878–1935)
Black Suprematist Square, 1914–15
Oil on canvas 79 x 79cm (31 x 31in)
Tretyakov, Moscow

Chiaroscuro

There are many examples of paintings dominated by the blacks, and in these paintings the colourless aspects contribute to the visual theme.

This style of painting is known as chiaroscuro – the contrast of dark against light. Rembrandt (1606–69) and Caravaggio (1573–1610) were masters of chiaroscuro and they used it in their paintings with great effect to heighten the tension and drama of both the subject and composition.

Rembrandt (1606–69)
Self-portrait aged 34
Oil on canvas 102 x 80cm (40 x 31½ in)
National Gallery, London

Absence of light and colour

American artist Ad Reinhardt (1913–67) produced a series of black paintings during the 1950s and 1960s. At first sight his canvases look completely black, demonstrating a total absence of light and colour.

On closer inspection, however, you can see a geometric composition of the most minimal variations of blackness, which are almost invisible to the spectator and certainly unreproducible here in a printed form. Reinhardt's black paintings can be seen in many collections around the world.

After Ad Reinhardt
Abstract Painting No. 5, 1962
Oil on canvas
152.4 x 152.4cm (60 x 60in)
Tate Modern, London

Comparing makes

Within the same price and quality range colours of the same name can vary in hue, pigment composition and behaviour from maker to maker. For example, some pigments may be more finely ground and may be less likely to granulate than others, some may be more intense and have stronger staining power, while others may be more transparent. There are general guidelines and standards relating to the behaviour of and expectation from the various kinds of blacks. The watercolour chart (right) shows that similarly named colours vary depending on the manufacturer. We have included Payne's Grey, Blue Black and Neutral Tint among the blacks here.

(From left to right, top to bottom)

Payne's Grey
Schmincke, PB29/PBk7

Payne's Grey Bluish
Schmincke, PB6/PB15/PBk6

Payne's Gray
Winsor & Newton, PB6/PB15/PBk6

Payne's Grey
Lukas, PB15/PBk7/PR17

Payne's Grey
Daler-Rowney, PB29/PBk7

Blue Black
Winsor & Newton, PBk6

Blue Black
Schmincke, PBk6

Ivory Black
Daler-Rowney, PBk9

Ivory Black
Lukas, PBk7

Ivory Black Extra
Old Holland, PBk7

Ivory Black
Schmincke, PBk9

Mars Black
Old Holland, PBk11

Ivory Black
Maimeri, PBk9

Ivory Black
Winsor & Newton, PBk9

Lamp Black
Winsor & Newton, PBk6/7

Lamp Black
Daler-Rowney, PBk7

Carbon Black
Maimeri, PBk7

Scheveningen Intense Black
Old Holland, PBk7/PBk11

Vine Black
Old Holland, PBk8

Neutral Tint
Lukas, PY83/PR122/PB15:1/PG7

Neutral Tint
Maimeri, PB29/PBk7

Neutral Tint
Winsor & Newton, PBk6/PB15/PV19

Payne's Grey

Nearly always listed with the blacks it is a composite pigment available in most media. The colour varies from maker to maker.

Experiment with the tremendous range of tints and shades to be obtained by mixing blacks with whites and other colours.

Tinting

Variation in the grey tints you achieve will be dictated by the choice of the type of black and white, and, of course, the medium (watercolour, acrylic, gouache, oil). You will notice how some blacks make warm brownish greys and others cool bluish greys, and how some are quite neutral.

Grey scale

A simple grey scale (above right) may be made using Ivory Black and opaque white gouache colours. A grey scale is a traditional basic teaching device. Its aim is threefold: to familiarize the student with handling materials, colour mixing and tonal values.

Shading

Experiment by mixing blacks with other colours, but be careful! Black used as a darkening ingredient in colour mixes can easily overpower and readily obliterate other colours.

Tone scale

A tone scale (right) also helps to familiarize students with colour mixing and handling. Here Lemon Yellow and Carbon Black acrylic paints have been used.

Coal tar

No article on the colour black would be well balanced without mentioning the importance of coal tar. Coal tar is a heavy, sticky, black liquid, a by-product of many industrial processes, particularly the manufacture of gas. It was considered to be fairly useless until a major discovery in the middle of the nineteenth century.

In 1856 industrial chemist William Perkin (1838–1907) announced the discovery of 'mauve', the first artificial colour to be derived from coal tar. This colour took the world by storm and became the height of Victorian fashion. Fifty years later there were two thousand artificial colours, known as aniline pigments, all stemming from Perkin's original experiments with coal tar.

'Coal-Tar Wizard Transmuted Dross To Gold'
HEADLINE, *NEW YORK HERALD*, AUTUMN 1906

The headline above, published on Perkin's arrival in New York to receive a professional medal of honour, testifies to the significance of his discovery and the lasting impact it made on the production of synthetic organic pigments.

Synthetic organic pigments were originally derived from coal tar.

Since black is regarded by artists as a fairly straightforward colour to mix, this leads to the question, 'Do I really need to spend good money on black paint?'

When used in combination with other colours on your palette the answer is probably no, and many artists make do without it. One criticism levelled at the ready-made pure blacks is that they tend to dominate the palette and deaden other colours when used in mixes.

Process Magenta

Cyan Blue

Cadmium Red Medium

Ultramarine Blue

Cadmium Red

Phthalocyanine Blue

Alizarin Crimson

Viridian

Black-mix combinations

You can make successful darks and replacement colours for black by mixing combinations of any of the above colours. The darker hues such as Alizarin Crimson and Viridian give the blackest results. When spread thinly as undertone, as seen in the right-hand column of the chart, the character of the mixing colours is revealed. If you add a dark earth colour such as Burnt Sienna or Burnt Umber the mixes can become even darker.

Intense darks

Add Burnt Sienna or Burnt Umber to the above combinations for even more intense dark mixtures.

London colours

Much London painting of the post-war years was tonal and subtle in colour, maybe even sombre. Many paintings from this period (1945–60) convey the austerity of the times and an atmosphere of discoloration caused by the widespread burning of coal.

British artist Lucian Freud (b. 1922), famous for his nude figure paintings, called his colours 'London colours'. To his whites and light colours he would add a little ground charcoal to create the slightly grubby colours of urban London. Ground charcoal, of course, is a pigment in its own right, identified as PBk8, and is used as an ingredient in paint.

Our Lady of Czestochowa
Painted wood panel
122.2 x 82.2cm (48 x 32½in)
*Monastery of Jasna Góra,
Czestochowa, Poland*

There is much debate as to the origins of this picture. Legend attributes it to the hand of St Luke the Evangelist, who painted it, from life, on a table top used by the Virgin. Evidence suggests that it may date from the fifth or sixth century, with extensive repainting in the fifteenth.

Dark hues
Many manufacturers offer colours similar to those shown below. They are mostly combination pigments made of blacks, blues, browns, greens and violets. The samples here are applied thickly as top tone and the inset colour shows how the colour behaves when a little Titanium White is added.

Nearly black
Along with Payne's Grey, manufacturers offer many serious, dark colours that at first glance could be mistaken for black. Among these are deep viridians and phthalos, violets, greys, neutral tints and burnt earth colours. When applied thickly these dark colours appear nearly black. Add the appropriate diluent (thinner) or medium, however, and the real character of these deep, dark colours becomes apparent.

Unreliable blacks
There are several examples of black-skinned depictions of the Virgin Mary, and some dispute as to why the Virgin Mary's original Caucasian features in these paintings have blackened. In some cases it is put down to the accumulation of centuries of candle smoke or the effects of fire damage. In others it is thought that the picture's underpainting, executed in a dark, blackish brown bitumen pigment known as asphaltum, has migrated to the surface over the years.

Bitumen or Asphaltum
This deep-shade brown, which is almost black in top tone, produces warm, earthy neutral tints when mixed with white. It is still available in oil paint from a number of makers.

Traditional darks
Samples above taken from Old Holland's Classic Oil Colour range.

(From left to right, top to bottom)

Paris (Prussian) Blue Extra
Blue Deep
Olive Green Dark
Neutral Tint
Van Dijk Brown
Sepia Extra

(From top to bottom)

Phthalo Turquoise
Dioxazine Violet
Virdian
Raw Umber

'Forcing yourself to use restricted means is the sort of restraint that liberates invention.'

PABLO PICASSO (1881–1973)

Greys may be produced by mixing black and white in varying proportions, or by mixing complementary colours. Adding red and yellow, or green and blue, produces warm, or cool, greys respectively. In oil painting grey was traditionally obtained by glazing with varnish mixed with a little paint. Greys are also obtained optically by placing small quantities of complementary colours side by side.

Greys in history

There are many descriptions of the specific use of grey in the history of painting.

Veneda

An old fresco, greyish black colour, Veneda was made from lime and a suitable black pigment. The term was also used to describe a mix of white lead and black for tempera on gesso panels or parchment. Veneda was used in medieval illumination.

Grisaille

This French word is used to describe the technique of painting in several shades of a single colour, usually grey, to build up sculptured relief. The technique is specially suited to architectural subjects. The term also describes underpainting in one colour, specifically grey, to produce a detailed monochromatic painting before colouring over with many layers of glaze. The technique was particularly favoured by the Northern Renaissance artists of Flanders and Germany. Grisaille is also a grey pigment used in stained-glass work.

Guazzo

This grey-in-grey tempera painting was employed by the Old Masters as preliminary exercises for oil painting. It is from the Italian *guazzo* that the French word 'gouache' is derived.

Greys are easy to mix and, using reliable pigments, may be more lightfast than some pre-mixed greys. A primary colour mixed with a secondary will provide a wide range of greys and the classic 'palette mud', the remnants of a day's work, provides a good neutral grey that is often reused.

Charcoal Grey

In oils this is ground charcoal. Watercolour is strengthened with carbon black and natural iron oxide. Lightfast, but often gritty. (See London colours page 82.)

Cool and Warm Greys

Used to describe the particular hue bias. Cool Greys are typically of a green or blue hue, while Warm Greys are of a red or yellow hue.

Graphite Grey

This blue-grey is dense and opaque. A soft, blackish form of crystalline carbon, it was first used in the eighteenth century to make lead pencils. It is named from the Greek *grapho* (meaning 'to write').

Payne's Grey

A blue-grey made from crimson, blue and black or ultramarine, ochre and black, the colour is lightfast and inert, but rather coarse. It is thought to have been named from William Payne (1760–1830), a British watercolourist.

Davy's Grey

Originally based on a special variety of powdered slate that tended to be gritty, this is a dull, yellowish grey. The colour is now strengthened and is based on a variety of ingredients – greens, browns, blacks, yellows and whites – but its lightfastness is still not always reliable. Davy's Grey is excellent for toning down mixes. The name was first suggested by Mr Henry Davy in the 1890s.

Naming grey

Greys may bear a descriptive name that gives an indication of their distinguishable hue or bias. There are also several Neutral Greys that are described as achromatic, having no distinguishable hue. These Neutral Greys are often identified by a numbering system – for example, Neutral Grey 1, Neutral Gray 2 etc. – which indicates the shade.

Bluish Grey
Brownish Grey
Charcoal Grey
Cold Grey
Cool Grey
Davy's Grey
Deep Grey
Dove Grey
Graphite Grey
Greenish Grey
Light Grey
Medium Grey

Mouse Grey
Neutral Grey
Olive Grey
Payne's Grey
Pebble Grey
Purplish Blue Grey
Reddish Brown Grey
Shade Grey
Shell Grey
Warm Grey
Yellow-Green Grey

☞ See also

Black 76–83	
Tinting and shading 81	
White 86–87	
Subdued colours 102	
Travelling colour 146	
Colour Index 176–177	

Prepared greys

Manufacturers offer several prepared greys. Many are simply composed of two pigments – black (PB) and white (PW), for example. Others are quite complex blends of many pigments.

(From top to bottom, left to right)
Davy's Gray (Winsor & Newton)
Graphite Gray (Tri-Art)
Warm Grey (Talens)
Neutral Gray N3 (Golden)
Warm Grey Light (Old Holland)
Cold Grey (Old Holland)
Warm Grey (Lukas)
Middle Grey (Daler-Rowney)
Neutral Gray N5 (Golden)
Neutral Gray N2 (Golden)
Davy's Grey (Old Holland)
Neutral Gray N7 (Golden)

Blended pigments

Makers offer many greys composed of many pigments. A warm grey could typically comprise white (PW4), green (PG36), yellow ochre (PY42), and brown (PBr33). A cooler grey, such as Payne's Grey, often contains three pigments.

Warm Grey   **Cool Grey**

'One of the most difficult problems I have been involved with … is that of warm and cold greys.'
BRIDGET RILEY (b. 1931)

Homage to Grey

'I don't know what I want,' stated Gerhard Richter, a German painter born in 1932. Richter grew up in Germany under the ideology of the Nazis, then in East Germany under the Communists and has subsequently expressed his resistance to any ideology. He was attracted to the inconspicuous neutrality of the colour grey and in the 1970s made a series of flat, grey paintings to express his feelings.

White lead stacking
The Dutch developed the modern stack process for making white, hence the name Dutch White (PW1). Lead white has been made by the stacking process since Egyptian times. White pigment was made by placing strips of lead in clay pots with a separate compartment that contained vinegar. The pots were packed tightly together on shelves and interspersed with animal dung to accelerate the chemical process, then sealed in a small outbuilding. A fermentation process took place over about three months, producing carbonate of lead, or lead white pigment. This method of manufacture only ceased in the 1960s.

☛**See also**

Choosing mediums 36–37

Tinting 81

Metallic & special-effect colours 88

Colour Index/White 179

If black is thought to be unnecessary in an artist's palette, then white is the opposite. It is indispensable to media such as oils, acrylics and gouache. A unique and unmixable colour, it provides the strongest expression of light on the palette. In watercolour the white of the paper performs the function of white pigment, but the versatility of white as a functional colour is well known too. Used as a primer, ground or base coat it is the essential foundation colour on which many a painting is built.

The earliest white

White lead is one of the earliest manufactured pigments on record. It was known in ancient China and is common in the earliest periods of European art. It was the only white oil colour available to artists until the mid nineteenth century and, although new white pigments have come along, it is still a popular choice among oil painters. It has many fine and, some say, unique qualities, producing a buttery paint with great opacity and covering power. It is an excellent mixer that gives fine tones and tints. It is very durable and permanent when applied properly following good oil-painting practice. But, it is poisonous if accidentally ingested, and in many cases has been superseded by less hazardous whites.

Flake White

This is the name you will find in manufacturers' catalogues for white lead (basic lead carbonate PW4). It is available as an oil medium only, as it does not work in other media such as acrylics. It is the traditional choice for the oil painter. Flake White is sometimes offered in two consistencies, one being stiffer. It is a comparatively quick-drying, flexible and durable white. It has two major drawbacks – its toxicity (see above) and its tendency to darken if in contact with sulphur, such as may be found in a polluted atmosphere.

Cremnitz White

This is an old-fashioned, high-quality white lead paint made with pure lead carbonate. It is more stringy than Flake White and yellower.

Titanium White

Titanium White is the modern, less hazardous replacement for white lead pigments, particularly for Flake White. It is a fairly slow dryer as an oil paint and popular as a mixing white. The most powerful of the whites, it is dense and opaque, and should be used with caution as it can overpower more transparent colours. In some catalogues it is suffixed Permanent White. It may be considered a neutral to warm mixer, compared to the cooler Zinc White.

Zinc White

In addition to oils you will find this colour listed with the water-soluble media too, particularly gouaches and acrylics. It is a very versatile white, but is less opaque than the other whites. It is an excellent mixer, particularly for glazing and making tints. In oil paint it is a slow dryer and is said to produce a colder, bluer effect when compared to Flake White. It is manufactured as a watercolour under the name Chinese White.

Chinese White

This is a specially prepared Zinc White and is the traditional watercolour white. It was introduced in 1834 by Winsor & Newton and is now available from many manufacturers. Purist watercolour painters shun the use of Chinese White, claiming the integrity of a watercolour painting relies on the transparency of the medium and the technique of reserving white paper for its unique effect.

Mixing White

Some manufacturers offer this colour in their acrylic ranges. It is a good general-purpose white that is excellent for lightening when used in glazes and for the general toning down of colours. It is quite translucent and mixes well to produce good transparent tints.

Iridescent White

This is composed of a Titanium White type pigment that is coated with mica. It has a pearlized appearance when seen neat. Iridescent White produces effective shimmer colours when used in admixture. Used in thin glazes over colour it produces unique effects of light interference. It is available in oil and acrylic media.

Underpainting White

A general-purpose oil-painting white, this white may be used for preparing grounds and for mixing with other colours. It is quick drying and when used alone produces a matt finish. It should be applied to previously sized or primed canvas.

Naming whites

As with blacks (see page 76) you will come across many descriptive names for types of white in books on art and in makers' catalogues and colour charts. Several of the names are old fashioned and may refer to outmoded brands and recipes. Other names are manufacturers' descriptive brand names. These days the naming of whites is fairly consistent across the different brands. However, a white bearing the same name may vary in behaviour and handling from one manufacturer to another. You will almost certainly find that students' quality whites have less pigment and covering power than artists' quality whites.

Baryta White

You may come across this name in old-fashioned or technical publications. The word is derived from barytes, an obsolete term for barium sulphate, which is a heavy, white inert pigment that is the main component of Baryta White.

Bismuth White

Used in the early nineteenth century as a less toxic substitute for white lead, this colour is now superseded by Zinc White.

Blanc Fixe

This is a later development of Baryta White, but made from artificial barium sulphate. Blanc fixe is sometimes used as a base during the manufacture of pigments. The term 'blanc fixe' has largely gone out of general use.

Permanent White

Originally used as an alternative name for blanc fixe, Permanent White is now used to describe the more modern Titanium White. It is also a name that is sometimes seen in school, student, designer and craft paint listings. It is commonly used to indicate opacity and non-yellowing characteristics.

Chinese White

An old-established name used to describe Zinc White. It has been manufactured as a prepared watercolour white since 1834. The name is still used today (see opposite).

Resists

Resists works on the principle that oil and water do not mix, and white areas can be created by this process. For example, a line drawing can be made with a candle or any greasy medium on a white ground. Subsequent areas of water-based colour may be washed over the initial greasy drawing, which remains as white line.

Reserved white

This is the effect of white in watercolour painting, created by leaving passages such as clouds, reflections and highlights as unpainted white paper. Masking fluid may be applied to achieve this.

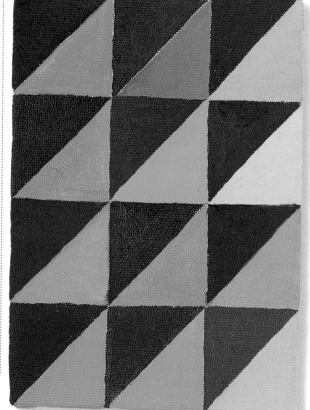

White magic

White can have a magical influence on the darkest and most sombre of hues. By adding white many colours are transformed.

(From top to bottom, left to right)

Indigo (Lukas)
Violet Dioxazine (Tri-Art)
Payne's Grey (Rowney)
Prussian Blue Extra (Old Holland)
Madder Lake Deepest (Lukas)
Van Dyke Brown (Winsor & Newton)
Burnt Umber (Winsor & Newton)
Sepia (Lukas)
Van Dyke Brown (Lukas)
Viridian Hue (Liquitex)
Phthalo Green Blue Shade (Golden)
Green Earth (Sennelier)

Traditionally, artists have achieved the illusion of metal or highly reflective and light-scattering surfaces in their paintings by skilful techniques using a base colour with white highlights and coloured ambient reflections.

Yellow is traditionally used to represent gold and copper. Various greys and blues can be seen for silver, while steel and pewter are treated similarly. Browns and ochres with subtle green glazes are often used for bronze.

The ancient and highly skilled craft of gilding is an important element in painting heraldry and historical decoration. This involves the application of very thin leaves of real gold to the surface of the artwork, then burnishing to a high sheen.

Nowadays most of the major art materials' manufacturers offer metallic colours to imitate gold, silver, bronze or steel. Most of these products use mica as one of the ingredients. Colour is coated onto the mica, then the pigment-coated mica is suspended in the appropriate vehicle, such as oil or acrylic.

Similarly, many light-scattering and iridescent colours are available that produce pearlized effects. These are often known as 'interference' colours and are so named because of the way that they disperse the light and create changing visual effects as the viewer moves.

NB: Due to limitations of the printing process it is not possible to show the full effect of metallic and iridescent paint samples. For greater accuracy refer to manufacturers' hand-painted colour charts.

Versatility
Most iridescent colours are very resistant to fading and will not oxidize or tarnish. They are therefore highly suitable for three-dimensional work, murals and outdoor applications.

Antique Bronze
Acrylic ranges provide the widest variety of metallic and iridescent colours. Here a plaster maquette has been painted to make a very convincing bronze. A base coat of Ivory Black carries a coat of Liquitex Antique Bronze, brushed on fairly dry to catch the raised relief of the surface, leaving the indentations solid black.

Metallic and iridescent colours

Metallic colours fall into a group known as iridescent pigments. Some are derived from metal and metal oxides, such as the colours named Iridescent Stainless Steel and Micaceous Iron Oxide that are manufactured by Golden in the USA.

Increasing brilliance
Iridescent pigments depend on light for brilliance. Adding glossy gels or mediums will allow more light to surround the pigments and increase their iridescent quality. A final top coat of gloss varnish can also increase the metallic look of an artwork, while matt varnishes tend to reduce brilliance and reflectivity.

Add ordinary yellows or browns to iridescent gold for antique gold.

Mixing
You can mix iridescent acrylics with ordinary acrylics to create a vast array of pearlescent colours – yellows or browns added to gold produce antique golds, blue plus iridescent pearl or iridescent white gives a blue pearl colour, and so on.

Base coats
Some iridescent colours appear to be transparent and low in pigment. This is because the physical paint formulation has to carry a high volume of the ingredient that creates the iridescent effect (such as mica flakes) in addition to the pigment colour. You can compensate for any weakness by applying a base coat of similar hue to the iridescent colour you wish to use. For example, Yellow Ochre acts as a good base coat for most gold colours and will save several layers of paint.

Red poliment

Poliment is a natural red iron-oxide pigment (PR102) and was the traditional base coat for gilding. There are many similar colours available. In acrylic ranges, for example, you may come across colours named Rich Transparent Red Oxide, Venetian Red or Red Iron Oxide. Used as a base coat for metallic gold colours, you can imitate the rich effect of traditional gold leaf by leaving a little of the red undercoat showing through.

Gold on Rich Transparent Red Oxide

Gold on Venetian Red

Gold on Red Iron Oxide

Anon
Vladimir Madonna, _c._ 1125
Pigment on panel
53 x 75cm (21 x 30in) (original size)

The illustration above shows a postcard reproduction (10 x 15cm, 4 x 6in) of the 'Vladimir Madonna', which dates from the twelfth century. Gold and red pigment combinations dominate the background. The later decorative frame has been given a faux poliment and gilding treatment to enhance the reproduction (see right).

Pearlizing colours
Many ranges offer pearl whites or iridescent whites that can be used very effectively to create pearlized colours. Use them directly in mixtures with regular paint or apply as transparent glazes over previously painted layers to create the effect.

Iridescent white used as a mixture and as a glaze

☛**See also**
Pigments in history 12–15
Brown and Red Earth 72–75
Colour Index 178–179

Flesh is never seen as a solid, even colour – it consists of a multitude of hues, tints, tones, textures and reflections. Art materials' manufacturers offer many ready-made skin colours that they identify as flesh or portrait colours. These colours usually depict light skin tones and historically were produced for a European market.

Ready-made colours

Flesh hues are usually made up of a combination of pigments and are good, convenient starting colours for painting bodies and portraits, and are ideal for colour sketching. These made colours provide useful basic flesh tones, and hues that can be put to purposes other than painting flesh. However, when it comes to capturing the quality of human skin, either in figure painting or portraiture, you may discover that mixing and blending colours from a variety of pure colours is the only effective way to convey the real nature of flesh.

Naples Yellow Reddish

Jaune Brillant

Unbleached Titanium

Flesh experiments
The colours here came straight from the tube and are from a variety of makers. Some of these colours are sold specifically for painting flesh. Others are single-pigment earth and ochre colours that, even when used alone, can be particularly useful for rendering flesh tones.

Straight from the tube
Colours sold specifically for painting flesh provide warm neutrals and useful pinks. Many other colours on offer, although suitable for flesh tones, are not labelled as such. Naples Yellow Reddish, Jaune Brillant and Unbleached Titanium are good examples of such useful colours.

Raw Umber   **Titanium White**

Warm neutrals
You can make warm neutral greys by mixing Raw Umber and Titanium White. This mix produces tints that are suitable for flesh tones.

A multitude of hues

These are Vincent van Gogh's own words on his technique for painting flesh, in a letter to his brother Theo:

'When I compare my painted study with those of others, it is curious to see that theirs have almost nothing in common with mine. Theirs have the same colour as the flesh, so that seen from nearby they are correct, but if you stand back a little they appear painfully flat – all that pink and delicate yellow, soft in itself produces a harsh effect. As I do it from nearby it is greenish-red, yellowish-grey – but when one stands back a little it stands out from the paint; there is atmosphere around it, and there falls on it a certain vibrating light.'

VINCENT VAN GOGH, LETTER

Vincent van Gogh (1853–90)
Italian Girl, 1887
Oil on canvas
81 x 60cm (32 x 23½in)
Musée d'Orsay, Paris

Selecting colours for mixing
For the colour-mixing experiments shown here acrylic paints were used and the following colours were chosen.

Basic five-colour mixing

Process Magenta

Process Yellow

Raw Sienna

Raw Umber

Titanium White

☛**See also**

Naples Yellow 64

Renaissance skin tones 112

Fast colour for flesh 106

A seven-colour palette 110

Colour Index/Flesh 160

Light flesh tones
For the purpose of the colour-mixing experiments Process Magenta and Process Yellow have been chosen, but you can experiment by substituting any reds or yellows you prefer.

Mixing combinations
● Process Magenta + Titanium White
● Process Yellow + Titanium White
● Process Yellow + Process Magenta + Titanium White

Toning down
Try adding different yellows and ochres, and earth colours such as umbers and siennas, to create less florid colours and richer, darker shades.

Mixing combinations
● Raw Sienna + Titanium White
● Process Magenta + Titanium White + Raw Sienna
● Process Yellow + Titanium White + Raw Sienna
● Process Yellow + Process Magenta + Titanium White + Raw Sienna

For darker colours
Experiment with the previous combinations, then replace Raw Sienna with Raw Umber for darker colours.

Mixing combinations
● Raw Umber + Titanium White
● Raw Umber + Titanium White + Raw Sienna
● Raw Umber + Titanium White + Raw Sienna + Process Yellow
● Process Yellow + Process Magenta + Titanium White + Raw Umber

The mixing process and combinations can go on practically ad infinitum. You can continue the experiments with Burnt Umber and Burnt Sienna and all kinds of ochres and other earth colours.

Combination pigments

The manufactured flesh colours shown here contain, in various degrees, red, yellow and blue ingredients. Some of the darker hues dispense with the white component altogether and others have added violet and orange pigments to enrich the depth of colour.

Prepared flesh colours

These colours are not exclusively for portraiture and life painting and may be used generally to extend the warm colour range on the artist's palette. Most of the prepared flesh colours shown in the sketchbooks and the colour charts (left), represent light skin shades. Some are combinations of red, yellow and white pigments that can easily be mixed, while others are more complex combination pigments.

(From top to bottom, left to right)

Flesh Tint, Schmincke Mussini **(rO)**
Flesh Tint, Schmincke Norma **(O)**
Flesh Colour, Lukas Studio **(O)**
Flesh Colour 2, Lukas Series 1 **(O)**
Flesh Colour 4, Lukas Series 1 **(O)**
Flesh Colour, Lukas Designers' **(G)**
Flesh Tint, Rowney Artists' **(O)**
Flesh Tint, Daler-Rowney Designers' **(G)**
Flesh Tint, Daler-Rowney Cryla **(A)**
Flesh Tint, Old Holland Classic **(O)**
Flesh Tint, Winsor & Newton Artists' **(O)**
Flesh Tint, Winsor & Newton Griffin Alkyd **(aO)**
Light Portrait Pink, Liquitex **(A)**
Portrait Tone, Tri-Art **(A)**
Flesh Ochre, Lukas Studio **(O)**
Flesh Ochre, Sennelier Extra Fine **(O)**
Flesh Ochre, Old Holland Classic **(O)**

(O) = oil
(rO) = resin oil
(aO) = alkyd oil
(G) = gouache
(A) = acrylic

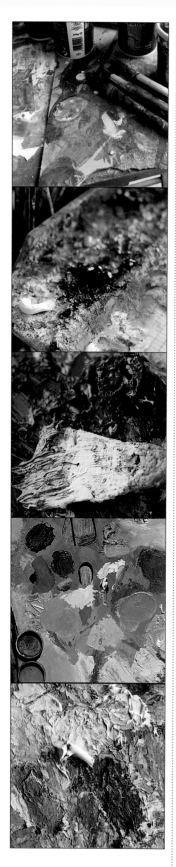

Colour produces a very personal reaction and there are as many creative directions and methods for using colour as there are individual artists.

In this section we have had the privilege of speaking with a number of artists who use a variety of techniques and a range of media. They have opened their homes and studios and given their time generously to bring us an insight into their approach and ideas about colour.

In discussion these artists have mostly said that there are no rules, and the ones who do acknowledge rules say that they are there to be broken. The notion of rules, although low on their list of priorities, clearly relates to style and aesthetic convention in art. In relation to colour, though, method and good practice were rated highly.

The artists all emphasized the importance of respecting their materials and of maintaining a disciplined approach to colour selection and palette layout, often with designated areas for mixing and blending. This was not always apparent when looking at their mixing surfaces and painting tables, which frequently seemed chaotic and uncontrolled. However, these do not give the true picture, for the artists agreed unanimously that without a sense of discipline towards colour, the results will be mud and confusion.

Palettes and painting tables
A selection (left, from top to bottom): Tim Riddihough, Desmond Haughton, George Rowlett, Daphne Jo Lowrie, John Reay.

Watercolour: straight and mixed | 98
Ray Balkwill

Putting more colour into watercolour

Subdued colours | 102
Joan Elliott Bates

Subtle colour and tone

Working without black | 104
Nick Bowering

Rich darks without using black

Fast colour for flesh | 106
Tim Riddihough

Expressive colour in a variety of media

A seven-colour palette | 110
Desmond Haughton

Many colours from a simple palette

Renaissance skin tones | 112
George Underwood

Tried techniques for glowing portraits

Massive colour in oils | 114
George Rowlett

Colour and the physical paint surface

Colour contained | 128
Daphne Jo Lowrie

Painted lines and colour contrasts

Colours from the mail | 140
Judith Chestnutt

Making colour from wastepaper

Colour on cloth | 148
Various artists

Applied colour with textiles and paint

Rich colour from acrylics | 118
Sue Fitzgerald

Getting acrylic colours to glow

Broken colour | 132
John Reay

A broken-prismatic colour effect

Colours for free | 144
Various artists

Experimenting with found colour

Smooth colour | 150
Various artists

Smooth-surface colour effects

Transparency and luminosity | 124
Marina Yedigaroff

A transparent colour dimension

Painting with non-art colours | 136
Carr & Dunsterville

Practical colours for large-scale work

Travelling colour | 146
Simon Jennings

Transporting colour on a small scale

Dry colour and line | 152
Various artists

Line and dry-colour materials

'My watercolour paintings have definitely become more colourful in recent years – probably due to introducing opaque media into them.'

Spontaneity in the studio
Watercolour's characteristics of translucency, expressiveness and unpredictability demand much forward planning by artists who use the medium. Energy is also vital in watercolour painting, and although this can come naturally when working outdoors, it can also be achieved in the studio by working quickly to ensure spontaneity. Ray Balkwill believes that the artist should take risks and allow watercolour to 'do its own thing'.

☛ See also

Choosing media/Watercolour 32–33
Mediums 36–37
Choosing palettes 40–41
Travelling colour 146

Ray Balkwill is an artist who has explored new ways of painting his maritime subjects, but he returns time and again to what he describes as 'the most wonderful medium of expression yet devised' – watercolour paints.

Watercolour explorations
Living in Exmouth, it is little wonder that the sea and its wealth of maritime subjects are the artist's main source of inspiration. The elemental forces in nature and the wide open spaces of sea, estuary and sky have long been an interest.

Mood and atmosphere play a big part in his paintings, and he finds that watercolour is the perfect medium to convey this. However, it is not an easy medium and for the first ten years of painting the artist worked solely in watercolour, trying to master its elusive and unpredictable qualities. These, he believes, are the secret of the medium's success and why it is so popular with artists.

When he is painting in pure watercolour he favours a limited and restrained palette. His usual colours include Ultramarine Blue, Cerulean Blue, Naples Yellow, Raw Sienna, Aureolin, Cadmium Orange, Permanent Rose, Light Red, Burnt Sienna and Burnt Umber. He chooses artists' colours for their transparency, lightfastness and purity, but finds the students' ranges of colours perfectly acceptable for the earth colours such as the umbers and siennas.

Contrast and tone
As a professional painter, the artist is continually looking for new ideas and more recently he has been making paintings that combine opaque media with watercolour.

Ray's palette varies according to the medium he is working in. In addition to his preferred watercolour palette he also uses colours such as Winsor Blue, Viridian, Sepia and Indigo – particularly in mixed-media paintings in which he combines pastel and particularly wants fiercer colours and stronger contrast.

Tone plays an important part in painting – especially in watercolour: 'When painting I concentrate on tone first, with colour in a supporting role. I find my black and white charcoal sketches an invaluable source for reference, when I am working in the studio.'

Ultramarine Blue and Burnt Sienna

Ultramarine Blue and Burnt Umber

Viridian and Sepia

Winsor Blue and Cadmium Orange

Cerulean Blue and Light Red

Ultramarine Blue and Light Red

For greys and browns
The artist mixes pairs of intense colours that oppose each other on the colour wheel. A favourite mix includes Winsor Blue, or Ultramarine Blue, and Cadmium Orange. For lighter greys, middle-value colours such as Cerulean Blue and Light Red, or watery mixes of more intense colours such as Cerulean and Rose Madder give clean, colourful greys.

Instead of black
Ray never uses black in his watercolours, preferring to mix darks using Ultramarine Blue and Burnt Umber, or Burnt Sienna. He sometimes uses Viridian mixed with Sepia when he wants a near black.

Ray Balkwill
Sheltered Moorings (detail)
Watercolour and mixed media

Mixing media
The artist often adds ink and gouache to the watercolour and pastel in his mixed-media paintings: 'I believe that there are only a few basic rules in painting. It's all about making your picture and expressing your own vision.'

The painting *Sunset on the Exe* is a typical example of how he has used the contrast of watercolour with other media to good effect. Here, by using colour counter-change, or complementaries, the warm areas of colour against cool ones create the intensity of tones that balance light against dark to their limit. The contrast of the two media working together makes for a much more vibrant picture than the 'softer' look of a pure watercolour. In this painting the watercolours used are Winsor Blue, Cadmium Orange and Raw Sienna.

Combining watercolour and other media
The artist feels it is important that every painter searches for interesting new ways to extend his or her experience and knowledge of technique, so he has also been experimenting in acylics, oils and pastels. More recently he has used mixed media – mainly watercolours and pastels combined. This seemed the natural progression from pure watercolour. The transparency and fluidity of watercolour and the opacity and vibrancy of pastel work extremely well together and their interplay produces paintings that are rich in a variety of marks, colour and technique.

With this method he still uses watercolour paper as the support, but aims to apply the watercolour more directly and loosely. He does this by using stronger colours – with plenty of paint – so that the colour is stated without the need for further washes, as in the more traditional method.

Ray Balkwill
Sunset on the Exe
Watercolour and mixed media
43 x 45.5cm (17 x 18in)

Palettes
Ray uses artists' quality watercolours. He prefers tubes rather than pans because it is easier to prepare large quantities of strong wash from them. In the studio old plates and saucers are employed for mixing colours. When working outside he uses a large plastic palette with plenty of deep wells.

Brushes
He uses four brushes, including a 25mm (1in) hake, a filbert, a no. 12 round and a rigger. He advises against using a small brush too early in a painting, otherwise it will all look too detailed.

Working with pure watercolour

Watercolour works best when it is expressed as simply and spontaneously as possible. When using pure watercolour the artist likes to paint in the traditional way by building up the picture gradually, applying washes and working from light to dark. One of the most important elements in a watercolour painting is the role of the paper itself and the artist makes good use of its qualities to retain translucency and 'sparkle'.

The painting *Quayside* (opposite) was built up using three or four washes, allowing each to dry before applying the next. By using masking fluid at the start, the artist could retain the whiteness of the paper as the lightest area. The use of some highly transparent colours – the essence of watercolour – also permits the white reflective surface to shine through.

Transparent watercolours have an attractive airy quality that is perfect for capturing the illusion of atmosphere, space and light. Of course, the opaque colours are also transparent when thinly diluted, but they impart a degree of opacity to other colours they are mixed with. White gouache is only added if necessary, to put in finishing touches such as rigging and seagulls, as here.

After masking fluid was applied with a brush on the boat and water, the artist applied a light wash of Cadmium Orange and Naples Yellow over the whole of the paper to set a warm mood, knowing that there would be cooler washes to follow. Naples Yellow is a semi-opaque colour that softens other colours, as well as adding warmth and mistiness.

When this was dry a mix of Cerulean Blue and Permanent Rose was washed over the distant hills and harbour wall. Both these colours have a cool bias. The artist repeated the wash, but dropped a mix of Ultramarine Blue and Raw Sienna into the background hills, merging it in places with a little Burnt Sienna. This 'wet-in-wet' technique is useful for suggesting distance, particularly if you wish to keep a painting simple. By using coolish colours the background tends to recede, while merging and moving these colours around helps keep the background lively to excite the eye without involving too much detail.

Burnt Sienna was dragged across the foreground with a 'dry brush' to suggest mud. This technique is a useful way of adding texture to contrast with the areas of soft washes. A further wash of the darker mixes was used in the build-up of darks for the wall and boat, letting some of the initial colours show through.

Light Red was used for the hull of the boat and a mix of Ultramarine and Permanent Rose for the shadows and distant water. Ultramarine and Light Red, and Ultramarine and Burnt Sienna, were added for further darks. Finally, the masking fluid was removed and any hard edges were softened with watercolour.

A painting is often spoilt by adding too much detail in the final touches and destroying its freshness. 'Letting go' of a painting is most difficult, particularly if you are enjoying it. In fact, the two most difficult aspects of painting, Ray Balkwill believes, are starting a painting – being faced with a sheet of white paper – and finishing one off.

Finishing touches
The finishing touches in *Quayside* involved adding a few flicks with a rigger for the rigging, ropes and seagulls using white gouache. Further darks were added in the wall, steps and boat.

Core colours and materials used
Artists' and students' quality watercolours: Ultramarine Blue, Cerulean Blue, Cadmium Orange, Permanent Rose, Light Red, Raw Sienna, Naples Yellow, Burnt Sienna and white gouache. In addition the artist used masking fluid and worked on 300gsm (140lb) Whatman (Not) watercolour paper.

Ray Balkwill
Quayside
Watercolour
12.5 x 17.5cm (5 x 7in)

The artist is a strong advocate of working 'en plein air'. He does much of his painting in the UK, where the atmosphere tends to soften the colours. This is why many of his paintings contain mellow mixes of blue-grey produced by the weather and climate. The view is taken from a pontoon at Dartmouth, Devon, and it was a difficult position to paint from. The inspiration for the painting was the late afternoon light and the strong contrast it created. *Quayside* is a good example of how colour can be used to suggest and accentuate the mood and atmosphere of a place.

'Whereas some think of colour as primaries, I tend towards the secondaries or tertiaries for my chords and harmonies.'

Sir William Coldstream (1908–87)
Coldstream was a member of the famous Euston Road School of painters, founded in the late 1930s, whose figurative work was subdued in colour.

White
The soft tonality of the artist's work relies on the use of a great deal of white. Joan Elliott Bates's choice is Flake White. This is a white that is traditionally used by oil painters and is probably one of the oldest known paint formulations. Being made from lead, Flake White is toxic and should be handled with caution.

Tonalism is a style of painting in which the artist strives to capture the effect of light and form through colour areas known as tonal masses, as distinguished from a linear approach. Joan Elliott Bates studied at the Slade School of Fine Art in London under Professor William Coldstream and her acutely observed landscapes display an instinctive awareness of colour and tonal values.

The artist recalls that 'William Coldstream was a fine Slade Professor, not least because he encouraged all kinds of different talents to emerge and prosper. Despite the fact that he had been a member of the Euston Road School there was no pressure on the students to work in that way.' However, students at the Slade were familiar with his work and that of other members of staff who followed that tradition.

Any painting is made up of composition, colour and tone. Joan Elliott Bates's drawings are often tonal, too, and she also produces linear etchings with tonal aquatints. She sees a landscape, still life or figure in terms of colour and tone, and regards these two elements as inextricably linked: 'I think this is instinctive. I once heard a notable teacher saying that colour mixing, composition and other elements can be taught, but not a sense of tonal values.' She much admires the work of Piero della Francesca, Rembrandt, late Turner, van Gogh, Bonnard, Vuillard, and Gwen John.

Personal palette
The artist believes that a limited palette results in a cohesive, unified painting – 'perhaps analogous to setting a key in music'.

Her favourite colours are White, Naples Yellow, Yellow Ochre, Cadmium

Naples Yellow

Light Red

French Ultramarine

Cadmium Yellow

Indian Red

Cerulean Blue

Yellow Ochre

Burnt Sienna

Cobalt Blue

Raw Sienna

Cadmium Orange

Black

Yellow, Raw Sienna, Light Red, Indian Red, Burnt Sienna, French Ultramarine, Cerulean Blue, Cobalt Blue and Cadmium Orange. She follows a set procedure in laying out her palette.

Only very occasionally does she pick perhaps three colours, probably black, white and one other, for more abstract painting – or she may try a completely different palette to force herself to rethink, lest her habitual palette is becoming too much of a cliché. She learns by doing this, but reverts with pleasure to her own familiar 'voice'.

The artist has no particular preferred brand of oil paint and the only additive she uses is genuine turpentine, never linseed oil. Colours are mixed rather than taken straight from the tube.

Colour and tone
Joan Elliott Bates describes her painting as close in tone and high in key. The terms 'tone' and 'tonalism' when used to describe the visible quality of colour in painting are used broadly. The hue may be described as yellow or reddish tone, for example; the value as pale or deep tone; and the degree of vividness, known as saturation, as bright or dull tone.

Palette choice and layout
Joan Elliott Bates will typically use only five or six colours. She lays her palette out in a set order, anti-clockwise from the thumbhole. She always uses White. For her yellows she will choose from Naples Yellow, Cadmium Yellow or Yellow Ochre, and always uses Raw Sienna. From the warm pigments she chooses Light Red, Indian Red or Burnt Sienna, and for coolness from the blues she selects from French Ultramarine, Cerulean and Cobalt. Occasionally she adds Black and Cadmium Orange to her palette.

See also ☛

Choosing media/Oils 30–31
Mediums 36–37
Choosing palettes 40–41
White 86–87

Joan Elliott Bates
East Anglian Estuary
Oil on board
15 x 25.3cm (6 x 10in)
*The painting
above is shown nearly
actual size.
(detail enlargement, right)*

'My paintings are often small but not always so. I often work directly from nature on a small scale and then continue with them or develop them in the studio. Most of my colours are in a high key and concerned with light. My brushwork is very much concerned with mark-making, which shows the individual hand of the artist – his or her calligraphy.'

'I find if you have thousands of colours to choose from it discourages the act of mixing.'

Nick Bowering is an artist who has exploited the potential of black. He has mixed darks to great effect from a limited palette, creating a series of boat paintings that convey subtlety of colour and specific mood. His work shows what can be achieved from the darker end of the spectrum with a limited selection of colours.

A controlled palette
Naples Yellow
Cadmium Yellow
Cadmium Red
Alizarin Crimson
Ultramarine
Prussian Blue

Monochrome experiments

Instinctively this artist views things monochromatically: 'I have spent a lot of time exploring the potential of black and white photography and I have been involved in single-colour printmaking. In both lithography and etching I have experimented with black ink.'

Recently he has become interested in glass painting, and has found black a particularly important graphic and tonal element in bringing an image together when painting on coloured glass.

Depth, body and subtlety

Blacks and darks can have so much depth, body and subtlety of colour. If you think of black and white as complete opposites with all those greys in between, it is this tonal range that interests him, and to a certain extent this has influenced his series of boat paintings.

He likes light and dark contrasts and 'all those halftones'. He has painted purely monochromatic studies and experimented with dark single-colour paintings that are virtually black, but has gradually introduced more colour into the boat pictures. He feels that it is the use of black that is the significant unifying element in these pictures.

Basic dark
A basic black from red and blue.

Warm
Adding more red and yellow creates a warmer mix and moves the colour towards a Burnt Umber colour.

Cool
Adding more blue increases darkness and takes the colour towards a deep slate grey.

Limited palette

Nick Bowering tends to use a palette limited to about five or six colours, and typically works with a palette of primary colours, but varies his selection. He may use Naples Yellow, Cadmium Yellow, Cadmium Red, Alizarin Crimson, Ultramarine and Prussian Blue, and white, but often lets the white of the primed background show through to brighten the mid tones.

Mixing colours

He never uses black straight from the tube, as it can be 'quite deadening and overpowering'. You can create a wide range of hues including dense, dark colours that appear to read as black, but on closer inspection carry plenty of colour.

The beauty of working with a limited palette is that you can steer the painting in any direction you want it to go: 'I will mix reds and blues to create a sort of base black. If I want a warm black I add more yellow. If I want a cool, deep black I add more blue.'

Different layers

He works in oils on either white-primed board or canvas, but his surface technique and brushwork varies. He seldom makes a drawing or outline sketch, but draws directly with the paint. Some areas are quite opaque. In other parts he may do a local-colour underpainting, then work with thinned paint. By adding layer on layer he builds up rich dark glazes and washes to create an overall mood and surface harmony.

Linear detail
Sometimes the artist scratches back into the paint using the end of the brush handle to reveal either linear underpainted areas of colour or the white of the canvas.

Nick Bowering
**Orange Boat
Essaouira**
Oil on canvas
25.5 x 30cm
(10 x 12in)

Nick Bowering
Beached Boats
Oil on board
(*below left*)
18 x 35.5cm
(7 x 14in)
(*below right*)
23 x 35.5cm
(9 x 14in)

Manipulating blacks

In these two small mono-
chrome studies the dark
colour has been steered
towards cool or warm by
adjusting the proportions
of the colours in the mix.

☛**See also**

Choosing media/Oils 30–31
Mediums 36–37
Choosing palettes 40–41
Blacks/Darks 76–83
Colour Index/Black 176

Tim Riddihough is an artist who has been through many phases in his approach to life painting and his attempts to capture the variety of hues and subtlety of tones to be seen in human flesh.

'Avoid getting into a rut with a particular technique or style. Try using new materials and new methods. Sometimes start with coloured outlines, sometimes start with coloured shapes.'

Seeing flesh
While at art school Tim first used a naturalistic approach to figure painting, trying to reproduce as accurately as possible the colours of the model in front of him.

His tutors encouraged him to be individual and less natural in style, and he went through a stage of painting colours that were totally different from the ones that he was seeing. He tried painting bodies red to contrast with the green of a sofa, or green because they were in a blue room, but found that this approach did not work for him.

'If I am painting a dark body or a pinkish one these are the colours that appear in my painting, but I will add all sorts of other colours too.'

Tim Riddihough
Red man, standing
Gouache and ink on paper
30 x 23cm (12 x 9in)

In this little abstracted study a random colour was laid first and then 'attacked' with ink lines.

He moved on to a more representational approach, and started to take note, probably subconsciously he thinks, of what the colour of flesh is, trying to convey these colours as they appear to him. He does not stick rigidly to attempting to reproduce the actual colours, though, but tries to create an impression of the image.

Supports and grounds
He sometimes works directly on plain white grounds and sometimes lays a tint first. Both approaches produce a specific kind of feel: 'I may try a big splash of Yellow Ochre with a bit of something else to make a warmish ground and then work into it with other materials. I am very messy when I paint and I splash it on.'

He uses thick, rough watercolour paper, of no specific make as long as it is heavy enough to remain reasonably flat when lots of moisture is put on it.

Mixing media
His mixed-media paintings usually consist of gouache, oil pastel, conté and water-soluble ink. He might decide to use ink for outline and structure, then oil pastel to highlight the background and certain areas of the form.

'If it has paint on it then it is a painting to me.'

Gouache is his main painting medium and the basic colours he would choose for a light-skinned person would be Yellow Ochre and White, and Alizarin Crimson or Cadmium Red. These are his basics for flesh mixes, but then he might add a colour that is more purplish, such as Rose Madder, but this depends on the particular figure and the background.

Working with colour and a reed pen

The artist often works with black or brown ink for his coloured figure studies. He uses a reed pen cut from *Phragmites* collected locally and cuts the nib with a penknife. He likes working with this tool as it gives an uncertain result. The ink sometimes runs out in mid line or goes scratchy and then blobs and he is never sure what is going to happen. It is this element of uncertainty that he finds creative. The unpredictable line brings more vitality to the end result.

Tim Riddihough
Check headband
Reed pen and ink, and mixed media on tinted paper
50 x 35cm (19¾ x 13½in)

'I find I can work all day on a painting, spending hours and even days on it, and sometimes the results are not very encouraging. The paintings that work best for me are the ones I have worked on as quickly as possible with as little conscious thought as possible. I am like a bull at a gate and just jump in. I would not recommend this approach for everyone. Some artists spend days, even years, on one painting.'

Working at speed

Tim Riddihough tries to vary his approach and not have a set routine as he finds this restricts the end result. Sometimes he starts with an ink outline and, as he uses water-soluble ink, the subsequent paint dissolves it and the ink starts to run.

Sometimes he reverses this approach and starts with a flat painted shape, then works on it with ink or pastel, or sometimes he will start with pastel. He does not just draw outlines and fill them in as this can become very stilted and flat, like painting by numbers, but always tries to paint the figure and the background together so that there is unity and harmony across the painting.

Exactly how his paintings work is a mystery to him: 'I am useless at talking about painting because I have not got a clue how it works. My most successful paintings seem to occur despite my best efforts, but in the past there has been a lot of work and practice put in.'

Painting and colour are now instinctive to the artist, but his method does not always work. He admits that he has a sort of scatter-gun approach and makes as many paintings as he can, as quickly as he can: 'I will often put a painting up on the wall for a week or two and contemplate it, but my rate of production is so great the display keeps changing. Then the paintings go in a cupboard, and come out after a month or two. Some of them I will like, some of them I will not. It's a big problem. I sometimes go back to paintings, but very rarely. If they do not succeed first time I abandon them.'

☞**Opposite page**

Tim Riddihough
Fast studies
Oil, acrylic and mixed media
Size range:
30 x 23cm (12 x 9in) –
50 x 35cm (19¾ x 13½in)

Just about all the paintings on the opposite page were done at top speed with the minimum of conscious thought. The bigger pictures take about half an hour, the smaller ones ten to fifteen minutes at the most.

Green-outlined figure
(top left)
The artist used hard conté pastel on a damp gouache-painted surface. Conté colour flows smoothly on a damp ground and dissolves and blends. White oil pastel applied first, with a dark colour over the top, creates a resist that indicates light coming through a screen behind the model.

Red man, crossed legs, leaning back
(bottom left)
Here is an example of using a random colour for flesh, one of those experiments intended to break with convention and loosen up the artist's thinking.

Straight paint
(top and bottom right)
These are pure paintings just using acrylic colour to define the shapes and forms of the figure.

☞**See also**

Choosing media 30–35
Flesh colours 90–93
A seven-colour palette 110
Renaissance skin tones 112
Dry colour and line 152–153

'My palette is limited, but not my colour range. The more colours you try to use, the more confusing a painting can become, unless you are a very experienced colourist.'

Core seven-colour palette
From top to bottom: French Ultramarine, Cadmium Red, Alizarin Crimson, Viridian Green, Lemon Yellow, Burnt Sienna. Tints are made with the seventh colour, which is Titanium White.

☞**See also**

Colours of the spectrum 24

Choosing media/Oils 30–31

Choosing palettes 40–41

Renaissance skin tones 112

Desmond Haughton's painting is about exploiting a few colours within a simple design. He always uses a seven-colour palette consisting of Titanium White, Lemon Yellow, Cadmium Red, Viridian Green, French Ultramarine, Alizarin Crimson and Burnt Sienna to bring a full-colour range to his work.

The artist moves between student and artists' colours with no particular brand preference, choosing his palette from what he refers to as the complementary primaries – colours that are directly opposite one another and those that he considers to be purest in hue.

For example, he chooses Viridian Green for being the purest of greens, without drifting towards yellow on the one hand or blue on the other. Similarly, he chooses French Ultramarine as the purest blue, one that does not veer towards green or red. He never uses black, but creates all his deep, dark and shadow areas from mixtures of his core palette of seven colours.

Desmond makes quite clear decisions about his colours and design before committing a painting to canvas and his colours are always mixed before laying them down.

In the self-portrait shown opposite the yellow waistcoat makes a striking element. The artist was drawn to the high contrast between the colours yellow and black, and the dramatic effect created by visual opposites. He used Lemon Yellow with Titanium White and Burnt Sienna to produce the yellow of the waistcoat, which is central to the composition. In turn, the yellow sits on a white shirt, which lifts and brightens the yellow colour even more. The brightly clothed torso is

sandwiched between the dark of the trousers and the face.

While making this painting the artist was thinking about complementaries and opposites and basic ways of bringing out the cools and purples of the skin tones to create an interesting atmosphere to the portrait.

Clarity of design and composition is also important to the artist. One of the reasons he was drawn to the waistcoat was its shape as well as its colour. Desmond describes his approach to composing the portrait as being one of simple design and simple colours, as if looking at a poster or a print – just well-balanced blocks of colour. He has tried to achieve a monumental composition by carefully placing his figure to fill the frame of the canvas with the arms just fitting in, pushing himself close to the picture frame.

The artist does not draw the composition first or employ underpainting techniques. He works straight away, drawing with the paint and creating blocks of colour that are at first abstract patterns and shapes. His technique is immediate and direct, applying neat paint to the picture surface, using only turpentine to thin it. He does not build up the colour with washes and glazes, trying to get the painting right first time. He favours round brushes, using a big brush to block areas in and a small one to draw details out.

'For a warm grey I mix white, Burnt Sienna and French Ultramarine. Buying grey paint is a waste of money as any two complementaries and white make grey. I never use black in my palette, but I always work on a black or brown primed canvas. One of the biggest mistakes is to use black as a mixing colour on the palette.'

'In my paintings there are no lines as such. Lines are defined where one area of colour stops and another starts.'

Desmond Haughton
**Self-portrait
with Yellow Waistcoat, 1994**
Oil on canvas
86.5 x 51cm (34 x 20in)

The choice of colour and style of costume influences the design and mood of a portrait painting and conveys a tremendous amount about the sitter. Desmond Haughton is an artist who has painted several self-portraits from a simple seven-colour palette. Lemon Yellow, used with Titanium White and Burnt Sienna for tints and shades, creates the yellow waistcoat around which the composition revolves.

'If you are not honest to the colours you see and the shapes you see, a painting can start to go wrong. It is all about logic, a logical sense of seeing. Ask yourself, what colour is this, what shape is that?'

The Italian Renaissance that flourished from the fourteenth to the sixteenth centuries is still recognized for its supreme artistic achievement and technique. These are some of the colours for painting flesh that you may come across when looking at paintings by masters of the Renaissance.

Verdaccio
A composite colour used in Florence made of Burnt Sienna, ochre, Lamp Black, chalk, green-brown and Raw Umber. Used for outlining and shading. In Siena a similar mixture was known as 'Bazzeo'.

Terre Verte
A common and inexpensive pigment used in admixture with white lead for underpainting flesh. Known in English as 'green earth'.

Sinopia
A name for a red iron-oxide pigment originating from the city of Sinope in Asia Minor. Similar colours are known today by names such as Red Iron Oxide, Venetian Red and Red Ochre.

Cinabrese
An ancient red pigment derived from mercuric-sulphide ore, also known as cinnabar. Used in admixtures with white lead to create warm flesh tones. Later superseded in popularity by the invention of the far superior Vermilion.

Michelangelo Buonarroti (1475–1564)
Madonna, Child and St John with Angels, *c.* **1506**
Oil on wood panel (detail)
105.4 x 76.8cm (41½ x 30¼in)
National Gallery, London

Cennino Cennini's advice on painting flesh on panel
'Take a little terre verte and a little white lead …, and lay two coats all over the face, over the hands, over the feet, and over the nudes … On a wall make your pinks with cinabrese, bear in mind on a panel they should be made with vermilion. And when you are putting on the first pinks, do not have straight vermilion – have a little white lead in it. And also put a little white lead into the verdaccio with which you shade at first – Make three values of flesh colour, each lighter than the other, laying each flesh colour in its place on the areas of the face; … do not work up so close to the verdaccio shadows as to cover them entirely; but work them out with the darkest flesh colour, fusing and softening them like a puff of smoke … Bear in mind that a panel needs to be laid in more times than a wall; but not so much as not to need to have the green, which lies under the flesh colours, always show through a little. When you have got your flesh colours down so that the face is just about right, make a flesh colour a little bit lighter and pick out the forms … until you finally come to touch in with pure white lead any little relief more pronounced than the rest, such as there would be on the eyebrow or the tip of the nose etc.'

THE CRAFTSMAN'S HANDBOOK (FIFTEENTH CENTURY)

Lay two coats of terre verte
In this partly finished work the technique of using the mixture of Terre Verte (literally, 'green earth') and white lead for underpainting flesh, as discussed by Cennini, above, can be clearly seen. The effect of using a complementary or contrasting ground colour in cool green enhances the warmth of the subsequent red-shade skin tones.

ee also
n Earth 67
colours 90–93

George Underwood
Portrait Fragments, 1997
Oil on canvas
10.2 x 10.2cm (4 x 4in) (actual size)
Collection of Simon Jennings

A traditional approach
In these small detail studies the artist has been influenced by Renaissance colouring techniques. Green is an unusual choice for underpainting skin colours, but here, as in fifteenth-century paintings, it is used to great effect to enhance the warmth and solidity of the skin tones.

'This is painting, not sculpture. If I could do it with thin paint, then I would – but I can't.'

Core palette
George Rowlett's palette consists of only four colours – Ultramarine Blue, Brunswick Green, Chrome Yellow (bulk-branded Lead-Free Lemon) and Cadmium Red Medium (bulk-branded Bright Red) – plus Titanium White.

☞**See also**
Choosing media/Oils 30–31

Entering George Rowlett's intimate London studio (he has a studio on the east Kent coast, too) is like getting right inside one of his paintings. The whole atmosphere is permeated by oil paint. The physical presence of it is everywhere – on the walls, the floor, the working surfaces and the equipment, but, most importantly, on the paintings themselves.

It is a privileged experience for anyone with an interest in painting to find themselves projected into this surprisingly well-organized world dripping with colours.

The artist is well known for his thickly painted views of London's river and for his seascapes and landscapes of the east Kent coast. A question people frequently ask him is: 'How long does it take for the colours to dry?'. The artist's answer is that a painting will skin over in one to two weeks, and the reds are the slowest colours to dry: 'I usually sell my paintings when they are touch-dry; they will bruise if you knock them at first. Then they take about four to six years to dry through, and become as hard as concrete.'

Another recurring question is: 'Do the paintings crack?'. George has seen a painting that he made thirty-five years ago and it is absolutely sound. One of the reasons for the longevity of his pictures is that they are painted on well-primed battened hardboard rather than canvas. Also, he uses a simple palette of colours and this means that there are fewer chemical reactions taking place between the pigments: 'I try to be absolutely honest and straight about colour.'

The artist has always applied his paint thickly, and his first inspiration was van Gogh. His sense of colour, he says, is drawn from the work of the Impressionists. He describes his own technique as drawing with colour, manipulating mass and bulk, and he has deliberately stopped using brushes.

The artist feels compelled to work by believing, literally and physically, in what he calls 'the deed' and acting instinctively as if 'running with the painting, following the dramatic weather and light changes'. By taking the 'losses' and the 'gains' in high concentration that such an approach produces he says that he becomes different, and totally absorbed, as he tries to connect with nature.

An act of self-censorship then takes place in which he scrapes back, removes, and rebuilds the paint, though he also accepts that every mistake is a small part of the whole painting. Most of his landscapes are started and finished in situ. Others are completed in the studio.

Method of working
George works on primed board, usually white, but sometimes grey or a neutral pink colour. He starts painting in the middle of the picture, towards the top, and then works outwards.

His main colours are mixed on a piece of board used as a palette. Again, he likens his way of working to running as hard as you can – mixing first, picking up pure colours, and working wet-in-wet. It is not an accidental process, but chance and error play a part when you are trying to push things to the extreme.

The paint is applied with spatulas, the kind used for scraping wallpaper, about 10cm (4in) wide for the broadest marks. He works in as broad areas as possible, laying in lights first, moving towards darks in the painting. Different sizes of spatulas – 2.5cm (1in), 5cm (2in), 10cm (4in) – are used to pick up the individual colours.

The thickness of the paint produces a powerful drawing, and the artist uses the edges of the spatula blades for marks and details.

George finds that he is applying increasingly larger amounts of paint and has discovered that he can do more with fewer marks and bigger drags of the spatula. He has also tried using pieces of hardboard as spatulas, and plasterer's trowels, but could not get on with them.

A 'long' paint

The artist uses a vast amount of paint at a ratio of about four tins of white to any other colour, so he buys the most economical, high-quality oil paint that is available.

His favourite is manufactured by Stokes in Sheffield in the north of England. He buys it in bulk and it is shipped directly to him in 5 litre (1 gallon) cans. Many professional artists use this paint, and George likes its quality and feel.

He has tried other brands, but the colours are different and the textures do not feel the same. It is important for his technique to have the elasticity provided by this paint. He is familiar with the pull and stretch of it. It is what is termed a 'long' paint, with the feel of an old-fashioned formula. Modern paints are 'short' paints and the artist finds them over-ground and too fine.

George Rowlett
Sunlit Walmer Beach, Deal Pier, Bathers and Crab Boat, 1997–98
Oil on board
76 x 122cm (30 x 48in)
Collection of University of St Andrews

Dripping with colours

An easel, paint-mixing table, spatulas, still-life objects and a painting in progress in the artist's studio are all encrusted with colour.

George Rowlett
Sudden storm over Thames, Rotherhithe Pier, 1996
(above and detail overleaf)
Oil on board
61 x 101.5cm (24 x 40in)
Private collection

Sue Fitzgerald's vibrant, multi-layered acrylic paintings reflect her passion for southern France and the Far East. She explores the richness of local culture and is inspired by an enveloping wealth of colour and texture, from exotic fruits to rich carpets and fabrics, to music.

Colour inspiration

Sue collects interesting china and textiles on her travels. She is particularly attracted by the sheen found on silks. Eastern fabrics are often threaded through with gold, and many cloths have mirrors and further patterns sewn into them. Sometimes she finds fabrics that are sewn from sections of old Indian bridal gowns, with a variety of patterns and textures, gold and silver thread all combined in one piece of material.

These treasures provide inspiration for her paintings: 'I never really know what I'm going to paint next, except I may see an interesting object or a piece of textile.' A find such as a yellow Moroccan teapot can suggest a picture that will feature yellow on a bright blue background: 'I've got a mind-store of subjects I'm going to paint.'

Acrylic paints

Like many artists, she has noticed the considerable improvement in the quality and range of artists' acrylic colours since their general introduction in the 1960s. Good artists' quality acrylics now compare favourably with oil paints.

She chooses colours such as Alizarin Crimson that are similar to the traditional oil-paint alizarins. Some of the cheaper 'hue' colours have white or other additives in them and seem to lack the intensity and clarity of oils. Sue is not averse to student colours, but thinks that 'when you spend time creating something a bit special, it's worth making the effort to use good-quality paints.'

She uses many different colours and brands, not particularly favouring one make over another, but in general likes artists' quality paints that 'have a nice buttery consistency'. She also uses a more liquid acrylic that comes in jars.

Mediums and methods

Mediums are sometimes useful if building up thick layers, but with the more buttery tube colours you can actually place a thick wedge of paint on the canvas, one that holds its shape, without using mediums. If you use gel mediums or texture pastes you have to make sure you use the correct acrylic-compatible ones to avoid any cracking. A little medium in the paint will build it up more and can give the surface dramatic ridges and textures. When the paint is dry Sue might rub a cloth over it, and actually polish some parts to give a shine, accentuating the texture and reflection of colour off the surface.

Equally, if the painting is not working, she rubs the picture over with a cloth, not to obliterate it but just to give it a bit of a 'knocking around': 'I throw paint at it, sometimes in blots, just shaking a loaded brush at it to disturb it. You can get too precious with a painting.' Sometimes she may work for three days and then destroy what she has done, because she cannot be bothered to continue working at an unsatisfactory painting.

'The reason why I describe my paintings as mixed media is because they are not just acrylic. In addition to a spot of watercolour they have some gold or silver leaf.'

Mixing media

Sue could never achieve the richness and depth she was after, so started using acrylic with watercolour. Now she mostly uses straight acrylic, which she applies quite thickly. Sometimes it is mixed with a gel medium and texture or modelling paste. She works on canvas, with a palette knife, laying paint on quickly and building up the textures. When the light catches the painting it reflects off different planes of texture, adding an extra colour dimension to the work. Brushes are used for broad areas and detail.

Occasionally she uses watercolour with acrylic to create a fluid-wash effect and then, finally, when everything is dry, works in a gold or silver metallic colour; this is a powder suspended in oil.

Sue Fitzgerald
Cardinal Grapes and Silken Shawl
Acrylic and mixed media on canvas
38 x 46cm (15 x 18in)
(detail, left)

'Do not be afraid of using colour in an unconventional way. Just because you think of leaves as green, break the preconceptions. If you think the leaves would look good blue then paint them blue. Quite often when people look at foliage they don't realize that leaves are really blue or red or purple anyway.'

Mixing colours

Sue Fitzgerald uses mostly pure colours, but they become blended and overlaid to a certain extent on the canvas as she paints. Sometimes a dinner-plate palette is used but, by and large, the colour effects and mixing, and the colour differences, are all made and blended wet-in-wet on the painting rather than on the palette. For instance, she might decide to add a bit of green over the top of another colour, even though the one underneath is still wet. Then she works them together. She has always used colour in this way, even when working in oils or watercolours.

Sue Fitzgerald
Two Dragons
Acrylic and mixed media on canvas
91 x 122cm (36 x 48in)

'Whenever I go into an art shop I think, "Oh! This is an interesting colour", and I buy it. Often it's just because of the colour, or I may be thinking of a piece of cloth or china I want to include in a picture. For example, I've got some saffron silks, and I was thinking to myself that I needed a really "saffron-like" colour; then I came across a slightly transparent yellow, one that would work well. I don't set out to buy a standard set of colours, but just pick them up as I go. It's a haphazard method, but this is the way I build up my repertoire of colours.'

Core colours
There are certain core colours that Sue always keeps in her studio, ones that she likes to return to in her paintings time and again.

☛ **See also**

Choosing media/Acrylic	33
Mediums	36–37
Metallic & special-effect colours	88
Colour Index	178

Colours and contrasts

Sue Fitzgerald likes contrast in painting, contrast between thin and thick line, large and small shapes, rough and smooth texture, dark and light, and bright and dull. She delights in the juxtaposition of precise pattern against big blocks of colour.

Her advice is not to be frightened of colour, but to experiment. Sometimes she might place a bright pink near a dark brown, for instance. Many artists like dealing with muted colours, but muted colours need not look dull. You can use Burnt Sienna or Indian Red and still get them to glow. Getting colours to glow depends on their context, what you put them against, and it all comes back to contrast. For example, placing Burnt Sienna next to purple works well. You might think that these are strong dark colours without much contrast, but you do not have to use bright reds or bright yellows to create a glow. 'People think of me as using really bright colours all the time, but I don't necessarily. I use an awful lot of dark purple and Burnt Umber and Raw Umber too.'

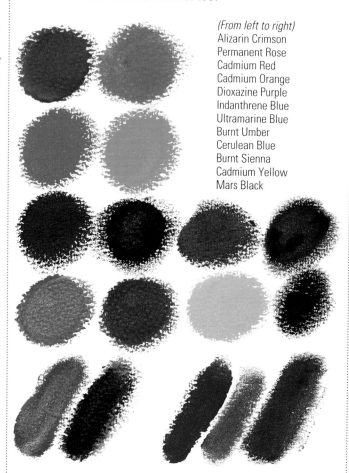

(From left to right)
Alizarin Crimson
Permanent Rose
Cadmium Red
Cadmium Orange
Dioxazine Purple
Indanthrene Blue
Ultramarine Blue
Burnt Umber
Cerulean Blue
Burnt Sienna
Cadmium Yellow
Mars Black

Essential colours
Alizarin Crimson is a particularly important colour for Sue. She also relies on Olive Green as a soft colour for glazing and layering, though this colour does not tend to be immediately evident in her paintings.

Siennas and purples
A colour such as Burnt Sienna can be used with purples to really vivid effect. Never think of colours like umbers and siennas as dull colours because they can be as bright and brilliant as, say, Cadmium Reds.

Improvised palettes
The artist uses old dinner plates as palettes to put her colours on. She has employed a proper palette now and again and tried to use it in an orderly fashion, but finds china plates more acceptable. Colours are not laid out in any particular order, but squeezed out, with two or three on one plate and some on another.

Organizing colours
Sue appreciates that a tidy studio would make her painting life easier: 'I know if I was more organized things would move along at a quicker pace and everything would be very precise, but that's not part of my nature. I have tried putting colours in order, the blues here, the earth colours there and so on, and it stays like that for about half an hour.'

Planning the composition

She never makes measured or preparatory drawings, or even initial colour sketches before starting a painting: 'I set up a still life, but only vaguely; it's not ruled or measured. If I want to do that blue cloth with that plant on it and those pots I'll set it up, but not in a very precise way because I might decide to change it around or begin to move away from it. I never draw, I just go straight in with brush or knife.'

Working on canvas

She works on pre-stretched and primed canvas. 'The type of surface weave doesn't really matter because the surface gets obliterated by paint and texture anyway.'

When she starts a new canvas she puts some colour on to break it up and get rid of the white. She may cover it all in Yellow Ochre, or just use up whatever is left on the palette. Sometimes more than one colour is brushed on.

Starting points

It does not really matter which colours are put on first. If two of the initial colours work well they might be left as part of the painting.

Next some texture is introduced onto the surface. To start Sue perhaps chooses one section to do some thick painting with a palette knife. This gives her some idea of how she might continue the painting, but she leaves it to dry before doing so.

Unifying texture
The overall textured surface brings a unifying element to the variety of colours and shapes in the painting.

Developing the painting

She might leave spaces for the objects, or just roughly paint in basic shapes on the canvas, then works over them, or she might put some white shapes in. Acrylic is a versatile medium that allows for many approaches. The underneath texture tends to unify the painting. She works over the top, going into details such as flowers and surface decorations, studying them and working them into the rough surface textures. Sometimes she works into wet paint with the tip of the handle of the brush, scratching into the paint.

Gold and silver
Sue uses gold or silver leaf most of the time in the final stages of a painting, not with every picture, but particularly for still lifes. 'I use it in powdered form mixed with oil. I suppose it is becoming my hallmark. I put it on with an old brush, or I might flick it on, or I might rub it on, or whatever – all very accidental, a happy accident, but sometimes you get an unhappy one.'

Brush care
Sue always washes her brushes scrupulously and makes sure after a day's painting that all the brushes are dry. Acrylic can ruin a brush even in a couple of hours.

Keeping brushes and colours clean

Sue is very keen on making sure that her brushes are always cleaned, dried off properly and standing up in a pot after use.

She is also fussy about changing the water frequently when painting: 'I have a big pot of water, no little jam jars. I always try and keep the water as clean as possible. I change the water a lot because if you've used one colour and then you start to use another colour you are sure to get elements of the previous one spoiling the subsequent colours.'

'I am trying to achieve a luminosity and transparency of light and colour. I call it see-throughness.'

Marina Yedigaroff is a painter who is fascinated by surface and beyond. She paints on paper, canvas, board, fabric, walls, doors, furniture, boxes and even wooden bowls. Moving from surface to surface, her techniques and her attitudes towards colour are constantly evolving. Her gallery paintings are executed in a variety of sizes and media.

Decorated house
One of Marina Yedigaroff's concerns as an artist is with what lies beyond the surface. Behind the painted doors and curtains of her house lies a wealth of colour and imagery.

Inspiration and media
The artist paints figures, birds, animals and flowers, creating intense decorative compositions that she describes as being in a 'mood-affective colourist style'. She is inspired by stained glass and the idea of light shining through objects from the back to the front – something that nature does all the time. The paint is applied extremely wet so that the work has fluidity and transparency. 'See-throughness' is an obsession and she is constantly seeking to achieve a luminosity in her painting.

Visual themes
Flowers, figures, birds and animals appear in the artist's work. Among her favourite subjects are tulips with their variety of petal shapes and inspirational colours.

Gouache, ink and technical pens

Working in gouache and ink

The artist uses a technique that is her own. She paints a picture in the normal way using gouache and when it is all done she draws all over it with a technical pen. The process is not quite as simple as it sounds as the idea is to create another dimension of see-throughness. This involves drawing a transparent veil over the painting. She starts from the bottom of the picture and progresses upwards, working in parallel, horizontal lines in coloured inks.

Marina Yedigaroff
Chrysanthemums
Gouache and ink on paper
51 x 91.5cm (20 x 30in)

The degree of transparency and colour of the ink changes as she proceeds: 'I work over the whole surface of the painting row after row, changing the ink colour and transparency as I go; it is all terribly time consuming. It is as if I am putting a fine gauze curtain between the viewer and the image.' She leaves parts untouched, too, so the pure colour of the gouache can still be seen underneath. In the painting *Chrysanthemums*, for example, areas of pure colour are left and a frame within a frame is created by leaving the border untouched.

The artist never knows what is going to happen as her technique creates further dimensions of diffusion: 'It just does something to the painting; you look through it and at it at the same time. It kicks the colours in and out.'

'Everything I do has this wish to get behind and beyond the surface and look through to something else, yet not see it absolutely.'

The point is not in the lines on the painting, but about the effect they have on the colours underneath. The colour of the ink changes from blue to black to brown. Although the lines are evident in the finished work the artist sometimes wishes they were not, as it is the altering effect that interests her rather than the physical appearance of the lines. She acknowledges that there may be some influence from textiles, describing her work as 'a kind of embroidery with a pen', but these are not textile designs, they are paintings.

These pictures come into the category of mixed-media paintings and a strong surface is needed to support the wet layers. She always uses a heavy 300–425gsm (140–200lb) watercolour paper with a smooth or Not surface and works in a variety of sizes. She is not particular about the make of gouache or ink she uses, simply judging by personal preference.

The artist usually works flat on a table. Colours are not set out in any particular order and rather than a conventional palette she uses an old china dinner plate. Favourite colours to which she likes to return time and again are Olive Green, Burnt Sienna, Payne's Grey and white. She makes numerous mixes of her colours, adding any colours that attract her and are to hand. However, she is careful to work methodically in order to preserve clean mixes.

Ink and gouache works are framed behind glass to protect them, but she is passionately averse to non-reflective glass as it seems to drain all the colour away from a painting.

'I mix and mix my colours, adding Alizarin Crimson, Bengal Rose, anything. I use small brushes and strong paper, but I am very organized. I have to be to maintain clean, pure colours.'

Working in oils

In some cases Marina Yedigaroff works from life and in others from her imagination. The tulips in *Red Tulips*, for example, worked in oils, are painted from life. She often chooses to paint tulips, but many of the flowers she depicts are from her head. Birds are another favourite subject.

Some people are surprised to find that these paintings are oils and believe them to be watercolours because of the transparency of the effect, but oil paint is the artist's main medium when working on board. Again, she paints extremely wet to maintain luminosity and transparency, mostly on MDF, first preparing the board with white acrylic primer.

She starts with the image, sometimes drawing it out first, but not always. With *Red Tulips* the flowers were painted on the board and looked 'rather ordinary' on a white background, so she started working into the background, using a brush in one hand and a hairdryer in the other. Her painting evolves subconsciously without a plan in mind, using very thin, diluted paint.

A painting such as this is worked flat, sitting at a table, but for larger paintings an easel is used. Oil painting is much faster than painting in gouache and ink. The artist's oil technique is quite precise as she is still aiming for transparency and movement. Colour is not flooded on, but she needs to work very fast and the hairdryer helps to move the paint, blowing it around the surface. Although working in oils, the paint tends to dry fairly quickly because it is so thin.

White spirit is used to dilute the colours: 'I have to keep my brushes clean to maintain clear, pure colours and have to frequently change the white spirit.'

The artist believes that oils settle. A finished painting is put straight up on a wall and after a few days it looks as if the surface has changed. If she thinks it looks awful she just paints over it.

'I am very driven and always planning what I am going to paint next.'

Marina Yedigaroff
Red Tulips
Oil on board
91.5 x 51cm (30 x 20in)

Choice of media
Oil paint, gouache and ink are the main mediums used. Occasionally the artist paints with acrylics, particularly for exterior mural work, but she dislikes this medium for conventional painting, finding it artificial and plastic-looking. The transparent effect that she achieves with oils, using dilute mixes of colours, is more usually associated with watercolour paintings.

☛**See also**

Choosing media/Oils	30–31
Choosing media/Gouache	34
Liquid colours	151
Dry colour and line	152

'My work is about simplification. I am trying to get to the essence of the subject by eliminating unnecessary detail which may confuse the eye and detract from the colours and shapes of the painting.'

Titanium White and Yellow Ochre

Cadmium, Alizarin and Venetian Reds

Cerulean and Cobalt Blue

Medium and Light Cadmium Yellow

Lemon Yellow and Aureolin

Daphne Jo Lowrie is an artist who moves freely between oils and watercolours. In her recent works she has used oils for painting still-life and landscape subjects and has concentrated on simplicity of colour, form and composition to convey the basic essence of her subjects.

Choosing colour

The artist does not necessarily choose expensive pigments, but she insists on having good-quality colours in her primary colour selection. She always has an artists' quality red, yellow and blue available, and there are two core colours that are essential to her palette and colour mixing range. These colours are white – usually a Titanium White is selected – and Yellow Ochre.

Colours are chosen from the primary colours depending on the subject or mood, but the artist often chooses her primary hues at random. Those she tends to use are Cadmium, Alizarin and Venetian Reds, Cobalt, Ultramarine and Cerulean Blues, and a medium and a light Cadmium Yellow, a Lemon Yellow and a rich yellow such as an Aureolin. For a blue-mauve effect, for example, she works with Alizarin Red and Ultramarine Blue.

Specific colour themes are often developed. A coastal series of paintings, for instance, uses Cadmium and Venetian Red, Cerulean and Cobalt Blue, and a Cadmium Yellow for warmth. Her foundation colours of white and Yellow Ochre are always included.

Working with oils

Daphne Jo loves working in oils. Oil paint is malleable and dries slowly and she particularly likes the way it can be moved around, allowing the artist to stroke it on smoothly or leave brushmarks and textures: 'It is sheer joy every time I dip my brush into this lovely buttery material. I enjoy its versatility and its sensuality.'

From an emotional, rather than practical, point of view the artist finds that oils have a quality that takes her mood. It is a positive medium, so she can take a gentle approach, yet within seconds become dramatic and forceful.

Getting it on clothing and having to clean brushes afterwards is a problem, but oils offer something that other painting media cannot.

Mixing colour

The artist works with two palettes, keeping her main colours on one palette and using another palette for mixing. It is all quite organized, though it sometimes does not look so. She may take half an hour to mix a colour and it is an important process for her: 'I sit quietly and think about my graduation of mixes that will create the harmony in the painting.' She mixes a lot of colour first in order not to stop work in mid flow.

Picking up individual colours to create a mix is equated to a marriage, with the colours regarded as a family. Bits of all those colours are taken from her basic palette through to her mixes. These are modified all the time, but as they are all from a common source, and related, this creates harmony in the painting.

'At the end of the day with the paints that are left over I can create a lovely grey. And I know that this grey is made up from all the relatives.'

The still-life paintings
The artist has been exploring a pictorial theme that is strong and graphic with blocks of colour contained within defined shapes. In these paintings the negative or background and in-between shapes are as important to her as the positive shapes of the objects. Her starting points are simple still-life arrangements set up on a table in front of a window. These become a basic colour, shape and compositional reference and from this the artist can quickly start interpreting and improvising.

Daphne Jo Lowrie
Siblings, 2001
Oil on canvas
55 x 45cm (21½ x 17¾in)

See also

Choosing media/Oils 30–31
Choosing palettes 40–41
Black 76–79

Daphne Jo Lowrie
Still Life with Orange Flower
Oil on canvas
55 x 45cm (21½ x 17¾in)

Varying intensity

The intensity of the colour and texture within a painting is changed by applying colour either thickly or very thinly in the way one would use watercolours. The artist works with paint straight from the tube without mediums except for turpentine or white spirit. Working over or around 'dribbly', thinly painted passages with thick, 'juicy' paint, she makes almost three-dimensional marks: 'I do not tend to build up surfaces and layers and transparent glazes. I like working directly and immediately. Processes and stages worry me.'

Daphne Jo Lowrie
Still Life with Bottles
Oil on canvas
55 x 45cm (21½ x 17¾in)

Exploring a theme

In these paintings the artist started by tinting the canvas with a thin mix of Burnt Sienna, then quite aggressively painted in the outlines of the objects. She made a dark-line brush drawing of the entire set-up. Black is not normally used as a mixing colour, but here she used pure black with a little Alizarin Crimson to take off the intensity.

When you look closely, though, you can see that the outline is not all black. Traces of other colours have been picked up, so the line wanes and softens. Sometimes there is a bit of red, making the outline brownish. Sometimes a little Raw Umber is added and this, too, makes the outline a little gentler. This brush drawing is used as a basis to give the picture its structure.

The artist originally thought of these still lifes as being quite conventional paintings of objects standing in space. Her plan was to fill the shapes right in and overpaint them, but she started painting up to the line, biting into it and occasionally obliterating it altogether, although always leaving it as part of the composition. On standing back and looking at the outlines in relation to the colours, she decided that she liked the line and that it worked in the painting. The outlines are very successful in defining both colour and shape, particularly in the way the colour bounces off the dark lines. The pictures evolved accidentally from here and she went on to paint a series of images.

Interpreting colour

The colours from the still-life set-up are interpreted to the painting in an emotional rather than an objective, observational way. For example, in *Still Life with Orange Flower* there is a clear-white bottle and a blue pot with an orange flower. It is the orange flower that attracted the artist in the first place and she wanted this to take her into the painting. So she played with colours until she found a combination that worked with the orange flower, mixing a blue for the vase that complements the orange of the flower. This approach makes a starting point and sets the code for the rest of the painting.

'As soon as I get my first colours down I am already sensing how to move the painting forwards in colour and tone. I sometimes go wrong with a painting and have to scrape it back to zero, but I realize quite quickly whether a painting is going to work or not.'

Daphne Jo Lowrie likes painting on paper and started the studies for the outlined still lifes on paper before moving on to canvas. The artist wanted the pictures to be simple and unframed, so the colour is carried around the edge of the canvas, too, and she started thinking about the whole painting as an object in itself. When you look into these paintings there is a lot of pattern and abstraction in the forms. Working in oils allows you to create lovely movements in the colour, which adds to the design. Getting excited about the paint and the colour overtakes concerns with the observation of the image. The forms and shapes become the vehicles that allow the artist to play around with colour and the texture of the surface.

'I sometimes pick up colours unintentionally. There are often happy accidents that take place, mishaps that can transform a painting from the mundane to the sublime.'

Vivid solid-ground colours

Sometimes the artist paints a whole canvas in a really strong, assertive ground colour, and then everything that goes on top of that colour involves a hard fight. You have to work hard to get your colours to register and in that process you can come up with some extraordinary and interesting hues. You are setting yourself a challenge by starting with dominant and powerful ground colours.

Solid-colour grounds drying, waiting for the first marks.

The artist may decide to paint some boats on one of these strong grounds, not boats with all their rigging and equipment, but the organic shapes and geometry of boats. These strong ground colours are painted as a challenge for when she does the final paintings, and enable her to create colour mixes and combinations that 'sock you in the eye'. Strong and powerful effects often cannot be achieved on a purely white ground.

Venetian Red ground
This painting in progress is painted on a solid Venetian Red ground and there is also some local underpainting in solid Burnt Sienna. The dark red and sienna peep through the subsequent colours; these little areas that are left attract the eye and create an excitement on the surface of the picture.

'I work mostly with oil paint straight from the tube, applying it with a knife. I like the simplicity of it. I do little preliminary work other than a basic simple line and brush drawing.'

Working with oilbar
Oilbar, also known as oil-painting stick, is used like a drawing tool. The basic drawing work can then be thinned and blended to make transparent lines and washes.

'I find this preliminary oilbar work can bring a glow to the colour. The underlying transparency brings a luminousness to the subsequent layers of pure opaque colour that I lay on with a knife.'

☛**See also**

Optical colour mixing 23

Choosing media/Oils 30–31

Choosing media/Oilbars 31

Dry colour and line 152–153

John Reay is an artist who works on large oil paintings. Many of his works are populated with hundreds of figures. Using a palette-knife technique, often worked over an oilbar underpainting, he creates what he calls 'a broken-prismatic effect' to produce luminous and vibrant surfaces of colour and light.

Working methods
The artist works on primed board, either hardboard, plywood or MDF. He likes working on board as its tough surface allows him 'to attack it when using a knife'.

Experience has shown him how to prime the board with the exact painting surface he wants: 'I use a coarse lambswool roller to give the surface a bit of tooth and, depending on the speed and density of primer application, I can lay down whatever surface texture I need.'

He then tints the prepared board with a thin wash of neutral-coloured acrylic or oils. He tends to keep to a consistent lilac-grey tint colour when painting directly. This neutral ground colour does not influence the outcome of the final picture greatly and there is little chance of it darkening and influencing the subsequent colours in later years. If he is underpainting with oilbars he often works onto a white-primed surface.

He uses good-quality oil paint, with no thinners or mediums except for paintings where he has employed oilbar (oil-painting sticks) to make the basic underpainting.

A lilac-grey tint colour provides a useful neutral ground.

Composing the painting
With these very crowded subjects the artist has an idea of the dynamics of the whole painting, but he does not draw each individual figure. If he started drawing all the figures one by one he could get in a terrible muddle, so it is essential to have an overall pattern and scheme in place.

Sometimes he makes a few rough preparatory sketches with a ballpoint pen to work out the dynamics of the composition, but he puts in the figures as he goes, reinventing them as he paints. He has an overall picture in his mind, but he does not draw it all out in detail: 'I put in a very basic brush-line drawing, but I do not stick to it when I get going. The idea of the drawing is just to indicate the basic size and position of the figures.'

If you look closely you will see that the application of colour, the knifework and brushmarks create the figures. The colour is not filled in between drawn outlines.

The artist knows roughly what sort of space the figures and groups need to occupy. With so many figures appearing in a painting correct perspective is important and the diminishing sizes must look right. He does not want some figures too small or others too big, so keeps an eye on where these people all are in space. The painting is improvised within a fairly tight mental plan as he works.

Oilbar for underpainting
John often uses oilbar as a basic drawing tool to make an underpainting and to draft in the forms and the composition. He makes a large drawing with oilbar that looks quite crude at this stage, then uses a round brush to blend the drawing with turpentine so that it looks more like a painting. The oilbar work becomes very thin and transparent and then he works over it with the painting knife.

He considers the oilbar technique as another way of drawing, as an intermediary stage to lay out the composition and lay in colour. Sometimes he reverses the colour; for example, he may have an underpainting of green and then work over it with red. Oilbar enables him to build up layers quickly and to get colour contrasts of one colour over another to create the broken-prismatic effect of the surface of his paintings.

John Reay
Lowestoft Beach
Oil on board
91.5 x 122cm (36 x 48in)

John Reay pursues techniques established by the Fauvists and Impressionists who expressed light not through tonal means but through colour contrasts and juxtaposition.

Light

For about five years John Reay worked exclusively outside, painting from nature. As a result his approach to light in a studio painting is now quite automatic and intuitive. In a complicated figure scene he finds that light is a unifying factor in a picture. It pulls everything together and brings a logic to the colour: 'It is not entirely this, of course. There are other factors to take into account, but light is so important for me. In all my paintings, whether single or massed-figure compositions, light and the way it strikes the forms is an important part of the painting.'

'I seldom mix colour on the palette. If I want a mid tone, for example, I pick up the component colours and mix them while spreading them on the canvas.'

'I often pick up two or three colours on the knife in one go and blend them wet-into-wet on the surface.'

Colours and paints

The artist usually works with more or less the same colour range. The reds are Alizarin Crimson, Cadmium Red and Vermilion. The yellows he chooses are Cadmium Yellow, Cadmium Yellow Light, Lemon Yellow, Yellow Ochre and, sometimes, Raw Sienna.

For blues he selects Cerulean Blue, Ultramarine Blue and sometimes a Cobalt Blue. He also likes Viridian, a ready-mixed green. He does not use black, preferring to mix Alizarin Crimson and Viridian to create a lovely dark that is full of colour.

A mix of Alizarin Crimson and Viridian creates a soft, rich dark.

He nearly always chooses Titanium White as it is a strong opaque white. He finds Flake White can often be a little too heavy and textured when used straight from the tube. Titanium White has a much smoother consistency for knifework.

The colour that he tends to use probably more than any other is Yellow Ochre. He describes it as 'a lovely, earthy colour and a medium range one, too, a warm glowing colour.' He finds it brings a bronze quality to flesh and an underlying earthy, yet human, warmth to figure painting.

Yellow Ochre is a warm, resonant colour.

Core colours

Alizarin Crimson
Cadmium Red
Vermilion
Cadmium Yellow
Cadmium Yellow Light
Lemon Yellow
Yellow Ochre Dark
Yellow Ochre
Raw Sienna
Cerulean Blue
Ultramarine Blue
Cobalt Blue
Viridian

A prismatic palette layout

He lays out his colours in a rough sequence. Since he does not stick too carefully to a set order some of the colours can become jumbled. Basically he follows a visual layout, from reds, grading through purples to warm blues, then through to cooler blues and on to yellows and greens.

Following this prismatic approach is useful, particularly as he works at quite a fast rate when he starts painting. It makes sense for the colours on the palette to have some kind of order and relationship, with the reds next to the oranges and the crimson closer to the ultramarine, for instance.

His palettes are disposable bits of board. He uses the same boards time and again, but they eventually reach the point where they are unusable and he simply throws them away. As the colour mixing takes place on the surface of the painting there is a good chance of colours contaminating one another on the palette. With the colours arranged prismatically there is less chance of contamination.

'Sometimes you find accidental colour mixes on the palette are more interesting than those that are happening in the work.'

Knife and brushwork

Most of the colour mixing takes place on the surface of the painting. The artist frequently blends his knifework with a brush, particularly in parts of the painting where the forms are small, and also where using pure knifework would overshadow the form and make it look clumsy.

The outline of a form is re-established with a brush and the inside attacked with a knife, creating a kind of visual dialogue of brushed and knifed marks: 'You cannot paint with a knife in a tight, limited way; it has got to be used in blocks and patches of colour.'

He finds that with a knife it is a process of defining, losing and redefining the form throughout the whole composition, going over it again and again with the knife.

'I find with a painting knife I can get amazing mixes because the individual colours never quite blend, particularly if you pick up two colours on different parts of the knife blade. They become blended in the mark that results.'

'In this technique of painting accident and chance can play a large part.'

John Reay
Lowestoft Beach
(same-size detail)

In this technique of painting interesting effects can occur quite by chance. It is very much part of painting with a knife that the artist can accidentally pick up a fleck of colour, but the colour does not blend in the same way as it does with brushwork. The colours showing through from underneath are important, making an interaction between the different layers of colour. Sometimes if an area of the painting has gone 'dead' the artist will deliberately change the colour. If someone is wearing a blue shirt, for instance, he may find that changing it to a red or green one brings some sparkle back into the painting.

How long does it take?

John never times how long a painting takes. It can be weeks or months, sometimes years: 'The initial laying in is usually done quite quickly, but when the picture has a lot going on I am redrawing it all the time, building up the colours and working to get a greater richness and balance.'

He tries to complete the knife-worked passages in one go, but it is not always possible. It is not so satisfactory to go over a painting again when it is dry. There is a different feeling and a different blend of paints when working over a dry, encrusted surface.

Sometimes he needs to go over a painting or parts of it again to make it work, but the best ones are often those done with minimum overworking. There is always a greater obvious freshness in the application of the colour.

'We tend to get through a lot of white; it's probably the greatest volume of any of the colours we use. When working on this scale we use a lot of tints – we don't need our colours to be too bright.'

Jessie Carr and Lucy Dunsterville are two artists who paint huge backdrops or 'cloths'. Their work is seen mainly in film, television and stage productions and is often used to decorate and provide atmosphere for special events. They are, in a sense, commercial artists working to order or commission, but they also create their own works, for sale or hire, which they post on their website. They choose household colours as a matter of course and use them with great success.

Bulk-volume colours

There are many kinds of colours – mainly with an acrylic base – that are available specifically for large-scale, scenic and mural painting. However, through experience these artists have found that ordinary household vinyl-emulsion paint suits their working methods best.

House and industrial paints

Household paints are inexpensive in comparison with artists' paint, but the artist needs to bear in mind that these paints are designed for a specific purpose. They are made for decorating rooms and houses where the colours will be changed, on average, every two to five years. Thus, these products are aimed at a market where extreme longevity is not the prime concern, so they are generally composed of ingredients that can eventually fail.

From an artist's point of view, the binders and fillers they contain, particularly in emulsion paints, can often make colours look flat and chalky and therefore lacking in intensity when used for painting a picture.

Sound technique

Paint specialists generally recommend that artists do not use industrial, household and decorating paints in their paintings and there are good reasons for this advice. The main one is that the pigments and binders used in these paints, compared to artists' colours, are less stable over time. Decorating paints, however, are perfectly good products in themselves. They offer a huge variety of colours and finishes, and are available in hundreds, perhaps thousands, of different hues, tints and shades.

For painters who use non-art colours the longevity of their work is an important consideration that requires them to follow sound technique. By staying with one medium – that is, not mixing oil-based and water-based paints – and working on appropriate supports, artists can avoid future problems. Works that are twenty years old can look as good as new after being hoovered, then sprayed with water to tighten them up.

Core colours

Decorating paints are given names that aim to create a mood and emotional response in the buyer. The same hue may be given one name one year and a different name the next. Sometimes a colour is deleted altogether, which can lead to difficulties with consistency. The core colours used by Jessie Carr and Lucy Dunsterville all have commercial names but they have fairly well-matched equivalents in artists' paint-colour ranges too. If you have a good eye and know your colours you can easily find hues that resemble artists' colours.

Choosing a palette

Their palette consists of ready-mixed paint bought directly from the supplier, and with a chosen set list of colours they can achieve a multitude of effects without having to resort to complex colour mixing in the studio. Obviously they mix and blend individual colours to achieve specific detail and the subtlety of effect they are after in certain passages of a painting, but, on the whole, they find their set palette of around twelve colours covers most of their requirements. The standard colours they use are: black, white, three blues, three browns, two reds, a pink, two greens and a yellow (see left).

Preferred finish

Just as artists working on conventional 'easel' paintings discover their preferred brand of colour, so these two artists have discovered theirs and always use the British paint brand Dulux. They only use the matt-vinyl finish, except for black, where they prefer the silk variety for its stronger pigmentation.

'We find this brand best for consistency and flow; the colours mix well and dry evenly. Some other brands can dry with a bit of a plasticky film.'

Trade Name	Generic Name
1. Regatta	Cerulean Blue
2. Aria	Cobalt Blue
3. Apothecary	Ultramarine Blue
4. Poppy	Cadmium Red Light
5. Fancy Dress	Naphthol Red Light
6. Monarch	Quinacridone Red
7. Gold Cup	Cadmium Yellow
8. Bracken	Yellow Ochre
9. Saddle	Burnt Sienna
10. VanDyke	Burnt Umber
11. Hollybush	Chrome Oxide Green
12. Goblin	Perm. Green Light

Mixing and painting

The medium the artists use for thinning their colours is water, and lots of it. At times their painting method almost becomes a staining technique as they brush and scrub the colour into the unprimed and absorbent support, flooding pure colour into the large areas with big housepainter's brushes, alternately picking up the shadow and detail with smaller brushes. They blend colours directly on the raw-calico cloth and create special colours by simply mixing their paints on the floor.

Colour on a large scale

The scale of the work is quite amazing when compared to a conventional painting. An average work would be 6m (20ft) long and 4m (13ft) high. The maximum scale the artists prefer to work to is dictated by the height of their studio – their current painting frame is limited to a 4m (13ft) height – but they have worked on massive pieces up to 37m (120ft) long and these have to be tackled in sections. If the height exceeds 4m (13ft) they have to allow the calico to extend down the wall onto the floor, and often paint sections working upside down. It tends to work out that Lucy, being the taller, works on the top sections, while Jessie tackles the lower ones.

Painting surface

The support used to paint on is artists' quality calico. This is a fairly lightweight cotton material and they work on it unprimed.

Studio techniques

Housepainter's brushes are used for painting large areas and the floor is used as an improvised mixing palette.

Planning a painting

On approval, after discussing details with the client, the artists transfer a preparatory sketch onto the calico support, using a measuring system, then draw the whole composition in with charcoal, modifying it as they go.

When painting the final canvas they keep colour references to hand, working from their own reference photographs or magazine and book references, depending on the commission.

In this case an Indian city was central to the commission and they had to work from photographic references for the scorched city and the dry, sandy earth colours of the landscape. The succulent green foreground foliage was taken from references made at the Royal Botanic Gardens, Kew, and the final success of the painting is left up to their skill and imagination.

Colour swatches

When painting the final canvas the artists make colour swatches, planning the hues, tints and shades they will require. They keep the selection of colours as simple as possible, having found through experience that if too many colours are mixed together the overall effect is deadened and the life taken out of the painting.

Teamwork

The artists work as a team – two people as one. They tend to paint their own sections, with different spurts of energy. A painting measuring 4 x 6m (13 x 20ft) takes two or three days to complete.

Preparatory sketch

If it is a commission the artists are working on it will start off as a fairly detailed small sketch painting that will be done to the exact proportions of the final required size. They may show some alternative colour variation sketches too, and the presentation sketches are accompanied by a colour swatch.

Judith Chestnutt describes herself as a papermaker, and the raw material of her work is junk mail that she makes into paper pulp. Judith utilizes the mountain of printed advertising material that accumulates in her home – the unsolicited coupons, leaflets and free sheets that are commonplace in every household. She rarely needs to buy any manufacturers' colours for her creative pursuits as her medium is delivered for free through her letterbox every day.

'I admire the recycling ethic and work with that in mind.'

Selecting the raw materials

Judith Chestnutt has developed a keen eye for the kind of junk mail she is looking for. Some printed papers perform better than others in the recycling process and produce a more successful finished work. When thinking of a new paper-pulp picture she sorts her papers for reuse using tried and tested criteria.

The artist avoids paper that has previously been recycled and she can usually tell through experience which papers these are. This usually precludes the use of newsprint, which is often, but not always, on recycled paper. The problems with such papers are that the fibres are too short: 'If you think about it, the paper has been shredded once before in the original recycling process; I get hold of it and shred it again and the fibres have become even shorter. The paper pulp does not blend easily and join together in the finished work.'

The papers should not be too shiny. Gloss art and machine-glazed papers and those with heavily varnished inks do not recycle into pulp easily. These papers do not absorb water readily and this makes the process of conversion to paper pulp more difficult than it needs to be.

This does not entirely exclude the reuse of shiny paper for recycling; it can be used, but it has to be soaked for an extremely long time. Alternatively it can be boiled since this helps accelerate the water-absorption process that is essential in making a good pulp, but boiling results in colour loss and, in turn, leads to a pulp that is of more subdued colour.

Selection of the raw materials for the paper-pulp medium is a continuous process and the artist sorts the junk paper systematically by colour into her storage system – reds into one drawer, blues into another, yellows into another, and so forth.

Shredding and pulping

The selected paper is torn and shredded colour by colour and from this selection of raw material the artist manufactures her paper pulp.

It is a simple enough process, but achieving a workable pulp that will blend and stick together in the final artwork requires experience and a good eye for the right raw materials.

Shredding

Having selected the papers for recycling, the next process is shredding. Hand shredding is best, and the artist simply tears the paper up into small pieces. Sometimes she uses a shredder, the type you can buy in an office-supply store for destroying documents. Using a shredder is less labour intensive and saves time when working on a large piece, but on the whole the artist has found hand shredding to be a more satisfactory method. Torn-edged paper breaks down more easily than paper with cut edges and the fibres tend to remain intact for the pulp-making process.

Recycling envelopes

Bank and junk-mail envelope interiors provide a wealth of blues for recycling to paper pulp.

Judith Chestnutt
Colour sample
Paper pulp
15.2 x 10.2cm (6 x 4in)

'I use whatever paper I can get. Bank envelopes with blue patterns printed inside make nice skies.'

Judith Chestnutt
Shoreline, 2001
Paper pulp
30 x 30cm (12 x 12in)

The artist is committed to conservation and the materials seen in her paper-pulp images of shorelines celebrate this passion. In recycling seemingly useless paper into individual artworks she combines her practical and creative skills to create pictures that she describes as paperworks. Her fresh, unpolluted shoreline studies make a positive stand against wastefulness and overt consumption.

'It is very important to use lots of water. My ingredients are very pure and simple. I do not use any glues, binders or chemicals and my final coloured pulp is stored in recycled plastic containers.'

Soaking and pulping

The shredded paper is then soaked in buckets with lots of water. After about three or four days the wet paper is ready for pulping and it is transferred in small amounts to an ordinary kitchen liquidizer. Again this is where the artist's experience comes into play and she has learned through trial and error the exact amount of shredded paper and the exact amount of pulping time – about five seconds – that is needed to make the perfect paper pulp.

It is very important that the pulp is the right consistency for working with on the final picture. If the shredded paper is pulped (that is, liquidized) for more than five seconds the short fibres will disintegrate and the work will not hold together. If it does not pulp after five seconds the paper has not been soaked for long enough.

'The pulped fibres have to stick together and lock into each other. If you over-process, nothing holds together.'

Working with coloured-paper pulp

Currently Judith is working on shoreline sea and sky compositions and from her collection of papers she selects various blues, and both cool and warm yellows, for shredding and pulping. Fortunately, she says, blue and yellow are predominant junk-mail colours, so she has a lot of colour choice for her subject matter.

Before she starts a pulp picture the artist thinks a lot about it and what she wants to do. She makes preparatory paintings and drawings and has a design for the composition in mind. All her themes – sea, sky and horizon – are inspired by nature.

She often works on a back piece, a pre-prepared piece of paper, to act as a support for the paper-pulp composition. This is particularly helpful if it is a larger work, but the pictures in the shoreline series are fairly small, about 30 x 30cm (12 x 12in), so for these the artist works directly with the paper pulp.

The artist works flat on a table, first laying down an absorbent surface, in this case tough, absorbent paper kitchen cloths. The work with the coloured pulp is started by using a fork to pick it up, the way one would use a paintbrush: 'I work with the coloured pulps, picking them up, laying them down on the absorbent cloth, laying and blending the pulp just as if I was using paint, until I feel the work is finished.'

Then she puts another absorbent cloth over the whole work, squeezes out the surplus moisture and lays it on one side to dry: 'I press really hard to take the water and compact the pulp, and then leave it to dry overnight.' The finished work is, by its very nature, highly textured, a handmade piece created with no grain or direction.

Once the completed picture is dry another process is employed to modify the surface and accentuate various parts of the composition. The artist often irons parts of the work to bring in another textural dimension. She uses a hot, ordinary domestic iron to flatten certain areas of the surface and uses the hot tip to indent small local areas to add to the texture and relief.

Using the liquidizer

If the shredded paper is liquidized for more than five seconds the paper fibres will break up and the work will not bind together properly.

Remnants of the original

'I like seeing some of the original material and being able to see what it is made of – a bit of type here, the lining pattern of an envelope there.'

Junk-mail colours

'In the sky and sea there are all sorts of colours. I can mix the pulps just like paint – I use them just like paint.'

Judith Chestnutt
Colour samples
Paper pulp
20.3 x 15.2cm (8 x 6in)

'It is a very simple process, using very simple equipment. Anyone can do it anywhere.'

Waste-paper collages

In addition to pulping junk mail, old newspapers and magazines are an endless free source of colours and materials for collage work. You will be surprised at the large areas of pure colour to be found that are uninterrupted by text or images. To avoid what is known as 'show through' – this is when print or type matter shows through from the back – paste the collages onto grey or black backgrounds.

Print editions
If you have a home PC set-up you can make convincing lithograph-like prints by scanning junk-paper collages and printing them onto heavy-quality papers or special printer-compatible canvas. Make short, signed and numbered editions, using archive-quality inks in the printer for longevity.

Collage samples
Magazine cuttings
and envelope interiors
12.7 x 15.2cm (5 x 6in) *(above)*
12.7 x 17.7cm (5 x 7in) *(above right)*
10.2 x 17.7cm (5 x 7in) *(right)*

☞**See also**
Colours for free 144–145

Many artists experiment with found materials and Primitive societies still use naturally occurring colours in their work. In developed societies, too, it is easy and fun to find colours from animal, vegetable and mineral sources around the house and garden.

Blood

Myths exist of deranged artists who painted with blood. It is said that El Greco (Domenikos Theotocopoulos) (1541–1614) used his own blood as he was often seen with bandaged hands, thought to be a result of drawing his own blood. It is more probable the bandaging was to protect skin damage caused by turpentine. It is common knowledge that blood is useless for painting as it becomes dark brown within a few days and eventually turns black.

Custom tinting

You can create warm tints using wine, tea, coffee and cola.

Natural complementaries

Autumn leaves of *Rhus trichocarpa*

☞**See also**

Yellow Ochre 66

Brown and Red Earth 72–75

Colours from the mail 140–143

El Greco (1541–1614)

Cochineal and vanilla essence

Fat, saliva, ash and charcoal

Early known examples of pigment used for images date back at least 35,000 years. Analysis of the famous cave paintings of south-west Europe, some 15,000 years old, reveals the use of animal fat, saliva, ash and charcoal. Pigments derived from the earth – colours that are now categorized as oxides, ochres and siennas – are also commonly found.

Cochineal mask

This graphite drawing is tinted with cochineal food colour. Foodstuffs and food colourings provide good sources of tinting materials.

Mustard powder in matt acrylic medium

Mustard powder in red wine

Mustard powder

English mustard in powder form makes a good transparent ochre.

Chilli powder in acrylic medium

Brick dust

Brick dust plus Titanium White

Sandstone in matt acrylic medium

Terracotta in matt acrylic medium

Mineral colours

Colours can easily be obtained by drilling into bricks and stones with a masonry drill bit. The resulting spoil, or dust, can then be bound in an acrylic medium and used like paint.

Vegetable colours

Colour can be obtained from vegetable matter. Grass, petals and berries can be rubbed into the surface of the paper to impart some of their original pigment. Many colours tend to go brown or quickly fade. However, the samples here are at least one year old.

Grass

Rose hip

Red-hot poker (Kniphofia)

Blackberry

Blackberry and Titanium White

Coal ash

Coal ash plus Titanium White

Soot

Simon Jennings
Dust to Dust
Teak wood dust
and acrylic medium on canvas
29.3 x 20.5cm (11½ x 8in)

Beach colour
The beach in this location was composed of grey volcanic pebbles, creating a mottled carpet of shadows and textures.

There is a great tradition of painting out of doors and observing light and colour directly from nature. When travelling it may be impractical to carry full-scale painting equipment, but successful results can be achieved with a limited selection of colours and materials.

Thinking ahead
If you will be painting in a sunny climate by the ocean, for example, obvious colour choices come to mind and you can pre-select your palette accordingly. Choose fast-drying media and good quality paper.

Primary Blue
An inexpensive and versatile middle blue. It is the most dominant colour in the picture above, but any mid blue would suffice. Primary Blue is fairly close in hue to Cerulean Blue.

Neutral Gray, value 5
An excellent neutral grey, used here for the beach and distant hills. It was mainly applied thinned with water, sometimes with a little white added.

Parchment
A very neutral lightish green, almost white; very useful when travelling light. It proved versatile here – applied thickly for the sea, in washes for the sky, and in admixture to lighten the other colours.

Naples Yellow (Hue)
An opaque lightish yellow; excellent for mixing. Subtle and not too dominant, here it suggests the transparency and reflective qualities of the sea. It was also used in its pure state for the distant shore.

.... **Sketchbook page join** (Sketchbook is 50 per cent actual size)

Travelling light

A colour sketching trip to the Mediterranean coast of the South of France necessitated travelling light. The artist, anticipating the opportunity to paint the sea and sky, took a small wooden box containing five tubes of acrylic paint – the four colours shown opposite, and white. In addition to a few brushes the travel-painting kit included a small watercolour box to provide a wider range of colours. A red came in handy for the sails of the dinghies and the roofs of distant buildings, and a touch of green depicted the foliage in the hills and the shoreline palms.

From Castel Plage
Acrylic and watercolour
in sketchbook
21 x 53cm (8¼ x 21in)

The beach scene above takes up a double-page spread of a sketchbook, and is shown here at about half size. Acrylics were the predominant materials used, but watercolour, applied fairly thickly, provided the small red and green colour accents that are shown in the actual-size details on the left.

Colour inspiration
Abandoned rope fragments from nets and boats are among the colours and textures to be found on most beaches.

☛**See also**
Choosing media/Acrylics 33
Dry colour and line 152–153

'I am a painter not a dyer.'

REMBRANDT'S RESPONSE TO THE CRITICISM THAT HE APPLIED HIS COLOURS TOO THICKLY

A strong relationship exists in the making of artwork between the use of colour in painting and in textiles. Cotton and linen canvas has always provided a traditional base for the artist's creations. Fabric dyes, too, share many colour sources and similarities with paints used in fine art painting.

In addition to straightforward painting, the techniques of dyeing, embroidery and appliqué can be used to great effect in making colourful art. In most manufacturers' catalogues today you will find textile and fabric paints, and general art materials suppliers even offer plain white cotton T-shirts for painting on. You will also find a wide range of silk and encaustic paints suitable for fabric applications.

Helen Banzhaf
(left and far left)
Vessels
Machine embroideries
Cotton thread on calico

Helen Dougall
(below)
Set Aside
Wall hanging,
Wax-resisted dyes on silk
47 x 64cm (18½ x 25¼in)

Australian bird species

Chris Perry is an artist whose background is in film animation, where he learnt about colours and colour mixing. These skills have infuenced his work as an illustrator, painter, paper sculptor and textile artist. For inspiration for his work he develops drawings and paintings from his sketchbook. Many of his images include people and animals, which he uses to communicate an environmental message.

Chris Perry
Homage to Paul *(left)*
Australian birds *(far left)*
Acrylic fabric paints on cotton

T-shirt designs

The artist washes the T-shirt to remove the starch used in the manufacturing process. He then inserts plastic-covered cardboard the same size as the shirt to act as a stiffener and barrier for the paint. A black marker sketch on white paper may be inserted under the shirt for a drawing guide. Otherwise, paint is applied directly onto the shirt.

Acrylic-based screen and fabric printing colours are used. The artist mainly treats the paint like watercolour, mixing it with water using sable brushes, but if he wants the colour to be flat and opaque he uses bristle brushes.

Sometimes black defining lines are required, so he leaves the areas of colour to dry overnight and paints the black next day. When dry, after two days, he irons the reverse of the fabric to fix the design.

Acrylic fabric paints are extremely bright and washfast. Chris limits his colours to Lemon Yellow, Brilliant Yellow, Vermilion, Crimson, Cobalt, Ultramarine, black and white and finds these are enough to produce a wide range of mixes. The artist is an ardent fan of primary colours and he particularly likes to use a watered-down Cobalt, which is excellent for sea and sky.

There are many textile paints on the market as well as a special textile medium that, when added to ordinary acrylic paint, renders it more flexible and increases washfastness.

'The advantage of painting on T-shirts is that one can wear and communicate one's art and message to the rest of the world. It feels like a mix of watercolour and canvas painting; it is cheap and fun. I have a love of nature and I work for a range of environment charities; on occasions I produce limited editions of approximately one hundred hand-painted shirts.'

Chris Perry
Homage to Vincent *(above and left)*
Acrylic fabric paints on cotton

Painting techniques are often associated with qualities of surface texture, involving impasto, mark making, glazes, washes and conscious brushwork. There are, however, many artists who practise a flatter, more controlled approach to colour. These methods of applying paint smoothly are sometimes born of necessity, and this is particularly so when colour images have to be considered for reproduction by photography or direct digital scanning.

In traditional animated-film cel painting techniques, before the use of computers, a special kind of liquid acrylic paint with strong pigments and good covering power, known as Cel Vinyl or Cartoon Paint, was the preferred medium. Thinner, more viscous colours of this type are still often favoured by artists who are pursuing a flatter, graphic or more fluid technique, and are also used by painters of large-scale murals as well as designers and illustrators whose work has to be photographed or scanned for reproduction.

Flatness and density
Although a little battered after nearly 35 years in storage, this original cel from the film *Yellow Submarine* (1968) shows the flatness and density of colour to be achieved by painting in opaque colours on the reverse of transparent materials such as glass and clear plastic. The detail above shows the not-so-smooth and more painterly effect on the reverse or working side of the cel.

Cel painting
Prior to the advent of computers nearly all animated cartoon films were produced by the 'paint and trace' method. This is where the design is traced in black outline onto transparent celuloid, hence the abbreviation 'cel'. Each cel was then passed to the painting department and the colours were filled in by hand. This process required a high degree of painting skill as the artists had to keep the paint extremely flat and flood it into the image, making sure the liquid paint did not overrun the traced outline. Painters had to work quickly, too, as cartoon films were composed of hundreds of thousands of individual cels, which were then photographed onto movie film.

To make certain of complete flatness and evenness of colour for photography the outline designs were traced on the front of the cel and the colour was painted onto the back. Painting opaque colours on the reverse of transparent materials is an invaluable technique that ensures an absolutely smooth surface effect.

Heinz Edelman
(Original character design)
Paul and Ringo
Hand-painted animation cel
32 x 41cm (12½ x 16in)
Collection of Rose Jennings
© King Features 1967

Enamel paint
In the paintings of the building fascias the flatness of the surface has been achieved using hobby enamel paints. The fluid consistency and easy brush application make enamel an ideal medium for painting details and flat areas alike. Often associated with decorative applications, enamel paints can also be mixed and blended for painterly effects, and take about 24 hours to dry.

Simon Jennings
Building Fascias
Enamel on board
61 x 61cm (24 x 24in)

Liquid opaque colours
Opaque colours similar in consistency to those favoured by traditional animation artists are available today and can be found in many manufacturers' catalogues in jar and bottle form. These paints are suitable for application to a wide range of surfaces and are made in acrylic, water-based or solvent-based enamel paint varieties. Most have strong pigments, good covering power and adhesion, are readily intermixable and are waterproof. Colours of this type are usually listed in the craft sections of catalogues, where similar, but more specialized, colours for painting onto glass, ceramics and textiles are often shown too.

☛**See also**

Communicating with colour 43

Painting with
non-art colours 136–139

Colour on cloth 148–149

There is a huge variety of dry media available that is easy to use and transportable, suitable for use alone or in mixed-media applications. These materials cross the divide between drawing and painting.

These two pages show some of the dry media that can be used for both colour and line: coloured pencils (regular and water-soluble), pastels, oil pastels, oilbars (sometimes known as oil-painting sticks), graphite and charcoal.

There are many other pencil and sticklike, dry-colour products available, such as wax crayons and conté sticks, that are highly suitable for creative colour expression. Much of this media is soluble in water or solvent and can be used to create fluid painterly effects. Many media that use liquids, such as pen and inks and fibre-tips for colour-linear techniques, are available too.

Colour availability varies from one maker to the next, but many of the pigments closely follow paint colours. Most major manufacturers offer high quality products in these media.

Coloured pencil and soft pastel selection

Blending and mixing with coloured pencils

Coloured pencils
These come in various thicknesses. Some brands are soft and free flowing. Others are thinner and of a harder consistency. There are many water-soluble types available, suitable for mixing and blending and for creating watercolour-like effects.

Charcoal sticks and pencil

Charcoal using linear and wash effects

Charcoal
The classic and time-honoured artist's drawing medium, charcoal comes in traditional sticks and pencil form in a variety of thicknesses and grades. A wide range of tones may be produced by blending and rubbing to create shades and soft greys. Charcoal is also soluble for use as washes.

Graphite pencil drawing

Graphite and charcoal
A selection of graphite and charcoal in pencil form. Graphite, like charcoal, is available in sticks too. Use a white paper stump or torchon for blending and gradating tones.

Mixing media
Oil pastel and graphite pencil are used here. Turpentine is used to blend the pastel, and pencil worked over the top.

Water-soluble coloured pencil selection

Line and tone effects using soft pastels

Oil pastels
These, too, can be used for linear and fluid techniques, enabling you to produce oil-like surface effects.

Water-soluble coloured pencil
You can move freely between linear and fluid techniques, creating wet and dry effects in the same piece.

Oil pastels are versatile and transportable, highly suitable for outdoor colour work.

Oilbar
Also known as oil-painting sticks, oilbars behave like oil paint. You can mix and blend them with solvent and use them to create surface texture and impasto effects.

Pastels
Soft pastels, or chalk pastels, are the artist's traditional choice when selecting a dry medium. Pastels come in hundreds of colours whose pigments match those of paints and most of the major manufacturers offer quality pastels in a wide colour range. They can be used to produce large areas of colour or finer lines. The technique of working in pastels is known as pastel 'painting'.

☞**See also**
Choosing media/
Pastels & coloured pencils 35

Sketchbook experiments
Experiment with mixing and blending water-soluble coloured pencils.

COLOUR
INDEX

& REFERENCE SECTION

The purpose of the Colour Index is to provide a visual reference source of the popular artists' colours, the ones you are most likely to see in the most common painting media – oils, watercolour, acrylics and gouache – in the various manufacturers' colour charts. This index is to help you get to know your colours and to demonstrate that, although artists' colours may be given the same name and contain the same basic ingredients, they can vary dramatically in appearance.

In the making and selecting of colours for the Colour Index the art editors have reviewed and sampled more than 1500 colours from 11 of the world's leading manufacturers. Of the 1500 colours reviewed over 400 have been selected for the index and the following criteria have been applied in the selection.

Colours have been reviewed by name. In certain circumstances you will see the same name repeated in the index – for example, Cadmium Red Deep. The purpose of this is to show how the same-named colour from two, or sometimes more, different manufacturers may vary in hue.

Colours have been reviewed by medium. The Colour Index also provides the opportunity for the reader to see variations in colours of the same name but in different media – for example, how Cadmium Red Deep will look in oil colour, gouache or acrylic.

Colours have been reviewed by pigment. All major manufacturers disclose the pigment content of their colours. It is now quite common to see this information printed on the tube or packaging. Failing this, the pigment declaration can usually be found in the maker's colour chart or catalogue. In the Colour Index you will find colours of the same name that

are composed of different pigments or, more importantly for an artist when considering colour, you will see colours with the same pigment content that vary considerably in colour.

Colours have been reviewed by hue. By 'hue' we mean colour or variation of colour (see Glossary of terms). As far as possible within the Colour Index colours have been grouped – for example, into Neutrals, Reds, Yellows, Blues, Greens, Browns, Earths and Ochres etc. This provides a direct visual comparison and enables you to see the differences between, say, a Cobalt Blue, a Phthalo Blue and an Ultramarine.

Colours have been reviewed for variety. In Chapter Two, 'Colour by Colour', we looked at the main colour groups and learned something of the history, background, character and handling of various hues and in many cases how professional artists have mixed and used colour in their work. However, it was not possible to show as many colours as we would have liked. The Colour Index acts as invaluable back-up reference.

Colour behaviour. The Colour Index has used flat colours for sampling and most of the colours have been shown in what is known as top or mass tone. In short this means they have been applied thickly as if seen straight from the tube or sitting as solid blocks in the watercolour pan. The true character of many pigments, particularly at the darker end of the scale, only becomes apparent when diluted or mixed with a medium. In some cases colour samples have been shown applied thickly as top tone and with a touch of white to create a tint to reveal something of the true character of the colour.

Colour accuracy. The only accurate colour charts are hand coloured, and most manufacturers supply these on request. Unfortunately, this book is restricted to the four-colour printing process. While this is a sophisticated and accurate technological process, bear in mind that the colours you see here are not actual pigments but are made up from printing inks (see pages 20–21), so there will be variations between the colours shown and the actual manufacturers' pigment colours.

☛Note
The following manufacturers have kindly supplied colours for use in the Colour Index and throughout this book: Winsor & Newton, Daler-Rowney, Golden, Tri-Art, Royal Talens, Sennelier, Schmincke, Liquitex, Maimeri, Lukas, Old Holland. *See pages 180–181 for details.*

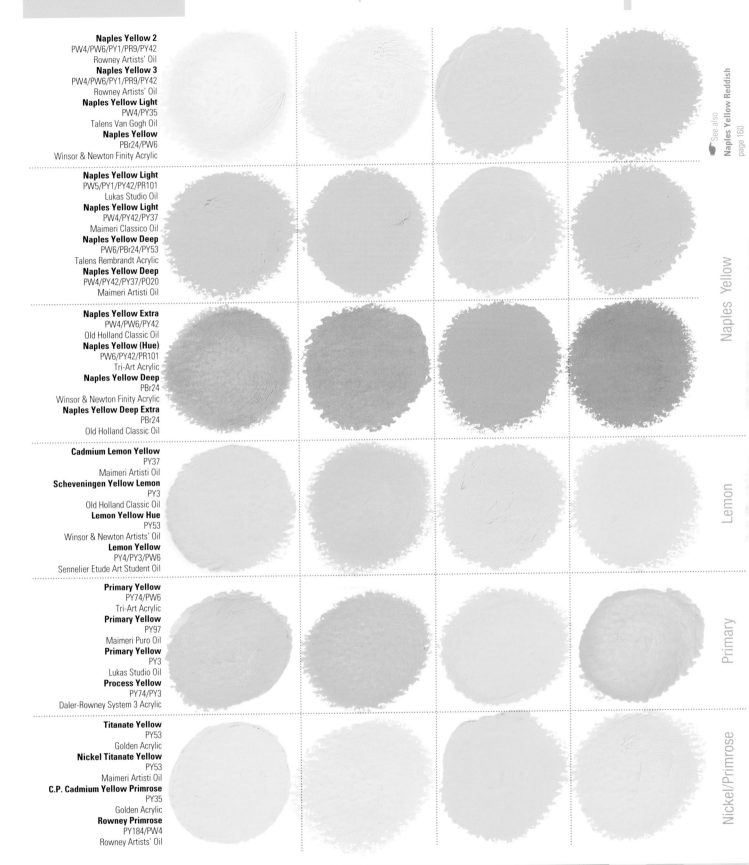

Naples Yellow 2
PW4/PW6/PY1/PR9/PY42
Rowney Artists' Oil
Naples Yellow 3
PW4/PW6/PY1/PR9/PY42
Rowney Artists' Oil
Naples Yellow Light
PW4/PY35
Talens Van Gogh Oil
Naples Yellow
PBr24/PW6
Winsor & Newton Finity Acrylic

Naples Yellow Light
PW5/PY1/PY42/PR101
Lukas Studio Oil
Naples Yellow Light
PW4/PY42/PY37
Maimeri Classico Oil
Naples Yellow Deep
PW6/PBr24/PY53
Talens Rembrandt Acrylic
Naples Yellow Deep
PW4/PY42/PY37/PO20
Maimeri Artisti Oil

Naples Yellow Extra
PW4/PW6/PY42
Old Holland Classic Oil
Naples Yellow (Hue)
PW6/PY42/PR101
Tri-Art Acrylic
Naples Yellow Deep
PBr24
Winsor & Newton Finity Acrylic
Naples Yellow Deep Extra
PBr24
Old Holland Classic Oil

Cadmium Lemon Yellow
PY37
Maimeri Artisti Oil
Scheveningen Yellow Lemon
PY3
Old Holland Classic Oil
Lemon Yellow Hue
PY53
Winsor & Newton Artists' Oil
Lemon Yellow
PY4/PY3/PW6
Sennelier Etude Art Student Oil

Primary Yellow
PY74/PW6
Tri-Art Acrylic
Primary Yellow
PY97
Maimeri Puro Oil
Primary Yellow
PY3
Lukas Studio Oil
Process Yellow
PY74/PY3
Daler-Rowney System 3 Acrylic

Titanate Yellow
PY53
Golden Acrylic
Nickel Titanate Yellow
PY53
Maimeri Artisti Oil
C.P. Cadmium Yellow Primrose
PY35
Golden Acrylic
Rowney Primrose
PY184/PW4
Rowney Artists' Oil

☞ See also
Naples Yellow Reddish
page 160

Naples Yellow

Lemon

Primary

Nickel/Primrose

Azo

Azo Yellow Medium
PY74
Winsor & Newton Finity Acrylic
Yellow Medium Azo
PY74 LF
Liquitex Acrylic
Azo Yellow Medium
PY74
Talens Van Gogh Acrylic
Azo Yellow Deep
PY74/PO43
Talens Van Gogh Acrylic

Bismuth/Hansa

Bismuth Yellow Medium
PY184
Tri-Art Acrylic
Bismuth Yellow Deep
PY184
Tri-Art Acrylic
Hansa Yellow Light
PY3
Golden Acrylic
Hansa Yellow Medium
PY73
Golden Acrylic

Cadmium Deep

Cadmium Yellow Deep
PO20/PY35
Winsor & Newton Artists' Oil
Cadmium Yellow Deep
PY37
Old Holland Classic Oil
Cadmium Yellow Deep
PO20/PY35
Rowney Artists' Oil
Cadmium Yellow Deep
PO20/PY35
Talens Van Gogh Oil

Cadmium Medium

Cadmium Yellow
PY35
Rowney Artists' Oil
C.P. Cadmium Yellow Medium
PY35
Tri-Art Acrylic
Cadmium Yellow Medium
PY37
Maimeri Artisti Oil
C.P. Cadmium Yellow Medium
PY35
Golden Acrylic

Cadmium Pale

Cadmium Yellow Pale
PY35
Daler-Rowney Cryla Acrylic
Cadmium Yellow Light
PW4/PY1
Lukas Studio Oil
Cadmium Yellow Light
PY35
Golden Acrylic
Cadmium Yellow Light
PY35
Talens Van Gogh Oil

Brilliant

Brilliant Yellow
PY83/PY97/PW6
Maimeri Brera Acrylic
Brilliant Yellow
PY83/PW6/PW4
Sennelier Artists' Oil
Brilliant Yellow Deep
PW4/PY83/PO43
Maimeri Classico Oil
Brilliant Yellow Light
PW4/PW5/PY1
Lukas Studio Oil

Chrome Yellow (Hue)
PY1
Rowney Artists' Oil
Chrome Yellow Light
PY34
Maimeri Artisti Oil
Chrome Yellow Hue
PY74/PO62
Winsor & Newton Artists' Oil
Zinc Yellow
PW5/PY3/PY42
Lukas Studio Oil

Aureolin
PY40
Rowney Artists' Oil
Aureolin
PY40
Maimeri Artisti Oil
Aureolin
PY40
Winsor & Newton Artists' Oil
Transparent Yellow
PY17
Maimeri Artisti Oil

Indian Yellow
PY100/PBk11/PR9
Rowney Artists' Oil
Indian Yellow
PY139/PR101
Winsor & Newton Artists' Oil
Indian Yellow
PY74/PR8
Lukas Studio Oil
Indian Yellow
PY110
Talens Van Gogh Oil

Indian Yellow Green Lake Extra
PY153/PY129
Old Holland Classic Oil
Indian Yellow Brown Lake Extra
PY153/PY42
Old Holland Classic Oil
Indian Yellow Orange Lake Extra
PY153/PR260
Old Holland Classic Oil
Indian Yellow
PY1:1/PO13
Rowney Designers' Gouache

Italian Pink
PY100/PR83:1/PBk9
Rowney Artists' Oil
Rowney Golden Yellow
PY53/PR101
Rowney Artists' Oil
Gamboge (Hue)
PY17/PY83
Maimeri Artisti Oil
Gamboge Lake Extra
PY153/PY3
Old Holland Classic Oil

Transparent Gold Ochre
PR101/PY43
Rowney Artists' Oil
Yellow Ochre Light
PY43/PW6/PY42
Maimeri Classico Oil
Yellow Ochre
PY42
Talens Van Gogh Oil
Yellow Ochre Light
PY43
Old Holland Classic Oil

Chrome/Zinc

Aureolin

Indian Yellow

Golden/Gamboge

Ochres

See also
Earths and Ochres
page 172

Flesh Colour
PW5/PY35/PO20
Lukas Studio Oil

Flesh Colour 2
PW5/PR108/PO20
Lukas Sorte 1 Oil

Flesh Colour 4
PW5/PR108/PO20
Lukas Sorte 1 Oil

Flesh Tint
PW4/PY42/PR101
Schmincke Mussini Oil

Flesh Tint
PW6/PW4/PY42/PR101
Schmincke Norma Oil

Flesh Tint
PW4/PR101/PY42
Rowney Artists' Oil

Flesh Tint
PY42/PR101/PW6
Daler-Rowney Cryla Acrylic

Flesh Tint
PW4/PY42/PV19
Winsor & Newton Artists' Oil

Flesh Tint
PW4/PW6/PY119/PR214
Old Holland Classic Oil

Light Portrait Pink
PR188/PO36/PW6
Liquitex Acrylic

Flesh Ochre
PR102/PY43/PW4
Sennelier Artists' Oil

Flesh Ochre
in Titanium White tint

Flesh Ochre
PY42/PR188/PR102
Old Holland Classic Oil

Flesh Ochre
in Titanium White tint

Naples Yellow Reddish
PW5/PY3/PY42/PO34
Lukas Studio Oil

Naples Yellow Reddish
in Titanium White tint

Naples Yellow Red
PW4/PY35/PR108
Talens Van Gogh Oil

Naples Yellow Reddish Extra
PW4/PW6/PY53/PO43/PR260
Old Holland Classic Oil

Naples Yellow Reddish
PW4/PW6/PO43
Maimeri Classico Oil

Naples Yellow Reddish
PW4/PY37/PR108
Maimeri Artisti Oil

Brilliant Yellow Reddish
PW4/PW6/PY53/PO69/PO43
Old Holland Classic Oil

Brilliant Yellow Light
PW4/PW6/PY83/PO69
Old Holland Classic Oil

Jaune Brillant
PY138/PY42/PR188/PW6
Winsor & Newton Artists' Oil

Sandstone
PR101/PY1:1/PW6
Daler-Rowney Designers' Gouache

Flesh Colour

Flesh Tint

Flesh Ochre

See also
Yellow Ochre
page 159

Reddish Yellows

See also
Yellows
page 157–158

Helio Genuine Yellow Deep
PO62/PO34/PY1
Lukas Sorte 1 Oil
Tangerine
PR4
Daler-Rowney Designers' Gouache
Benzimidazolone Orange
PO62
Winsor & Newton Finity Acrylic
Azo Orange
PY74/PO34
Talens Van Gogh Acrylic

See also **Cadmium Yellow Deep** page 158

Cadmium Orange
PO20
Schmincke Horadam Gouache
C.P. Cadmium Orange
PO20
Golden Acrylic
Cadmium Orange
PO20
Old Holland Classic Oil
Naphthol Orange
PY65/PR112
Tri-Art Acrylic

Cadmium Orange

Helio Genuine Orange
PO62/PO13
Lukas Sorte 1 Oil
Pyrrole Orange
PO73
Tri-Art Acrylic
Chrome Orange
PW5/PO36
Lukas Studio Oil
Chrome Orange Deep (Hue)
PO34/PY74/PY42
Daler-Rowney Georgian Oil

Red-Orange/Orange

Coral Orange
PO67
Old Holland Classic Oil
Translucent Orange
PO71
Schmincke Mussini Oil
Winsor Orange
PO73
Winsor & Newton Artists' Oil
Cadmium Red Orange
PO20
Maimeri Artisti Oil

Red Orange
PR4/PO13/PW6/PY42
Daler-Rowney Designers' Gouache
Vermilion Red Light
PO34
Lukas Studio Oil
Vermilion
PO34/PR57:1
Talens Van Gogh Oil
Vermilion Red
PR4/PR9
Daler-Rowney Designers' Gouache

Scarlet/Vermilion

Naphthol Red Light
PR112/PO34
Talens Van Gogh Acrylic
Scarlet Lake
PR255
Winsor & Newton Artists' Oil
Scarlet Lake Extra
PR168/PR209
Old Holland Classic Oil
Pyrrole Red Light
PR255
Golden Acrylic

Light Cadmium Red

Cadmium Red Lightest
PR108
Lukas Sorte 1 Oil
Cadmium Red Light
PR108
Winsor & Newton Finity Acrylic
C.P. Cadmium Red Light
PR108
Tri-Art Acrylic
Cadmium Red Light
PR108
Old Holland Classic Oil

Middle Red

Quinacridone Red Light
PR207
Golden Acrylic
Helio Genuine Red
PR9/PO35
Lukas Sorte 1 Oil
Old Holland Bright Red
PR168
Old Holland Classic Oil
Bright Red
PR254
Winsor & Newton Artists' Oil

Medium Cadmium Red

Winsor Red
PR255/PR254
Winsor & Newton Artists' Oil
Quinacridone Red
PR209
Winsor & Newton Finity Acrylic
Lukas Red
PR9
Lukas Sorte 1 Oil
Pyrrole Red Medium
PR254
Tri-Art Acrylic

Cadmium Red
PR108
Daler-Rowney Cryla Artists' Acrylic
Cadmium Red Medium
PR108
Liquitex Acrylic
Cadmium Red Medium
PR108
Maimeri Artisti Oil
Cadmium Red Middle
PR108/PW21
Schmincke Mussini Oil

Deep Cadmium Red

Scheveningen Red Medium
PR188
Old Holland Classic Oil
Permanent Red
PR112
Talens Van Gogh Oil
Naphthol Red Medium
PR5
Golden Acrylic
Perylene Red
PR149
Winsor & Newton Finity Acrylic

Cadmium Red Deep
PR188/PR112
Lukas Berlin Water-Mixable Oil
Cadmium Red Deep
PR108
Maimeri Artisti Oil
C.P. Cadmium Red Dark
PR108
Golden Acrylic
Cadmium Red Deep
PR108/PW21
Schmincke Mussini Oil

Old Holland Red Gold Lake
PY153/PV19R
Old Holland Classic Oil
Chinese Vermillion
PR108/PR242
Sennelier Artists' Oil
Scarlet Lake
PR9/PR5
Rowney Artists' Oil
Scarlet Alizarin
PR4/PR83:1
Rowney Artists' Oil

Geranium Lake
PR8/PY74
Lukas Studio Oil
Ruby Red
PV19/PR48:2
Sennelier Gouache Extra-Fine
Cadmium Red Purple
PR108
Sennelier Artists' Oil
Cadmium Red Purple
PR108
Old Holland Classic Oil

Alizarin Carmine
PV19/PR206
Maimeri Classico Oil
Permanent Alizarin Crimson
PR117
Talens Van Gogh Acrylic
Alizarin Madder Lake
PR83:1
Schmincke Mussini Oil
Alizarin Crimson
PR83
Winsor & Newton Artists' Oil

Antique Rose Madder
PR122/PY83
Maimeri Artisti Oil
Madder Lake Red
PR112/PR176
Lukascryl Artists' Acrylic
Madder Lake Deep
PR101/PR176/PBk11
Lukas Berlin Water-Mixable Oil
Madder Lake Deepest
PR83/PR176
Lukas Sorte 1 Oil

Carmine
PV19/PR83:1
Rowney Artists' Oil
Carmine Deep
PR12/PV19
Talens Van Gogh Acrylic
Carmine Lake Extra
PV19B/PV19R/PR83/PR88
Old Holland Classic Oil
Permanent Carmine
Quinacridone/Pyrrol
Winsor & Newton Artists' Oil

Maroon
PR12/BV10:BR2/PV1
Daler-Rowney Designer's Gouache
Permanent Maroon
PV19/PR101/PB15:3
Tri-Art Acrylic
Caeser Purple
PV19
Schmincke Mussini Oil
Purple Lake
PR83:1/PR88
Rowney Artists' Oil

Darks/Deeps

Alizarin

Madder

Carmine

Maroon/Purple

Rose/Pink

Magenta

Pink
PR4/PV2
Lukas Designer Gouache
Deep Pink
BV10:BR2/PR3
Daler-Rowney Designers' Gouache
Rose Pink
BV10:BR2/PR3/PW6
Daler-Rowney Designers' Gouache
Brilliant Pink
PW4/PW6/PR188
Old Holland Classic Oil

Rose Dore (Madder Lake Antique Extra)
PR175/PR168/PR83
Old Holland Classic Oil
Quinacridone Rose
PV19
Maimeri Artisti Oil
Permanent Rose
PV19/PR122
Daler-Rowney Cryla Artists' Acrylic
Scheveningen Rose Deep
PV19R
Old Holland Classic Oil

Permanent Rose
PR122/PV19
Talens Van Gogh Oil
Permanent Rose
PR122
Lukascryl Artists' Acrylic
Brilliant Rose Light
PR4/PV2
Lukas Designer Gouache
Brilliant Rose
PR112/PR176/PV2
Lukas Designer Gouache

Light Magenta
PR112/PW6/PR207
Golden Acrylic
Magenta Light
PR122/PW6
Tri-Art Acrylic
Medium Magenta
PR122/PW6
Liquitex Acrylic
Primary Red
PR122
Maimeri Classico Oil

Primary Magenta
PV19
Golden Acrylic
Process Magenta
PV19/PR122
Daler-Rowney System 3 Acrylic
Process Magenta
BV10:BR2/PR3/PR9
Daler-Rowney Designers' Gouache
ACRA© Magenta
PR122
Liquitex Acrylic

Deep Magenta
PR122/PV19DL/PW6
Liquitex Acrylic
Magenta
BV10:BR2/PR3/PR9
Daler-Rowney Designers' Gouache
Magenta
PV23/PR122
Winsor & Newton Artists' Oil
Magenta Lake
PV19/PR81
Maimeri Artisti Oil

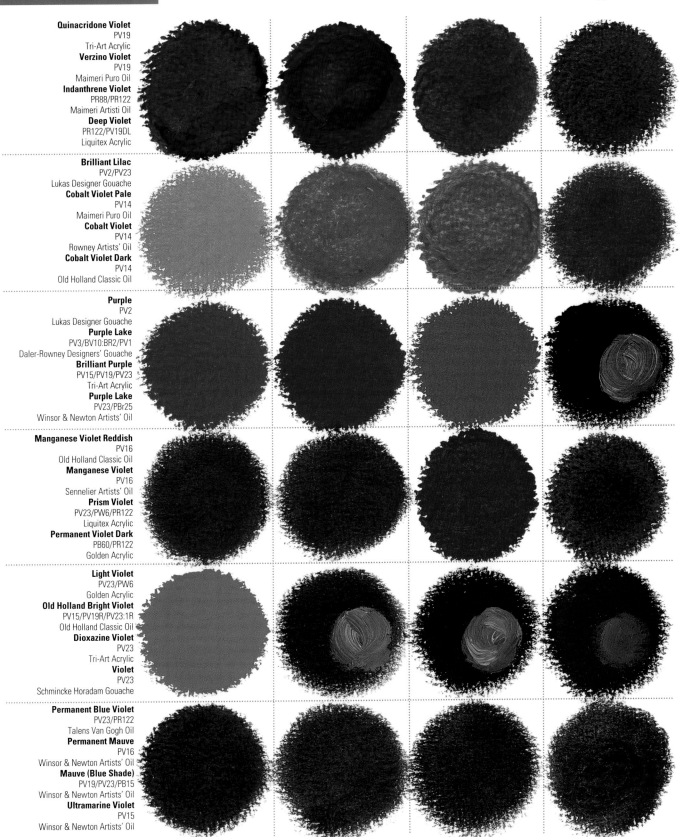

Quinacridone Violet
PV19
Tri-Art Acrylic
Verzino Violet
PV19
Maimeri Puro Oil
Indanthrene Violet
PR88/PR122
Maimeri Artisti Oil
Deep Violet
PR122/PV19DL
Liquitex Acrylic

Red Violet

Brilliant Lilac
PV2/PV23
Lukas Designer Gouache
Cobalt Violet Pale
PV14
Maimeri Puro Oil
Cobalt Violet
PV14
Rowney Artists' Oil
Cobalt Violet Dark
PV14
Old Holland Classic Oil

Cobalt Violet

Purple
PV2
Lukas Designer Gouache
Purple Lake
PV3/BV10:BR2/PV1
Daler-Rowney Designers' Gouache
Brilliant Purple
PV15/PV19/PV23
Tri-Art Acrylic
Purple Lake
PV23/PBr25
Winsor & Newton Artists' Oil

Violet/Purple

Manganese Violet Reddish
PV16
Old Holland Classic Oil
Manganese Violet
PV16
Sennelier Artists' Oil
Prism Violet
PV23/PW6/PR122
Liquitex Acrylic
Permanent Violet Dark
PB60/PR122
Golden Acrylic

Light Violet
PV23/PW6
Golden Acrylic
Old Holland Bright Violet
PV15/PV19R/PV23:1R
Old Holland Classic Oil
Dioxazine Violet
PV23
Tri-Art Acrylic
Violet
PV23
Schmincke Horadam Gouache

Violet

Permanent Blue Violet
PV23/PR122
Talens Van Gogh Oil
Permanent Mauve
PV16
Winsor & Newton Artists' Oil
Mauve (Blue Shade)
PV19/PV23/PB15
Winsor & Newton Artists' Oil
Ultramarine Violet
PV15
Winsor & Newton Artists' Oil

Blue Violet

Note
Dark pigments are also shown with a white tint detail to bring out the true character of the colours

Prussian/Parisienne

Helio/Phthalo

Deep/Ultramarine

Old Holland Blue Violet
PB15:1/PV23:1R
Old Holland Classic Oil
Faience Blue
PB60
Maimeri Puro Oil
Indanthrene Blue
PB60
Daler-Rowney Cryla Artists' Acrylic
Old Holland Blue Deep
PB29/PB60/PBk7
Old Holland Classic Oil

Indigo
PG7/PBk7/PB29
Rowney Artists' Oil
Paris Blue
PB27
Lukas Studio Oil
Prussian Blue
PB27
Rowney Artists' Oil
Prussian Blue
PB27
Liquitex Acrylic

Prussian Blue (Hue)
PB15:1/PV23
Tri-Art Acrylic
Prussian Blue Phthalo
PB15:4/PBk11
Talens Van Gogh Acrylic
Old Holland Blue
PB15
Old Holland Classic Oil
Winsor Blue (Red Shade)
PB15
Winsor & Newton Artists' Oil

Phthalo Blue (Red Shade)
PB15:1
Tri-Art Acrylic
Phthalo Blue (Red Shade)
PB15:1
Winsor & Newton Finity Acrylic
Scheveningen Blue
PB15
Old Holland Classic Oil
Phthalo Blue
PB15
Talens Van Gogh Acrylic

Phthalo Blue (Green Shade)
PB15
Daler-Rowney Cryla Artists' Acrylic
Rowney Blue
PB29/PB15
Daler-Rowney Designers' Gouache
Helio Genuine Blue
PB15:3
Lukascryl Artists' Acrylic
Helio Blue
PB15:3
Schmincke Horadam Gouache

Ultramarine Deep
PB29
Maimeri Puro Oil
Ultramarine Deep
PB29
Talens Rembrandt Oil
Ultramarine Deep
PB29
Schmincke Horadam Gouache
French Ultramarine
PB29
Winsor & Newton Artists' Oil

Ultramarine
PB29/PB15
Daler-Rowney Designers' Gouache
Ultramarine Blue
PB29
Golden Acrylic
Ultramarine Middle
PW5/PB29
Lukas Designer Gouache
Ultramarine Light
PB29
Lukas Designer Gouache

Permanent Blue
PB29
Rowney Artists' Oil
Ultramarine Blue (Green Shade)
PB29
Liquitex Acrylic
Cobalt Blue Deep
PB29/PB16
Lukas Studio Oil
Cobalt Blue Deep
PB74
Winsor & Newton Artists' Oil

Cobalt Blue Deep
PB28
Maimeri Artisti Oil
Cobalt Blue
PB28
Talens Van Gogh Oil
Cobalt Blue
PB28
Rowney Artists' Oil
Cobalt Blue
PB28
Golden Acrylic

Cobalt Blue Hue
PB29/PW6
Liquitex Acrylic
Cobalt Blue Light
PB28
Schmincke Mussini Oil
Cobalt Blue Light
PB28
Maimeri Artisti Oil
Cobalt Blue Light
PB28
Schmincke Horadam Gouache

Delft Blue
PB29/PB15/PW6
Daler-Rowney Designers' Gouache
Brilliant Blue
PB29
Daler-Rowney Designers' Gouache
Cerulean Blue
PB36:1
Tri-Art Acrylic
Cerulean Blue
PB35
Talens Van Gogh Oil

Cerulean Blue
PB35
Winsor & Newton Artists' Oil
Cerulean Blue
PW4/PB15/PB16
Lukas Studio Oil
Cerulean Blue Deep
PB36
Old Holland Classic Oil
Cerulean Blue Deep
PB36
Golden Acrylic

Ultramarine

Cobalt/Permanent

Cerulean/Delft

Light Blue

Manganese Blue
PB33
Old Holland Classic Oil
Azure Blue
PB15:4/PG7
Sennelier Artists' Oil
Scheveningen Blue Light
PB15/PW4/PW6
Old Holland Classic Oil
Powder Blue
PB29/PW6
Daler-Rowney Designers' Gouache

Kings Blue Deep
PB29/PW4/PW6
Old Holland Classic Oil
Light Ultramarine Blue
PB29/PW6
Golden Acrylic
Royal Blue Light
PB29/PW5
Lukas Sorte 1 Oil
Sky Blue
PB29/PB15:1/PW4
Lukas Berlin Water-Mixable Oil

Sky Blue
PW4/PB15
Talens Van Gogh Oil
Sky Blue
PB15:3/PW4
Maimeri Classico Acqua Oil
Primary Blue
PB15:1/PBk7
Lukas Designer Gouache
Primary Blue
PB15:3
Lukas Berlin Water-Mixable Oil

Primary/Process

Primary Cyan
PB15:3/PW6
Tri-Art Acrylic
Process Cyan
FB2:1
Daler-Rowney Designers' Gouache
Primary Blue-Cyan
PB15:3/PB16
Maimeri Classico Oil
Brilliant Blue
PG15/PG7/PW6
Talens Van Gogh Acrylic

Caribbean Blue
PB16
Old Holland Classic Oil
Turquoise Deep
PB15:3/PG7
Liquitex Acrylic
Phthalo Turquoise
PB15:3/PG7
Tri-Art Acrylic
Phthalo Turquoise Light
PW6/PG7/PB15:3
Tri-Art Acrylic

Turquoise

Turquoise
PB15/PG7
Daler-Rowney Designers' Gouache
Turquoise Blue
PW4/PB15/PG7
Talens Van Gogh Oil
Permanent Light Blue
PB15:3/PG7/PW6
Maimeri Brera Acrylic
Turquoise Blue
PW4/PG7/PB16
Maimeri Classico Oil

Cobalt Blue Turquoise
PB36
Old Holland Classic Oil
Cobalt Turquoise (Hue)
PB15/PW4/PG7
Daler-Rowney Cryla Artists' Acrylic
Cobalt Turquoise
PB36
Golden Acrylic
Brilliant Green Blue
PB16
Lukas Designer Gouache

Cobalt Turquoise
PB36
Liquitex Acrylic
Cobalt Blue Turquoise Light
PG50
Old Holland Classic Oil
Ultramarine Green
PG29/PG7
Maimeri Artisti Oil
Cobalt Teal
PG50
Tri-Art Acrylic

Bright Aqua Green
PG7/PB15/PW6
Liquitex Acrylic
Light Turquoise (Phthalo)
PB15:4/PW6/PG7
Golden Acrylic
Winsor Green
PG7
Winsor & Newton Artists' Oil
Emerald Green
PW5/PG7
Lukas Studio Oil

Emerald Green
PG7/PY74/PW4
Winsor & Newton Winton Oil
Emerald Green
PY3/PB15/PW4
Maimeri Artisti Oil
Rowney Emerald
PW4/PG7/PY3/PY53
Rowney Artists' Oil
Barite Green
PG7/PY3/PW6
Sennelier Artists' Oil

Viridian
PG7
Sennelier Etude Art Student Oil
Monestial Turquoise (Phthalo)
PB15
Rowney Artists' Oil
Viridian
PG18
Rowney Artists' Oil
Viridian
PG7/PY43
Talens Van Gogh Oil

Cobalt Green Light
PG50
Maimeri Puro Oil
Cobalt Green
PG26/PG50
Winsor & Newton Artists' Oil
Cobalt Green
PG50
Liquitex Acrylic
Cobalt Green Deep
PG26
Old Holland Classic Oil

Cobalt/Turquoise

Emerald/Turquoise

Viridian

Cobalt Green

Brilliant etc.

Brilliant Green
PG7/PY3
Daler-Rowney Designers' Gouache
Helio Green Yellowish
PG36
Schmincke Horadam Gouache
Winsor Green (Yellow Shade)
PG36
Winsor & Newton Artists' Oil
Phthalo Green
PG7
Talens Van Gogh Oil

Permanent

Permanent Green Light
PG7/PY74
Talens Van Gogh Acrylic
Permanent Green
PW4/PW6/PY151/PB15
Old Holland Classic Oil
Permanent Green Medium
PG7/PY74
Talens Van Gogh Acrylic
Permanent Green Deep
PY138/PG7/PW6
Winsor & Newton Artists' Oil

Cadmium

Cadmium Green Pale
PY35/PG18
Winsor & Newton Artists' Oil
Cadmium Green
PG18/PY37
Maimeri Artisti Oil
Cadmium Green
PY35/PG18
Winsor & Newton Artists' Oil
Cadmium Green Deep
PY37/PG18
Old Holland Classic Oil

Vivid/Bright

Saffron Green
PG7/PY3
Daler-Rowney Designers' Gouache
Vivid Lime Green
PY97/PG7/PW6
Liquitex Acrylic
Bright Green
PG7/PY3
Daler-Rowney Cryla Artists' Acrylic
Light Green (Yellow Shade)
PG7/PY3/PW6
Golden Acrylic

Yellowish

Light Green
PG7/PY3
Daler-Rowney Designers' Gouache
Yellow Green
PG7/PY3/PW6/PY42
Daler-Rowney Designers' Gouache
Yellowish Green
PG7/PY74/PW4
Talens Van Gogh Oil
Yellowish Green
PG7/PY74
Talens Rembrandt Acrylic

Cinnabar

Cinnabar Green Lightest
PY1/PG7
Lukas Designer Gouache
Cinnabar Green Light Extra
PY35/PG18/PB29
Old Holland Classic Oil
Cinnabar Green Light
PY1/PB15
Maimeri Artisti Oil
Cinnabar Green Deep
PY1/PB16
Lukas Designer Gouache

Opaque Oxide of Chromium
PG17
Daler-Rowney Designers' Gouache
Chrome Oxide Green
PG17
Maimeri Puro Oil
Chromium Oxide Green
PG17
Liquitex Acrylic
Chrome Green Deep Hue
PB15/PG7/PY42
Winsor & Newton Artists' Oil

Sap Green Light
PY42/PG7
Tri-Art Acrylic
Sap Green
PB60/PY150
Schmincke Mussini Oil
Hooker's Green No. 2
PY3/PR101/PG7
Rowney Artists' Oil
Hooker's Green Lake Deep Extra
PR101/PG7/PBk7
Old Holland Classic Oil

Stil De Grain Yellow
PY1/PG10
Maimeri Artisti Oil
Green Gold
PY150/PG36/PY3
Golden Acrylic
Old Holland Golden Green
PY129
Old Holland Classic Oil
Old Holland Green Deep
PY129/PG36
Old Holland Classic Oil

Green Earth
PG23
Old Holland Classic Oil
Bohemian Green Earth
PY42/PG17
Lukas Designer Gouache
Terre Verte
PY43/PBr7/PB15
Talens Van Gogh Oil
Bohemian Green Earth
PY42/PR101/PBk11/PG7
Lukas Studio Oil

Rowney Olive
PY153/PG7
Rowney Artists' Oil
Olive Green
PG7/PY17
Talens Van Gogh Oil
Olive Green
PG7/PY3/PO13
Daler-Rowney Designers' Gouache
Olive Green
PB60/PO49
Winsor & Newton Finity Acrylic

Olive Green Dark
PY129/PB60/PG7/PBr7
Old Holland Classic Oil
Greenish Umber
PY42/PBk11
Talens Rembrandt Oil
Green Umber
PY42/PBk11/PG17
Lukascryl Artists' Acrylic
Green Umber
PY42/PR101/PBk11/PG7
Lukas Studio Oil

Oxide

Sap/Hooker's

Golden

Earth Green

Green Umber/Olive

See also
Ochres page 159
Flesh Ochre page 160

Yellow Ochre

Gold Ochre

Mars Yellow

Bronze/Oxide

Sienna

Yellow Ochre
PY43
Winsor & Newton Artists' Oil
Yellow Ochre
PY43
Winsor & Newton Finity Acrylic
Yellow Ochre
PY43/PW4/PY42
Maimeri Classico Oil
Yellow Ochre
PY42
Talens Van Gogh Acrylic

Yellow Ochre Light
PY42
Lukas Studio Oil
Attish Light Ochre
PY42
Schmincke Mussini Oil
Yellow Ochre Pale
PY43/PW4
Maimeri Artisti Oil
Yellow Ochre Light
PBr24
Talens Van Gogh Acrylic

Gold Ochre
PY43
Old Holland Classic Oil
Gold Ochre
PY42/PR101/PBk11
Lukas Studio Oil
Gold Ochre
PY42
Winsor & Newton Finity Acrylic
Golden Ochre
PY53/PR101
Daler-Rowney Cryla Acrylic

Mars Yellow
PY42
Rowney Artists' Oil
Gold Ochre
PY42
Winsor & Newton Artists' Oil
Mars Yellow
PBr6
Golden Acrylic
Mars Yellow
PY42
Old Holland Classic Oil

Bronze Yellow
PY42/PBr7
Liquitex Acrylic
Bronze Yellow
PY42/PBr7
Daler-Rowney Cryla Acrylic
Yellow Oxide
PY42
Liquitex Acrylic
Yellow Oxide
PY42
Golden Acrylic

Raw Sienna
PY43
Talens Van Gogh Oil
Raw Sienna
PY42
Lukas Studio Oil
Raw Sienna
PY42/PR101 Trans/PBk9
Daler-Rowney Cryla Acrylic
Raw Sienna
PY42
Rowney Egg Tempera

Red Ochre
PR102
Old Holland Classic Oil
Red Ochre
PR101
Maimeri Puro Oil
Brown Ochre Light
PBr7
Old Holland Classic Oil
Brown Ochre
PR101/PBk11
Talens Rembrandt Oil

Brown/Red Ochre

Deep Ochre
PR102
Old Holland Classic Oil
Terra Rosa
PR101
Winsor & Newton Artists' Oil
Mars Orange
PY42
Maimeri Artisti Oil
Pouzzoles Red
PR101/PY154
Sennelier Artists' Oil

Orange/Deep Ochre

Quinacridone Gold
PO49
Winsor & Newton Finity Acrylic
Quinacridone Gold
PO48/PO49
Golden Acrylic
ACRA© Gold
PO48/PY83
Liquitex Acrylic
Chinese Orange
PR83/PY13
Sennelier Artists' Oil

Burnt Orange/Gold

Quinacridone Burnt Orange
PO206
Winsor & Newton Finity Acrylic
Transparent Oxide Orange
PY42/PR101
Talens Rembrandt Acrylic
Transparent Oxide Red
PR101
Talens Rembrandt Acrylic
Translucent Red Oxide
PR101
Schmincke Mussini Oil

Orange/Red Oxide

Transparent Brown
PBr25
Tri-Art Acrylic
Italian Brown Pink Lake
PR101/PY83
Old Holland Classic Oil
Transparent Mars Brown
PR101
Maimeri Puro Oil
Transparent Oxide Red Lake
PR101
Old Holland Classic Oil

Brown Pinks

Light Red Oxide
PR101
Talens Van Gogh Oil
Red Oxide
PR101
Liquitex Acrylic
Red Oxide
PR101
Golden Acrylic
Red Earth
PR5/PR8/PR101
Daler-Rowney Designers' Gouache

Red Oxide/Earth

English Red

English Red Light
PY42/PR101
Lukas Designer Gouache
English Red
PR102
Maimeri Artisti Oil
English Red
PR101
Old Holland Classic Oil
English Red Deep
PY42/PR101
Lukascryl Artists' Acrylic

Indian Red

Indian Red
PY101/PY43
Maimeri Artisti Oil
Indian Red
PR101
Rowney Egg Tempera
Indian Red
PR101
Talens Rembrandt Acrylic
Indian Red
PR101
Winsor & Newton Artists' Oil

Venetian/Mars Red

Venetian Red
PR101
Rowney Egg Tempera
Venetian Red
PR101/PY42
Maimeri Artisti Oil
Mars Red
PR101
Rowney Artists' Oil
Caput Mortuum Light
PR101
Lukas Studio Oil

Deep Violet

Violet Oxide
PR101
Golden Acrylic
Mars Violet
PR101
Maimeri Puro Oil
Mars Violet
PR101
Rowney Artists' Oil
Mars Brown
PR101
Old Holland Classic Oil

Burnt Sienna

Burnt Sienna
PR101/PR206
Daler-Rowney Cryla Artists' Acrylic
Burnt Sienna
PR101
Winsor & Newton Finity Acrylic
Burnt Sienna
PBr7
Maimeri Classico Oil
Burnt Sienna
PBr7
Lukas Berlin Water-Mixable Oil

Burnt Sienna
PY42/PR101
Lukas Designer Gouache
Burnt Sienna
PBr7/PR101/PBk11
Daler-Rowney Designers' Gouache
Burnt Sienna
PR101
Lukascryl Artists' Acrylic
Burnt Sienna
PBr7
Liquitex Acrylic

Brown Madder (Alizarin)
PBr7/PR83:1
Rowney Artists' Oil
Burnt Umber
PR101/PBk11
Talens Van Gogh Acrylic
Burnt Umber
PY42/PR101/PBk7
Lukascryl Artists' Acrylic
Burnt Umber Light
PBr7
Golden Acrylic

Red Umber
PBr7
Old Holland Classic Oil
Burnt Umber
PBr7
Liquitex Acrylic
Burnt Umber
PBk11/PBr6
Maimeri Brera Acrylic
Burnt Umber
PBr7
Maimeri Puro Oil

Vandyke Brown (Hue)
PY42/PBr7
Daler-Rowney Designers' Gouache
Vandyke Brown
PBk11/PR101
Talens Van Gogh Acrylic
Vandyke Brown
PY42/PR101/PBk11
Lukascryl Artists' Acrylic
Vandyke Brown
NBr8/PBr7
Winsor & Newton Artists' Oil

Cassel Earth
PR176/PY74/PBk7
Lukas Studio Oil
Cassel Earth
PBr7/PBk7
Maimeri Artisti Oil
Bitumen
Bk6
Maimeri Artisti Oil
Sepia
PR101/PG7
Tri-Art Acrylic

Sepia Warm Extra
PBk7/PR102/PBr7
Old Holland Classic Oil
Sepia
PY42/PR101/PBk11
Talens Rembrandt Oil
Raw Umber
PY42/PBr7
Daler-Rowney Designers' Gouache
Raw Umber
PY42/PR101/PBk11
Lukascryl Artists' Acrylic

Raw Umber
PY42/PBk11
Talens Van Gogh Acrylic
Raw Umber
PBr7/PG17
Maimeri Artisti Oil
Raw Umber
PBr7
Winsor & Newton Artists' Oil
Neutral Tint
PB15/PV19B/PBr7
Old Holland Classic Oil

☛**Note**
Dark pigments are also shown with a white tint to bring out the true character of the colour.

Umbers

Bitumen/Cassel Earth/Vandyke Brown

Neutral/Raw Umber/Sepia

Note
Dark pigments are also shown with a white tint to bring out the true character of the colour

Black

Blue Black

Green Black

Vine Black
PBk7
Lukas Sorte 1 Oil
Vine Black in Titanium White tint

Mars Black
PBk11
Maimeri Puro Oil
Mars Black in Titanium White tint

Ivory Black
PBk9
Talens Van Gogh Oil
Ivory Black inTitanium White tint

Lamp Black
PBk7
Rowney Artists' Oil
Lamp Black in Titanium White tint

Payne's Grey
PBk11/PB15/PV19
Talens Van Gogh Oil
Payne's Grey in Titanium White tint

Payne's Grey
PB29/PBk7
Golden Acrylic
Payne's Grey in Titanium White tint

Blue Black
PB29
Winsor & Newton Artists' Oil
Blue Black in Titanium White tint

Graphite Grey
PBk10
Tri-Art Acrylic
Graphite Grey in Titanium White tint

Atrament Black
PBk31
Schmincke Mussini Oil
Atrament Black in Titanium White tint

Davy's Grey
PG23/PW4/PBk9/PBr7
Old Holland Classic Oil
Davy's Grey in Titanium White tint

Davy's Gray
PBk19/PY42/PBk7
Winsor & Newton Artists' Oil
Davy's Grey in Titanium White tint

Davy's Gray
PBk19/PY42/
Winsor & Newton Finity Acrylic
Davy's Grey in Titanium White tint

Titan Buff
PW6
Golden Acrylic
Unbleached Titanium
PBr7/PY42/PW6
Liquitex Acrylic
Buff Titanium
PY42/PW6
Winsor & Newton Finity Acrylic
Old Holland Warm Grey Light
PW4/PW6/PBk7/PBr7
Old Holland Classic Oil

Warm Grey 1
PBr7/PBk9/PW6
Daler-Rowney Designers' Gouache
Warm Grey 2
PBr7/PBk9/PW6
Daler-Rowney Designers' Gouache
Warm Grey 3
PBr7/PBk9/PW6
Daler-Rowney Designers' Gouache
Grey 1 (Warm Grey)
PW5/PBk7/PY42
Lukas Sorte 1 Oil

Scheveningen Warm Grey
PW4/PW6/PBk9/PBr7
Old Holland Classic Oil
*Scheveningen Warm Grey in
Titanium White tint*

Warm Grey
PW4/PR101/PBr9
Talens Rembrandt Oil
Warm Grey in Titanium White tint

Middle Grey
PW6/PBk9/PBr7
Daler-Rowney Cryla Acrylic
N5 Neutral Gray
PW6/PBk9/PBr7
Golden Acrylic
N4 Neutral Gray
PW6/PBk9/PBr7
Golden Acrylic
Neutral Gray 1
PBk7/PW6
Daler-Rowney Designers' Gouache

N8 Neutral Gray
PW6/PBk9/PBr7
Golden Acrylics
N6 Neutral Gray
PW6/PBk9/PBr7
Golden Acrylics
Grey 2 (Cold Grey)
PW5/PBk9/PY42
Lukas Sorte 1 Oil
Old Holland Cold Grey
PW4/PW6/PBk7/PB29
Old Holland Classic Oil

Cold Grey 3
PW6/PG7/PBk7
Lukas Gouache
Grey 1
PW6/PBk9
Lukas Gouache
Cool Grey 2
PB29/PBk9/PW6
Daler-Rowney Designers' Gouache
Cool Grey 3
PG7/PBk9/PW6
Daler-Rowney Designers' Gouache

See also
Earths & Ochres
page 172

Warm Grey/Buff

Neutral/Middle

Cold/Cool

Gold

Rich Gold
Mica-coated titanium dioxide/Iron oxide
Liquitex Acrylic
Iridescent Gold Deep
(Mixed pigment/vehicle content)
Tri-Art Acrylic
Renaissance Gold
Titanium dioxide-coated mica/Iron oxide
Winsor & Newton Finity Acrylic
Pale Gold
(Mixed pigment/vehicle content)
Daler-Rowney Designers' Gouache

Copper

Iridescent Rich Bronze
Mica-coated titanium dioxide/Iron oxide
Liquitex Acrylic
Iridescent Bronze (Fine)
Iron oxide coated mica particles
Golden Acrylic
Antique Bronze
Mica-coated titanium dioxide /Iron oxide/PBk9
Liquitex Acrylic
Bronze (Imitation)
(Mixed pigment/vehicle content)
Daler-Rowney Cryla Acrylic

Bronze

Copper
(Mixed pigment/vehicle content)
Daler-Rowney Designer's Gouache
Copper (Imitation)
(Mixed pigment/vehicle content)
Daler-Rowney Cryla Acrylic
Iridescent Copper (Coarse)
(Mixed pigment/vehicle content)
Golden Acrylic
Iridescent Copper
(Mixed pigment/vehicle content)
Tri-Art Acrylic

Silver

Iridescent Bright Silver
Mica-coated titanium dioxide/Iron oxide/Stainless steel
Liquitex Acrylic
Silver
(Mixed pigment/vehicle content)
Daler-Rowney Designer's Gouache
Dark Silver
Titanium dioxide-coated mica/Iron oxide
Winsor & Newton Finity Acrylic
Iridescent Stainless Steel (Coarse)
(Mixed pigment/vehicle content)
Golden Acrylic

Interference colours

Interference Violet (Fine)
(Mixed pigment/vehicle content)
Golden Acrylic
Interference Red (Coarse)
(Mixed pigment/vehicle content)
Golden Acrylic
Interference Blue (Coarse)
(Mixed pigment/vehicle content)
Golden Acrylic
Interference Green (Fine)
(Mixed pigment/vehicle content)
Golden Acrylic

Spectral colours

Spectral Fuchsia
(Mixed pigment/vehicle content)
Tri-Art Acrylic
Spectral Brilliant Red
(Mixed pigment/vehicle content)
Tri-Art Acrylic
Spectral Brilliant Blue
(Mixed pigment/vehicle content)
Tri-Art Acrylic
Spectral Brilliant Green
(Mixed pigment/vehicle content)
Tri-Art Acrylic

SAMPLE WHITES
(From left to right, top to bottom)

Cremnitz White
PW1
Old Holland Classic Oil
Flake White
PW1/PW4
Old Holland Classic Oil
Zinc White
PW6
Winsor & Newton Artists' Oil
Titanium White
PW6/PW4
Rowney Artists' Oil
Mixed White
PW6/PW4
Talens Van Gogh Oil
Underpainting White
PW6/PW4
Winsor & Newton Artists' Oil
Mixing White
PW6
Rowney Artists' Oil
Opaque White
PW4
Lukas Studio Oil
Warm White
PW6
Tri-Art Acrylic
Iridescent White
Mica-coated titanium dioxide
Liquitex Acrylic
Iridescent Pearl
Mica-coated titanium dioxide
Tri-Art Acrylic
Iridescent Pearl (Coarse)
Mica-coated titanium dioxide
Golden Acrylic

☛**Note**
Whites given the same name can vary considerably in opacity, consistency, mixing and handling properties. There are commonly two types of white seen in manufacturers' colour charts. These are Zinc White and Titanium White in oils and acrylics. In watercolours you will come across Chinese White, and in many artists' quality oil-colour ranges you will see the traditional Cremnitz White and Flake White. Many products are labelled as 'mixing' whites and 'underpainting' whites, and in acrylic ranges pearl and iridescent whites are available too. See pages 86–87 for details.

☛ **NOTE: Metallic and Special-effect colours**
All metallic and special-effect samples (opposite) are shown against black for tonal variation. It is impossible to show the true light-scattering effects of these samples. Refer to manufacturers' hand-painted colour charts and see more details on pages 88–89.

There are hundreds of art materials manufacturers, ranging from small specialists who produce traditional pigments using time-honoured methods, to well-known brands that are household names recognized throughout the world. Many European and North American manufacturers have assisted with images, materials and information in the making of this book and the following have been particularly generous in supplying samples.

Daler-Rowney

Daler-Rowney's reputation as a manufacturer of art materials dates back more than 200 years. Turner and Constable are said to have used Daler-Rowney colours and to this day the company offers a comprehensive range of high-quality art materials throughout Britain, continental Europe and beyond.

Daler-Rowney Ltd
Bracknell, Berkshire RG12 8ST, UK
Telephone: 01344 424621
Fax: 01344 486511
www.daler-rowney.com

Winsor & Newton

The William Winsor and Henry Newton partnership was founded in London in 1832 and over the years the names Winsor & Newton have become universally synonymous with many ranges of reliable and quality fine art materials.

Winsor & Newton
Whitefriars Avenue
Harrow, Middlesex
HA3 5RH, UK
Telephone: 020 8427 4343
Fax: 020 8863 7171
www.winsornewton.com

Royal Talens

Talens, founded in 1899, is a prestigious producer of artists' materials and is a name that is known throughout the world. Royal Talens is based in The Netherlands and produces colour materials under the brand names Rembrandt, Van Gogh and Amsterdam.

Royal Talens
PO Box 4, 7300 AA Apeldoorn
The Netherlands
Telephone: (+31) 55-52.74.700
Fax: (+31) 55-52.15.286
www.talens.com

Golden

Golden have gained a worldwide reputation for their heavy-body acrylic colours and mediums. In the 1980s Golden heavy-body acrylics were available only in jars and sold directly to professional Manhattan artists. As they gained in popularity Golden started to manufacture heavy-body acrylic colours in tubes for a wider and ever-growing market. They now produce a range of 94 different colours, shades and tints.

Golden Artist Colors Inc.
188 Bell Road,
New Berlin, NY 13411-9527, USA
Telephone: (+1) 800-959-6543
Fax: (+1) 607-847-6767
www.goldenpaints.com

Maimeri

Painter Gianni Maimeri was an artist who ground his own colours. His methods were so satisfactory that in 1923 he and his brother, a chemist, founded the company Maimeri to produce fine art colours in a competitive domestic market. Eighty years later, Maimeri is still a family company and has developed into a major player in the world of artists' colours and materials.

Maimeri S.p.a.
Via Gianni Maimeri 1
20060 Bettolino di Mediglia
Milan, Italy
Telephone: (+39) (02) 906981
Fax: (+39) (02) 90698999
www.maimeri.it

Lukas

Lukas was founded in 1862 by Dr Franz Schoenfeld in Düsseldorf and the company has enjoyed prominence as a manufacturer and supplier of colours and materials since the nineteenth century. Van Gogh requested colours from Schoenfelds in his letters to his brother Theo. Saint Lukas is the patron protector of painters and the brand name Lukas came into being in 1900, becoming the trademark of all products from the manufacturer Dr Fr. Schoenfeld. Lukas now enjoy an international reputation as suppliers of quality art materials.

Lukas
Dr Fr. Schoenfeld GmbH & Co
Postfach 10 47 41
40038 Düsseldorf, Germany
Telephone: (+49) 0-211-7813-0
Fax: (+49) 0-211-7813-24
www.lukas-germany.de

Schmincke

In 1881 the chemists Herman Schmincke and Josef Horadam imported raw materials, particularly ultramarine, to produce high-quality artists' colours. A reputation was established particularly for resin-oil formulations, which before the invention of the tube had been difficult to store and transport. The resin-oil formulations are based on old-master recipes obtained from Prof. Cesare Mussini of Florence and the Mussini name along with Horadam has become synonymous with quality art materials fom Schmincke.

H. Schmincke & Co. GmBH & Co. KG
Otto Hahn Strasse 2
40699 Erkrath, Germany
Telephone (+49) 0-211-2509-0
Fax: (+49) 0-211-2509-461
www.schmincke.de

Old Holland

The Old Holland Oil Colour Association was established in 1664 and is still continuing a tradition of nearly 300 years in the oldest artists' paint factory in the world. Old Holland paints are still manufactured according to seventeenth-century methods using natural oils and pigments ground on stone rollers to create strong pure colours that are a little more expensive than other brands. Old Holland enjoys an international reputation and their classic oil and watercolours are exported to over 56 countries.

Old Holland
Nijendal 36
3972 KC Driebergen
The Netherlands
www.oldholland.com

Liquitex

The first water-borne acrylic, the kind of acrylic colour we use today, was developed and launched in 1955. Combining the words liquid and texture, the product was named Liquitex. Liquitex as an artists' material was developed by Henry Levinson in the USA in a family-owned business named Permanent Pigments, a firm with a pedigree dating back to the early 1930s, and one with an impressive record in the development of permanence and lightfastness in pigments. Liquitex has become known worldwide as the original heavy-bodied, solvent-free artists' medium.

Liquitex UK
Colart Fine Art & Graphics Ltd
Whitefriars Avenue, Harrow
Middlesex HA3 5RH, UK
Telephone: 020 8424 3249
www.liquitex.com

Sennelier

The company of Sennelier have been producing artists' materials in France since 1887. Gustave Sennelier was a chemist who developed a distinctive and meticulous process for manufacturing colours and soon his palette became a benchmark of quality and reliability among artists. Sennelier products are now admired worldwide for combining nineteenth-century traditions with twenty-first-century innovations.

Sennelier
Max Sauer S.A.
2 Rue Lamarck BP204
22002 Saint-Brieuc cedex France
Telephone: (+33) 02 96 68 20 00
Fax: (+33) 02 96 61 77 19
www.max-sauer.com

Tri-Art

Tri-Art is a modern Canadian-based company established in 1984. They have been manufacturing new-generation acrylic paints in Canada and North America since the mid 1990s and are now exporting to ten countries. In addition to liquid acrylics and inks Tri-Art produce 92 colours in artist-quality, high-viscosity acrylic colours. They use 100 per cent acrylic emulsion to produce many colours with drastically improved properties that mimic the rich, transparent hues of older lake pigments.

Tri-Art
Woolfitt's Art Enterprises Inc.
1153 Queen Street West
Toronto, Ontario M6J 1J4, Canada
Telephone: (+1) 416 536 7878
Fax: (+1) 416 536 4322
www.woolfitts.com

Acrylic paint
A paint that contains acrylic resin obtained by the polymerization of acrylic acid. Acrylic colour can be mixed with water, but dries to a hard, plasticky film.

Additive mixing
The mixing of coloured light. When the three primary additive colours of red, green and blue are mixed together they produce white light.

Advancing colours
Colours that appear to move towards the front of the picture plane. These tend to be the 'warm' colours such as reds, yellows and oranges. (See also Receding colours)

Aerial perspective
This is the technique of using cooler, lighter colours towards the back of the picture plane to give an impression of recession and depth. Sometimes also known as 'atmospheric perspective'.

Alizarin
One of the constituent dyes of the madder root, produced synthetically from the 1860s.

Alkyd resin
A synthetic resin, usually clear, used in paints and mediums. Alkyd resins are soluble in most solvents.

Alla prima
(Italian for 'at the first')
Used to describe a painting made in one session, with no underpainting.

Aniline pigment
A dye synthesized from coal tar. Aniline dyes, first produced in the 1850s, were in the mauve, purple and red range.

Archive-quality
A term particularly applied to paper that is acid free with a neutral pH rating that ensures it will not yellow with age. The term may also be applied to paints and inks with respect to their permanence.

Artists' quality colours
Paints made with best quality ingredients. They contain maximum purest pigments and binders.

ASTM
Acronym for the American Society for Testing and Materials. Provides an independent and international paint qualities standard recognized by major manufacturers.

Azo
Descriptive word pertaining to synthetic organic pigments, short for 'diazotized amines'.

Backrun
A term used mainly in watercolour to describe an irregular unwanted blotch that may occur when wet paint is introduced into a previous layer that has not fully dried.

Balance
The overall arrangement and distribution of shapes, colours and tones in a painting.

Base coat
Layer of paint that acts as a ground for a painting.

Bice
Descriptive word pertaining to colours obtained from combining copper carbonates with silver. Used in the seventeenth century, these blue or green colours were also referred to as 'ashes'.

Binder
A liquid medium mixed with powdered pigment to form a painting or drawing material. In watercolour and gouache the binder is gum arabic, in oil paints it is oil and in acrylics it is acrylic resin.

Bleeding
A colour moving past its required limit or leaking into another colour, sometimes from a previous layer.

Blending
Merging the edges of two adjacent colours together to create a smooth gradation at the join.

Blocking in
The initial process in painting a picture when the basic shapes of colour and tone are broadly placed. This provides a foundation for refining the composition.

Blue wool scale
An international standard that measures the lightfastness of dye colours by dyeing samples of blue wool. The highest rating of 8 is regarded as permanent. Originally used in the textiles industry, the blue wool scale is now also used as a measure in commercial paint and print environments.

Board
Prepared artists' board covered with canvas or cotton, usually ready-primed for use with oils or acrylics.

Body colour
Opaque water-based paint, particularly gouache, also known as designers' colour. 'Body' can also refer to the density of a colour.

Broken colour
Applying colour so that previous layers of other colours show through to maximum optical effect.

Brushwork
The characteristic way that an artist applies paint with a brush.

Canvas
Traditional ground or support used for oil painting and acrylics. The term may refer to the actual fabric used, such as linen, cotton or jute canvas, or calico, or it may be used for the whole support of stretched canvas on a frame.

Cartoon
A full-size drawing from which a final fresco or tapestry is copied. The term particularly applies to Renaissance fresco works.

Charcoal
Carbonized, burnt wood specially prepared for art use. Charcoal sticks produce a dark mark and are available in different grades and sizes. The best quality is soft and non-gritty, often made from willow, but also from vine wood. Charcoal is also available in pencil form. This medium smudges easily and drawings made in charcoal need to be sprayed with fixative.

Chiaroscuro
(Italian for 'light/dark')
The use of light and shade in a painting where strong tonal contrasts are a feature, particularly applied to oil painting.

Chroma
A term used to designate the purity of a colour. A colour with high chroma contains little or no grey. (See also Saturation)

CMYK
Acronym for cyan, magenta, yellow and black, the four colours used in the printing process. (See also Four-colour process)

Cockling
The unwanted wrinkling or puckering of a paper support when too heavy a wash is painted on. It particularly occurs with watercolour when the paper has not been stretched.

Cold-pressed paper
Watercolour paper that has a slightly textured surface. Also known as CP or Not paper (that is, paper that is not hot pressed).

Collage
Artwork composition in which pieces of paper, fabric or other items are pasted onto a support.

Colour cast
Mainly a printing term referring to a particular bias of colour in an image.

Colour field painting
Style of abstract painting developed by American Abstract Expressionist artists of the 1950s. Artists such as Mark Rothko painted large areas of pure colour to give the sensation that the field of colour seemed to go beyond the picture plane.

Colour swatch
A small sample of a particular colour that can be used for matching, experimenting or reference purposes.

Colour temperature
Colours may be described as 'warm' or 'cool'. Colours within a hue may also be described as warm or cool in relation to each other. (See also Warm colours and Cool colours)

Colour
The visual sensation and attributes of distinguishable wavelengths of refracted or reflected light.

Colour wheel
The arrangement of primary and secondary colours into a circle in the order of the spectrum. Intermediary colours may be added to enlarge the circle. Used as a basic device to explain colour theory.

Complementary colours
Colours that are opposite each other on the colour wheel. Red is the complementary of green, yellow of violet, and blue of orange. Similarly, on the enlarged colour wheel, red-orange is the complementary of blue-green, yellow-orange of blue-violet, and yellow-green of red-violet.

Composition
The arrangement of subject matter within a picture. It involves the planning of colour, use of light and shade and considered placing of the various elements.

Conté crayons
Similar to pastels, conté crayons are sticks made from pigment and graphite bound with gum and a little grease. They have a harder consistency than pastels.

Contrast
The degree of difference between the light and dark tones in a drawing or painting. Low contrast has fairly even tones throughout, while high contrast has bright highlights and dark shadows.

Contre-jour
(French for 'against day')
A photographic term, meaning a painting or drawing in which the light is behind the subject.

Cool colours
Colours in the green/blue/violet sector of the colour wheel are generally described as cool.

Crosshatching
A method of indicating tone and shading by criss-crossing close parallel lines. (See also Hatching)

Cyan
A bright greenish blue that is used with magenta, yellow and black in the four-colour printing process. (See also CMYK and Four-colour process)

Dead colour
Sometimes used to refer to the underpainted colours in a painting.

Diluent
A liquid used to thin down paint. For oil paints liquids such as turpentine and white spirit are used. The diluent for water-based media is water.

Dot screens
Screens from which regular patterns of dots are produced for each separate colour in the four-colour printing process. (See also CMYK and Optical mixing)

Dry brush
A technique in which a minimum amount of paint is brushed lightly across the painting surface for a slightly textured effect. Can be used in any medium, but with watercolour the brush is literally kept dry.

Dye
A colouring agent that dissolves in water, used for colouring fabrics. Dyes are also used to colour white powder to produce pigment 'lakes' and 'pinks'. (See also Lake and Pink)

Earth colours
Colours traditionally produced from naturally occurring pigments such as oxides, ochres, umbers and siennas. Though regarded as the most stable pigments, many earth colours are now replicated by synthesized ingredients.

Egg tempera
Pure pigment bound with egg yolk and distilled water. As the paint dries it leaves a hard, silky surface and traditionally this paint was applied to wooden panels over a gesso ground. The term tempera actually refers to binder and it is also sometimes used for other bound paints such as gouache or 'body' colour.

En plein air
(French for 'in open air')
Used to describe a painting made outdoors, and usually directly from the subject in the landscape.

Encaustic
A technique in which the pigment is bound with wax. When melted the wax binds the pigment to the ground or support.

Etching
A print or impression produced from a drawing scratched into a metal plate. Areas of tone and texture may be added by dipping the plate into acid. The plate is then inked and passed through a printing or etching press.

Fat
Used to describe the oil content of oil paint, particularly when it has not been thinned. Fat, oil-rich paint takes a long time to dry and shrinks as it does so. To prevent the problem of the surface cracking, fat layers are traditionally applied on top of lean, thinned paint that is likely to dry first. (See also Lean)

Faux
(French for 'false')
A paint effect that gives the illusion of being real.

Fixative
A thin varnish-like solution that is sprayed by aerosol or mouth diffuser onto pictures worked in a medium likely to smudge, such as pastels, charcoal or graphite. It enables the particles of pigment to adhere fully to the support.

Flocculation
An effect particularly found in watercolour where particles of pigment settle in groups. The appearance of the dried paint is grainy rather than evenly dispersed.

Form
The three-dimensional appearance of a subject that produces its shape.

Format
The size and proportions of a painting or drawing. The two most popular are traditionally landscape and portrait, but square and round are frequently also chosen. (See also Landscape format and Portrait format)

Found colours
Colours that may be obtained from non-paint sources such as natural materials, liquids and foodstuffs.

Four-colour process
The printing process that uses three process colours – cyan, magenta and yellow – and black to produce a full-colour effect. (See also CMYK and Dot screens)

Fresco
(Italian for 'fresh')
A method of painting using water-based colours applied to wet plaster.

Fugitive
Description given to pigments and dyes that are liable to fade with exposure to light. Modern methods of manufacture have reduced this problem considerably. (See also Lightfast and Permanence)

Genre
(French for 'kind')
The type of painting that a picture can be categorized as by its subject matter, such as still life, landscape or portrait. The term 'genre' is particularly applied to paintings that have domestic subjects.

Gesso
A mixture of chalk whiting and glue size used traditionally as a ground and primer in tempera and oil painting. The term is also used to describe modern acrylic primers.

Gilding
The application of thin gold leaf, which may be burnished to give a high sheen.

Glaze
A transparent or semi-transparent layer of colour painted over another colour to modify or enhance its effect.

Gouache
Opaque water-based body colour, also known as designers' colours. In inexpensive student ranges also known as poster paint.

Granulation
An effect particularly found in watercolour where coarse particles of pigment give a speckled appearance when dry.

Graphite
A form of carbon used in pencils, graded from soft to hard. Also available in solid stick or as powder.

Gridding up
A means of transferring a drawing or composition to another support. By drawing a grid over the original and a larger or smaller grid onto the new surface the drawing can be copied section by section to an enlarged or reduced size. Also sometimes called squaring up.

Ground
A layer of priming or preparation that protects the support and provides a surface for painting. It may be coloured to set a key for the subsequent painting.

Ground colour
A colour applied to a prepared support to give a more sympathetic background to a painting rather than brilliant white.

Gum arabic
A water-soluble gum made from certain acacia trees, added as a binder for watercolour pigment. It can also be used as a medium for watercolour to increase gloss and transparency.

Harmonious colours
Colours that are near each other on the colour wheel, generally involving no more than two primary colours.

Hatching
A method of indicating tone and shading using close parallel lines.

Highlights
The lightest areas of tone within a painting or drawing, generally describing reflected light.

Hot-pressed paper
Watercolour paper that has a smooth surface. Also known as HP paper. (See also Cold-pressed paper)

Hue
The general name for a colour, such as red or green. Hue may also be used to describe the comparative character of a colour; for instance, Vermilion and Cadmium Red may be said to be similar in hue. Modern colour manufacturers also use the term to denote that a synthetic pigment has been used to replicate the colour of a traditional one.

Icon
A stylized image of Christ, the Virgin Mary or a saint, particularly as painted in Byzantine style. Now also used to describe a figure who has become symbolic or representational of a particular era or fashion.

Impasto
A technique of painting in oils or acrylics where the paint is applied thickly to create a textural surface. Mediums may be added to the paint to enhance the effect.

Impressionism
A movement in painting in France that developed in the 1870s. Among the principal artists were Monet, Renoir, Sisley and Pissarro, all of whom were interested in painting the changing impressions of light perceived when working out of doors.

Imprimatura
A coat of diluted colour applied to a primed surface to tone down its brightness prior to painting.

Intensity
The brightness and strength of a colour, also called saturation. Intensity also links to purity of colour.

Interference colours
Paints that disperse the light in such a way that they give a varying effect as the viewer moves.

Iridescent colours
Paints that mimic the effect of iridescence typical of an insect's wing or bird's feather. Also known as interference colours, they produce a pearlized effect. (See also Interference colours)

Key
The dominant tone of a painting, whether light or dark. Key may also refer to the process of abrading the surface to receive a heavier layer, such as for mural painting when the wall must be prepared by adding a layer of plaster.

Lake
The pigment colour produced by dyeing a white inorganic mineral powder such as gypsum or chalk with organic colouring matter through the use of a mordant. (See also Pink)

Landscape format
A painting or drawing where the height is narrower than the width. This is the traditional shape for painting a landscape or vista. (See also Portrait format)

Lean
Used to describe thinned oil paint, applied in the underlayers of an oil painting. (See also Fat)

Lifting out
This technique relates particularly to watercolour and involves removing paint from the paper with a damp brush or a tissue. It can be used to create highlights or to soften edges, or to create effects such as clouds.

Lightfast
Description of pigments that are not liable to fade after exposure to light.

Limited palette
Term applied to a particular choice of colours that an artist chooses to use, usually a small number of colours so that there is control over the colour balance in a picture. Also known as a 'restricted' palette. (See also Palette)

Local colour
The actual colour of an object with no added effects of light or shade or reflected colour.

Luminosity
The quality of reflecting light, particularly in watercolour, where areas of white paper show through the layers of paint.

Magenta
Bright violet-red aniline colour, named in 1859 after the battle in Italy. It is one of the three primary colours used in the four-colour printing process. (See also CMYK and Four-colour process)

Maquette
Initial sketch or model for a painting or sculpture.

Mars colours
Applied to colours with iron oxide as their source. Mars was the alchemical name for iron.

Masking
The covering of an area in a painting to protect it or reserve it for further applications. In watercolour a rubbery solution called masking fluid is often applied to reserve the white paper as highlights. When the paint is dry the protective coat is simply rubbed off or peeled away with the fingers.

Medium
The type of drawing or painting material used, such as oil, acrylic, watercolour or pastel (plural 'media'). Medium is also used to refer to the various substances that may be added to paint to change its character in use (plural 'mediums').

Mica
Silicates used in particle or flake form in metallic and iridescent paints. The paint is coated onto the mica to give a varying effect when viewed.

Mixed media
The use of two or more different media in a painting, such as watercolour with pastel or ink.

Monochrome
An image made using different tones of either black and white or a single colour.

Munsell scale
A three-dimensional scale used in specifying colour, developed by Albert Munsell (1858–1918), where colour is shown in both degrees of saturation of hue and brightness.

Mural
A painting made directly on a wall, as with fresco.

Negative shapes
The shapes around or between the main objects in a drawing or painting. (See also Positive shapes)

Not paper
Slightly textured watercolour paper. (See also Cold-pressed paper)

Oilbars
Oil colours in solid stick form, made by combining pigment and oil with waxes. Also called oil-painting sticks. They may be applied as drawing instruments, but the oil worked into with knife or brush.

Opacity
The degree to which a medium or colour can obliterate what is underneath. Different media and colours within them vary in their covering power.

Optical mixing
The technique of painting small areas or dots of colour close to each other so that they appear to mix when viewed from a distance. This is the method used in four-colour printing where colours are screened to be reproduced in dot form. (See also Dot screens and Four-colour process)

Palette
The tray or surface on which colours are arranged and mixed. Palette also refers to the particular selection of colours that an artist chooses.

Pantone®
A proprietary system of colour standards and quality that describes each colour in terms of its composition in percentages. The system thus provides a method that enables the printer to match an exact specified colour.

Pastels
Sticks of colour made from a hardened paste of pigment bound together with chalk or clay and gum. They are available as soft (chalk) or hard sticks, or in pencil form. Oil pastels are made from pigments, fat and wax, so have a different character in use.

Permanence
The degree to which a pigment is lightfast or liable to fade on exposure to light. Art materials' manufacturers supply details as to the permanence of individual colours in their ranges. (See also Lightfast)

Perspective
A method of establishing space and depth in a painting or drawing by describing objects in the distance as smaller than those in the foreground. Parallel lines converge to a vanishing point as they meet the horizon (eye level). Also called linear perspective. (See also Aerial perspective)

Phthalocyanine
A pigment synthesized from copper in the 1930s. It provides the base for a number of modern blue colours, mainly greenish, but sometimes with a reddish bias.

Picture plane
The vertical surface or area of a drawing or painting in which the composition is placed.

Pigment
The colouring agent in drawing and painting media. Originally from natural plant and mineral sources, most pigments are now synthetic. Pigment also refers to pure colour in powder form.

Pink
A colour produced by dyeing a white inorganic powder such as chalk with natural materials such as berries and plants. Many yellows were produced by this method and the term 'pink' was used to describe these colours. (See also Lake)

Pointillism
A style of painting in which dots of colour are juxtaposed so that they mix optically when viewed from a distance. The nineteenth-century French artist Georges Seurat used the technique greatly (see page 23).

Poliment
A red iron-oxide pigment that is applied as a base for gilding.

Portrait format
A painting or drawing where the height is taller than the width. As its name suggests, this is the traditional shape for painting a portrait. (See also Landscape format)

Positive shapes
The actual shapes of the objects in a drawing or painting. (See also Negative shapes)

Primary colours
The three primary colours – red, yellow and blue – are so called because they cannot be mixed from other colours. In theory, however, all other colours can be mixed from primaries. All three primaries mixed together produce 'black'. (See also Subtractive mixing)

Primer
A base coat, usually required for oil and acrylic painting to protect the support and to provide a suitable foundation for paint. Gesso is traditionally used to prime surfaces for oils, but synthetic preparations are now available for both oil and acrylic paints.

Process colours
The colours used in the four-colour printing process. (See also CMYK)

Receding colours
Colours that appear to move into the distance within the picture plane. These tend to be the 'cool' colours, particularly blues. (See also Advancing colours)

Recession
The impression of depth in a picture. This can be achieved both through linear perspective and aerial perspective, involving the use of lighter, cooler colours.

Reduction
Mixing a colour with white paint.

Reflected colour
The light reflected from a coloured surface onto another object, so modifying the object's own local colour. (See also Local colour)

Relief
Usually a sculpture or carving in which the image stands proud of its background, described as high or low relief depending on the extent to which this is apparent. The term may also be used to describe the effect of paint applied thickly, as with impasto. (See also Impasto)

Renaissance
A period of history in Europe that lasted from the fourteenth to the sixteenth centuries. The Renaissance was a rebirth and flowering of the arts, science and culture, much of which was associated with the great master Italian painters.

Resist
A material such as wax placed on a support to repel water. The technique is used effectively in watercolours for texture and highlights.

Rough paper
Unpressed watercolour paper, perhaps hand-made, which has a rough, indented surface texture.

Saturation
The degree of vividness and purity of a colour. A light colour or tint may be regarded as of low saturation, while pure colour is termed fully saturated or of high saturation. (See also Chroma and Intensity)

Scumbling
A technique originally applied to oil painting, but now used with all opaque media. It consists in dragging dryish paint over the surface of a painting so that the layers underneath show through.

Secco
(Italian for 'dry')
A wall painting made on dry plaster or plaster that is slightly dampened. (See also Fresco)

Secondary colours
Colours obtained by mixing two primary colours. Orange is produced from red and yellow, green from yellow and blue, and violet from blue and red.

Series no.
A number that denotes the quality and price range of the pigment.

Sfumato
(Italian for 'smoked' or 'misty')
A gradual transition from light to dark with no noticeable change from one to the other.

Sgraffito
(Italian for 'scratched')
A technique where the top layer of colour is scratched or incised to reveal the layer or ground beneath.

Shade
A colour that has been darkened by the addition of black.

Shaped canvas
A canvas that is not rectangular.

Sinopia
A red iron-oxide colour used by Renaissance artists to make a preliminary drawing prior to painting, itself referred to as the sinopia.

Size
A glue-like liquid that is applied to a canvas support to make it impermeable before applying a layer of gesso or primer.

Sketch
A rough drawing, sometimes made as a preliminary to a composition.

Solvent
Agent or medium that thins or dissolves neat paint or pigment.

Spectrum
The arrangement of colours produced when white light passes through a prism. Seven separate colours are distinguished – red, orange, yellow, green, blue, indigo and violet.

Split complementaries
These are colours that are adjacent to the true complementary of a colour. For instance, the split complementaries of blue are red-orange and yellow-orange.

Staining colours
A term that refers particularly to watercolours. Some colours are made from very finely ground particles of pigment and may not be completely 'lifted out' from the paper.

Stretcher
The wooden frame on which canvas is stretched and fixed to provide a support for painting in oils or acrylics.

Study
A detailed drawing or painting of a part or parts of a composition.

Subtractive mixing
The mixing of pigments. When the three primary pigment colours of red, blue and yellow are mixed together they produce black.

Support
The surface on which a drawing or painting is made, such as paper, canvas, board or wood panel.

Tertiary colours
Colours produced by mixing equal proportions of a primary colour with its adjacent secondary colour. For instance, yellow mixed with green gives yellow-green.

Thinner
A liquid added to paint to dilute it and make it easier to apply to the support. Many are available, depending on the medium used and the consistency required. The traditional thinner for oil paint is turpentine.

Three-dimensional
The impression given in a drawing or painting of objects having depth or volume as well as height and width.

Tint
A colour that has been lightened by the addition of white.

Tinting strength
The degree to which a pigment can dominate in colour mixtures.

Tondo
A circular easel painting or relief carving.

Tone
The lightness or darkness of an element in a drawing or painting, irrespective of its local colour. Also called value. The term tonal value is also used to describe the relation of one tone to another.

Tonking
A means of removing surplus paint by pressing a sheet of paper over the surface of the painting, used particularly in oil painting.

Tooth
Term used for the surface texture or interweave of fibres of the paper. A paper with pronounced tooth is required when painting with pastels so that the dry pigment may be held.

Top tone
The obvious hue of a colour, such as red or blue. (See also Undertone)

Torchon
A tightly rolled paper stump used for blending pastels and charcoal. The pointed end can be used for detail.

Transparency
The degree to which light can pass through a colour. Watercolour is a transparent medium, but thinned glazes of oils and acrylics may also allow transparency.

Trompe l'œil
(French for 'deception of the eye') A painting that is so realistic that the viewer is fooled into thinking the objects or a scene are real.

Underdrawing
A drawing made on a surface or support to indicate the basic positions or guidelines for the composition.

Underpainting
The early stages of a painting when the colour balance, tone and composition are laid down.

Undertone
The underlying tone of a colour, which may veer towards another hue. For instance, a blue may be reddish or yellowish. (See also Top tone)

Vanishing point
In perspective the point at which parallel lines converge as they meet the horizon. There may be several vanishing points in a picture.

Varnish
A transparent liquid applied to the surface of a painting, which dries to form a transparent protective film. Varnishes are available in matt or glossy finishes and specific formulations are available for the medium used in the painting.

Vehicle
A liquid, including the binder and additives, which holds pigment in suspension so that it can be applied to a surface in the form of paint.

Vignette
A painting or drawing of which the edges are shaded off or fade away, often in the shape of an oval.

Volume
The space filled by an element or object in a drawing or painting.

Warm colours
Colours in the red/orange/yellow sector of the colour wheel are generally described as warm.

Wash
A layer of transparent or thinly diluted paint or ink, usually applied in broad sweeps. Colour may be built up by layering one wash over another.

Water-soluble pencils
Coloured pencils and crayons that may be used with water to produce watercolour effects.

Watercolour
The term mainly applies to pigment bound with a water-soluble substance, such as gum arabic, which gives transparent colour when dry. However, opaque watercolours, known as gouache or 'body' colour, which contain fillers such as chalk, are also applied by diluting with water. (See also Gouache)

Wet-in-wet
A technique in watercolour in which a wash is applied on top of another while the first is still wet.

Wet-on-dry
A technique in watercolour in which a wash is applied on top of another after the first is fully dry.

Wetting agent
A liquid such as ox gall added to watercolour that enables it to flow more easily on the paper.

White light
This effect is produced when red, blue and green light are combined in equal proportions. (See also Additive mixing and Subtractive mixing)

Whiting
Ground and washed white chalk used to make whitewash and gesso.

Yellowing of paint
An effect of yellow discoloration on oil paintings that may occur if too much linseed oil is added to the paint. Some varnishes may cause a painting to take on a yellow tinge or the surface of the varnish may become grimy. Oil paintings kept in the dark also tend to take on a yellowish look.

Yellowing of paper
Gradual darkening of paper towards a yellowish or brownish shade. This is especially noticeable in acidic papers, such as those made from wood pulp.

Much of the material contained in this manual was informed by first-hand experience, curiosity and experimentation, and through talking to practising artists and manufacturers of artists' colours. Many hundreds of books have been browsed too, and the following were of particular interest. Some are standard works of reference on colour and some just tell a fascinating story. Many of the older works contain practical information on colouring techniques from bygone ages and may encourage more curious readers to experiment for their own amusement.

Advice to Artists
Leonardo da Vinci
Edited/Annotated by Emery Kelen
Running Press, Philadelphia, 1990

The Art of Colour
Johannes Ittens
Van Nostrand/Reinhold, New York, 1961
[Original German Edition, Kunst der Farbe, Studienausgabe, 1961]

The Artist's Handbook of Materials & Techniques
Ralph Meyer
Fifth Edition, Faber & Faber, London, 1991
Revised and expanded by Steven Sheehan

Artists' Materials
Which, Why and How
Emma Pearce
A&C Black (Publishers) Limited, London, 1992

Artists' Pigments
F. W. Webber
Van Nostrand, New York, 1923

Bright Earth
The Invention of Colour
Philip Ball
Viking, London, 2001

The Craftsman's Handbook
Il Libro dell 'Arte, Cennino d'Andrea Cennini
Translation: Daniel V. Thompson Jr.
Yale University Press, 1933
Dover Publications Inc. (paperback), New York, 1960

Colour
How to Use Colour in Art and Design
Edith Anderson Feisner
Laurence King, London, 2001

Colour
Making and Using Dyes and Pigments
François Delamare & Bernard Guineau
Translated by Sophie Hawkes
Thames & Hudson, London, 2000
[Original edition, Gallimard, Paris 1999]

Colour
Travels Through the Paintbox
Victoria Finlay
Sceptre/Hodder and Stoughton, London, 2002

Colour for the Artist
A Pocket How To Do It
Hans Schwarz
Studio Vista, London, 1980

Colour and Culture
Practice & Meaning from Antiquity to Abstraction
John Gage
Thames and Hudson, London, 1993

Colour and Meaning
Art, Science and Symbolism
John Gage
Thames and Hudson, London, 1999

Concerning the Spiritual in Art
Wassily Kandinsky
Dover, New York, 1977
[Original edition, trans. from German, 1914]

The Elements of Colour
A treatise based on the Art of Colour
Johannes Ittens
Edited by Faber Birren
John Wiley & Sons Inc., 2001

Interaction of Color
Josef Albers
Yale University Press, 1963

Lights and Pigments
Colour Principles for Artists
Roy Osbourne
John Murray, London, 1980

Living Colours
The definitive guide to colour palettes through the ages
Margaret Walch and Augustine Hope
Chronicle Books, San Francisco, 1995

The Materials of the Artist and their use in Painting
With notes on the techniques of the old masters
Max Doerner
Harcourt Brace & Company, 1949
Harvest Paperback edition, 1984
[Original German edition, Maltmaterial und seine Verwendung im Bilde, 1934]

The Materials and Techniques of Painting
Jonathan Stephenson
Thames and Hudson, London, 1989

Mauve
How one man invented a colour that changed the world
Simon Garfield
Faber & Faber, London, 2000

Methods and Materials of Painting
of the Great Schools and Masters
Sir Charles Lock Eastlake
[Two volumes bound as one, paperback],
Dover Publications, New York, 2001
[Original edition, Materials for a History of Oil Painting, Longmans, London, 1847]

Notes on the Composition and Permanence of Artists' Colours
Winsor & Newton
ColArt Fine Art & Graphics Ltd, 1997

The Oxford Companion to Art
Edited by Harold Osborne
Oxford University Press
First published 1970, Nineteenth Impression 1999

The Painter's Handbook
A Complete Reference
Mark David Gottsegen
Watson Guptill, 1993

Painting Materials
A short Encyclopaedia
Rutherford J. Gettens & George L. Stout
Dover Publications, New York, 1966
[Original edition, D. Van Nostrand Co. Inc. New York, 1942]

The Primary Colours
Three Essays
Alexander Theroux
Picador, London 1995
[Original edition, Henry Holt & Co Inc., New York, 1994]

What Every Artist Needs to Know about Paint & Colors
David Pyle
Krause Publications, Wisconsin, 2000

A

Abbé Breuil 12
Abstract Expressionism 59
Abstract Painting No. 5, 1962
    (After Ad Reinhardt) 79

acrylics artists' colours 156–79
    brushmarks 33
    diluents 33
    Douglas Wilson 38
    drying times 33
    flow improvers 37
    impasto 33
    industrial development 33
    liquid 33
    mediums 33, 37
    mistakes 33
    palettes 40
    permanence 33
    portable 147
    resin 33
    starter palette 33
    Sue Fitzgerald 118–23
    versatility 33

additive colour mixing 25
additive primary colours 25
additive secondary colours 25
additives 36
Adriatic Sea 74
Afghanistan 51
alkyd oils 31
alkyd resin 36
alla prima 30, 31
Altamira cave paintings 62
American Society for Testing
    and Materials (ASTM) 17
aniline pigments 58, 81
animation 150, 151
appliqué 148
aquarelle pencils 35
Armenian stone 50
arsenic 14, 68, 70
art masking fluid 32
artists' colours 30, 156–79
ash 144
Asia 68
Asia Minor 67
asphaltum 75, 83
atmosphere 42, 43, 98
Australian Birds (Chris Perry) 149
azo dyes 64
Aztecs 54, 58
azurite 12, 50, 51, 68

B

backdrops 136
Balkwill, Ray 38, 98–101
Beached Boats (Nick Bowering) 105
bitumen 75, 83

black Animal Black 77
    asphaltum 83
    bitumen 83
    Bone Black 77
    charcoal 82
    chiaroscuro 79

CMYK 21
coal tar 81
Colour Index 176
dark hues 83
Elephant Black 77
experimenting with 78
Flame Black 77
Gilsonite 75
granulation 80
Grape Black 77
grey scale 81
history 77
intense darks 82, 83
Ivory Black 30, 32, 77, 78
Kernel Black 77
Lamp Black 77, 78
London colours 82
making 76
manipulating 105
Mars Black 77, 78
mixing 82
nearly black 83
Oil Black 77
Payne's Grey 77, 78, 80
pigments 76–83
shades 76, 78, 81
shop-bought darks 83
staining power 80
tints 76, 78, 81
transparency 80
undertone 78
variations 80
Vine Black 77, 78
watercolour 32
working without 104–05

Black Suprematist Square,
    1914–15 (Kasimir Malevich) 79
blackberry 145
blanc fixe 34
bleeding 16
Blind Girl, The
    (John Everett Millais) 24
blood 144

blue Alexandrian Blue 50
    Antwerp Blue 52
    azurite 12, 50, 51, 68
    azzurro della magna 50
    Berlin Blue 52
    Blue Bice 55
    Cerulean Blue 13, 52, 53
    chemical blues 53
    cobalt 51
    Cobalt Blue 13, 52, 53
    Colour Index 166–69
    core 53
    cyan 21, 50, 53
    Egyptian Blue 12, 50
    Egyptians 50
    French Ultramarine 13, 52
    frit 50
    fugitive 51
    Greeks 50–51
    history 50–51
    Indanthrene Blue 52–53
    indigo 51
    Indigofera tinctorum 51
    industrial technology 52

International Klein Blue 53
Isatis tinctoria 50
lapis lazuli 15, 50–52
lazurite 51
Leyden Blue 51
Manganese Blue 53
Middle Ages 50, 51
Monastral Blue 14, 15
Mountain Blue 50
obsessions 53
Paris Blue 52
Phthalo Blue 14, 52–53
pigments 50–53
Primary Blue 53, 146
Prussian Blue 13, 32, 52
Renaissance 50, 51
Romans 50, 51
Smalt 51
Ultramarine 13, 50–53, 77
woad 50

Blue Horse 1, 1911 (Franz Marc) 53
blue jeans 51
Blue Rider group, The 53
boat paintings 104–05
Book of Kells 50
Bowering Nick 104–05
brick dust 145
British Standards Institute 17
Britons 50
broken-prismatic effect 132–35
bronze 88

brown Bistre 75
    bitumen 75
    Brown Madder 74, 75
    brown ochre 72
    Burnt Sienna 12, 72, 75
    Burnt Umber 13, 72, 75
    Caput Mortuum 74
    Cassel Brown 74
    Cologne Earth 74
    crocus martis 74
    history 72–73
    Kassel Earth 74
    Mars Black 74
    Mars Brown 72, 74
    Mars colours 74
    Mars Violet 74
    Mars Yellow 74
    Mummy Brown 75
    pigments 72–75
    Raw Sienna 72, 75
    Raw Umber 72, 75
    Rubens' Brown 74
    Rubens' Madder 75
    Sepia 74
    Spanish Brown 72
    Vandyke Brown 72, 74
    Violet Oxide 74

brushes 123, 138
brushwork 132, 135
Building Fascias (Simon Jennings) 151

C

cadmium 12, 13, 59, 60, 64
Caesar, Julius 50
calico 138
canvas123, 148
Caravaggio,
    Michelangelo Merisi da 79
carbon black 84
Cardinal Grapes and Silken Shawl
    (Sue Fitzgerald) 118–19
carmine 15, 58
Carnevale di Venezia
    (Jackie Simmonds) 38
Carr, Jessie 136–39
cars 14
Cartoon Paint 150
cave paintings 12, 72, 144
Cel Vinyl 150
Celadonite 67
Cennini, Cennino 57, 61, 62, 63, 68,
    72, 73, 77, 112
ceramics 30, 35
chalk 35, 56
charcoal 82, 84, 139, 144, 152
charcoal pencils 35
Check headband
    (Tim Riddihough) 38, 107
chemistry 13, 14, 15
Chestnutt, Judith 38, 140–43
chiaroscuro 79
chilli powder 144
Chinese 12, 56, 68
chlorophyll 68
chrocoite 69
chromium 58, 60, 64, 69
Chrysanthemums
    (Marina Yedigaroff) 125
Churchill, Winston 74
Cinabrese 112
cinnabar 12, 57, 69, 112
clay 72
CMYK (cyan/magenta/yellow/black) 21
coal ash 145
coal tar 70, 75, 81
cobalt 51, 54
cobalt aluminate 52
cobalt oxide 13
cobalt pigments 13
cochineal 15, 58, 144
coffee 144
cola 144
Coldstream, Sir William 102
collages 143

colour additive colour mixing 25
    animal sources 144
    artists' 156–79
    atmosphere 42, 43
    bias 16, 26
    bleeding 16
    blending 96
    broken 132–35
    cadmium 12, 59, 60, 64
    clean 123
    cloth 148–49
    code 42–43
    communication 42–43
    complementary 26, 27

complementary
    primaries 110
contained 128–131
contrast 122, 133
control 21
cool 27
creative directions 96
designers' 30, 34, 37
diagrammatic 26
dry 152
earth 14, 56, 72
experimenting 26, 45
fabric 35, 148–49
fast work 108–09
flesh 90–93, 106–09
for free 144-45
fugitive 51, 56, 58
ground 131
harmony 27, 128
household paints 136–39
identification 26
information 42–43
inspiration 118
intensity 130
interference 88
interpreting 44-45, 131
iridescent 25, 88
juxtaposition 133
language 42–43
large scale 114–17, 138
light-scattering 88
limited range 110–11
luminosity 124–27
manufacturers'
    colour charts 156–79
media 96
mediums 36
metallic 88, 178
mineral sources 144–45
mixing 23, 26, 35, 121, 128
modern 14
mood 42, 43
natural 146
non-art 136–39
opaque 150, 151
optical mixing 23
organizing 122
paper pulp 140–43
pearlizing 88–89
portable 14, 146–47
practical use of 42
prehistoric primary 62
printing 20–21
process 20–21, 23
Renaissance
    skin tones 112–13
reproduction 20–21
selection 96
six-colour division 26
smooth 150–51
special-effect 88
spectrum 24
subdued 102–03
subtractive
    colour mixing 25, 26
techniques 96
tertiary 27
texture 130
themes 128, 130

three-dimensional 43
top tone 27
traditional 14
transparency 16, 31, 32,
    36, 37, 124–27
twelve-colour division 26
undertone 27
vegetable sources 67,
    144–45
warm 27
wheel 25, 26–27

Colour field painting 59
Colour Index 156–79
Colour Index International 16, 18–19
Colour samples
    (Judith Chestnutt) 140, 143
colour wheel 25, 26–27
coloured pencils 30, 35, 152
columbine 67
communication 42, 43
composition 110, 123, 132
Constable, John 58, 180
contrast 122, 133
conté sticks 34
copper 68, 69, 70
copper carbonate 50, 51
copper phosphate 54
copper silicates 50
corrosion 74
crimson 15, 58
cuttlefish 74
cyan 21, 50, 53
Cyprus 67

D
Daler-Rowney 156, 180
dammar resin 31
Dark Side of the Moon, The
    (George Hardie) 24
darks 27, 83, 104–05
da Vinci, Leonardo 76
Dead Sea 75
Delacroix, Eugene 72
Delftware 51
Derain, André 59
designers' colours 30, 34, 37
Diesbach 13, 52
digital scanning 150
Doerner, Max 20
dot screen 22–23
drawing 152–53
Dresden 74
dry painting media 34–35
drying times
    16, 30, 31, 33, 36, 37, 40
Dunsterville, Lucy 136–39
Dust to Dust (Simon Jennings) 145
dye 51, 56, 58, 64, 148

E
earth colours 56, 72, 172–75
earth pigments 12, 14, 72, 73, 144
East Anglian Estuary
    (Joan Elliott Bates) 103
egg tempera 30, 34, 84
Egyptians 12, 34, 50, 56, 68, 75, 86

El Greco 144
Elliott Bates, Joan 102–03
embroidery 148
en plein air 146
enamel paint 151
Euston Road School 102

F
fabric paints 148–49
fabrics 30, 35, 51, 70, 118, 148–49
fast work 108–09
fat 144
'fat over lean' 36
Fauvists 59, 133
felt tips 35
ferric ferrocyanide 52
Field, George 15, 58
Field's *Chromatography* 68
Fitzgerald, Sue 118–23

flesh   combination pigments 93
colours   Green Earth 67
              Jaune Brillant 90
              mixing 92
              Naples Yellow Reddish 90
              pigments 90, 92, 93
              prepared 93
              Renaissance
                skin tones 112–13
              shop-bought 90
              Tim Riddihough 106–08
              Unbleached Titanium 90
              warm neutrals 90

flint 37
floral artists 33
flow improvers 37
four-colour printing 20–21
France 66, 72
fresco 72
Freud, Lucian 82
Friedlander, P. 12
frit 50
From Castel Plage
    (Simon Jennings) 147
fuchsin 58
fugitive colour 51, 56, 58

G
Gauguin, Paul 70
Germany 74
gesso 34
gilding 88–89
Gilsonite 75
Girlfriends, 1965–66
    (Sigmar Polke) 23
glass painting 30, 35, 104
Glauconite 67
glazing 31, 34, 36, 58, 77, 84, 86
glycerine 37
gold leaf 63, 88, 123
Golden 156, 180

gouache   artists' colours 30,156–79
             body colour 34
             design studios 34
             gum arabic 37
             Marina Yedigaroff 125–26
             poster paints 34
             Tim Riddihough 106
             students' quality 30

Graebe, Carl 58
Graham, Peter 28–29
granulation 16, 32
graphic reproduction 20–21
graphite 84, 152
grass 145
Graves, Robert 68
Greeks 12, 43, 50, 56, 57
Green-outlined figure
    (Tim Riddihough)109

green   arsenic 13, 68, 70
           Cadmium Green 70
           Chrome Green 70
           Chromium Green 69
           Chromium
               Oxide Green 69, 70
           chrysocolla 68
           cinnabar 69
           Cinnabar Green 70
           Cobalt Green 13, 70
           Colour Index 169–71
           complementary 71
           copper 69, 70
           copper green 68
           Creta viridis 67
           Emerald Green 13, 70
           experimenting 71
           Green Earth 67, 70
           Green Umber 67
           history 68–69
           Hooker's Green 70
           Hungarian Green 68
           malachite 68
           Mineral Green 68
           mixing 71
           Mountain Green 68
           Munich Green 70
           Naphthol Green 68, 70
           Olive Green 70
           Paris Green 70
           Permanent Green 70
           Phthalo Green 68, 70
           pigments 66–71
           Royal Green 69
           Sap Green 69, 70
           Scheele's Green 68
           Schweinfurt Green 70
           Terre Verte 13, 67, 112
           vegetable greens 69
           verdigris
           Verona Green Earth 67
           Vert-antique 69
           Vienna Green 70
           Viridian 68, 71
           Viridian Green 70
           Winsor Green 15
           Yellowish Green 70
           Zinnober Green 69

grey
Colour Index 176–77
Cool Grey 85
Davy's Grey 84
Gerhard Richter 85
graphite 84
grisaille 84
guazzo 84
history 84
homage to 85
Neutral Grey 84
Payne's Grey 84
pigments 84–85
veneda 84
Warm Grey 84–85

Gries, Patrick 25
ground colour 131
Guimet, J.-B. 13, 52
gum arabic 37
gypsum 56

H
Hand of Nature, The
 (Patrick Gries) 25
hard pastels 34
hardboard 34
Hardie, George 24
Haughton, Desmond 96, 110–11
Helios 63
hematite 72–73
highlighting 31, 32
Hirst, Damien 43
Hoechst 15, 64
Homage to Paul (Chris Perry) 149
Homage to Vincent (Chris Perry) 149
Hooker, William 70
Höpfner 52
Hopi Indians 54
Horadam, Josef 180
household paints 136–39
hue 14, 27, 156
Hunt, William Holman 58
Hymn (Damien Hirst) 43

I
ICI 14
illustrators 33, 34
impasto 31, 37, 153
impasto gel 37
Impressionists 30, 70, 133
India 51, 56, 66, 67
Indigo 51
industrial paints 136
Industrial Revolution 13
information 42–43
Ingres paper 35
ink 74, 107, 108, 125–26
iridescence 25, 88
Iridescent Stainless Steel 88
iron oxide 14, 66, 67, 72, 73, 74
Italian Girl, 1887
 (Vincent van Gogh) 91
Italy 66, 67
Iznik tiles 51

J
Jennings, Simon 8, 145, 151
'Judas hair' 57
junk mail 140, 142

K
Kandinsky, Wassily 51, 53, 60, 61, 65
kermes insect 56, 58
Kiss of Judas, The
 (Giotto di Bondone) 57
Klee, Paul 9
Klein, Yves 53
knifework 37, 132, 134, 135

L
lac insect 56
lake making 12–13, 56
landscapes 102–03, 131
lapis lazuli 13, 15, 50, 51, 52
Lascaux cave paintings 62
layering 104
Le Chahut, 1889–90
 (Georges-Pierre Seurat) 23
lead chromate 69
Lemon (Douglas Wilson) 38
Levinson, Henry 180
Libri Colorum – Jean Lebegue 52
Liebermann, Carl 58
Lichtenstein, Roy 22
life painting 106–08
light 86, 134, 146
lightfastness
 13–15, 16–17, 35, 66, 70, 84, 180
limonite 66, 73
linear techniques 104, 152–53
linseed oil 30, 31, 34, 36, 40
Liquin 31
Liquitex 156, 180
London colours 84
Lowestoft Beach
 (John Reay) 133, 135
low-odour thinners 30, 36
Lowrie, Daphne Jo 96, 128–31
Lukas 156, 180
luminosity 124–27

M
madder 15, 58, 74, 75
Madonna, Child
 and St John with Angels
 (Michelangelo Buonarroti) 12, 112
magenta 14, 21, 58
magnetite 73
Maimeri, Gianni 156, 180
malachite 12, 68
Manhattan (Peter Graham) 29
manufacturers' colour charts 156–79
marble dust 37
Marc, Franz 53
Mars colours 14, 74
massicot 62
Masterpiece 1962
 (Roy Lichtenstein) 22
materials' suppliers 180
Matisse, Henri 59

mauve 81
mauvine 13
media 30–35, 39, 45

mediums
acrylic 33, 37, 118
additives 36
alkyd 36
colour 36
drying 37
flint 37
flow improvers 37
gloss 37
gouache 37
gum arabic 37
impasto 37
interference 37
iridescent 37
marble dust 37
matt 37
oils 36
ox gall 37
paint characteristics 36
pearlescent 37
retarding 37
sand 37
special-effects 37
texture 36
texture gels 37
texture pastes 37
watercolour 37

Mesopotamia 56
metallic colours 88, 178
mica 86, 88
Micaceous Iron Oxide 88
Michelangelo Buonarroti 12, 112
Millais, John Everett 24
minerals 66, 72
mistakes 30, 33
mixed media 39, 45, 98–99,
 106, 119, 125–26, 152
Monet, Claude 55
Monfreid, George Daniel de 70
monochrome painting 104
mood 42, 98
Morning mist (Ray Balkwill) 38
moulding 37
Mussini, Professor Cesare 31, 180
mustard powder 144

N
Naples 75
Napoleon Bonaparte 13
Navajo Indians 54
Neutral Gray 146
Newton and the Prism
 (After George Romney) 24
Newton, Henry 180
Newton, Sir Isaac 24
Newton's Rings 24
Night Café (Vincent van Gogh) 71
non-art colours 136–39

O
ochre 12, 14, 62, 63, 65, 66, 72–74

oils
alkyd 31
artists' colours 156
cracking 36, 37
Daphne Jo Lowrie 128–31
diluents 31
drying times 30
George Rowlett 38, 114–17
Joan Elliott Bates 102–03
John Reay 132–35
linseed oil 30, 31, 34, 36, 40
Marina Yedigaroff 38,
 126–27
mediums 36–37
Nick Bowering 104–05
oil pastels 35, 153
oilbars 30, 31, 132, 153
oil-painting sticks 132,153
palettes 30, 40
resin oil colours 31
safflower oil 31, 37
solvents 31
starter palette 30
students' quality 30
sunflower oil 30, 37
thinners 36
walnut oil 37
water-mixable 31
white 31
yellowing 36, 37

Old Holland 156, 180
optical illusions 20
optical mixing 23
Orange Boat Essaouira
 (Nick Bowering) 105

orange
Benzimidazolone
 Orange 60
cadmium 60
Cadmium Orange 60
Chrome Orange 60
chromium 60
Colour Index 161
history 60
Mars Orange 74
Perinone Orange 60
pigments 60–61
Pyrrole Orange 60
realgar 60, 61

Oranges, 1863 (Antonio Mensaque) 60
orpiment 62, 63, 64
Our Lady of Czestochowa (Anon) 83
ox gall 37

P
paint
acrylics 33, 118–23
cel 150
characteristics 36
egg tempera 30, 34, 84
enamel 151
fabric 148–49
fat 31
flow 36

generic name 137
gouache 34
household 136–39
industrial 136
long 115
oil 30–31
short 115
trade name 137
watercolour 32

palette acrylics 40
bun-tin style 40
choosing 40–41, 102
colour range 41
core 114, 122
home-made 41
kidney-shaped 40
layout 96, 102
light to dark colours 41
limited 104
linseed oil 40
mahogany 40
management 41
mixing area 40
'mud' 27
non-art colours 137
oils 40
plastic 40
priming 40
prismatic layout 134
seven-colour 110–11
spectrum order 41
starter 30, 32, 33, 41
Stay-Wet Palette 40
tear-off paper 40
thumbhole 40
traditional 40
travelling 147
warm to cool colours 41
watercolour 40
white porcelain 41

paper pulp 140–43
paperworks 140–43
parsley 67

pastels buying 35
charcoal pencils 35
colour choice 35
colour mixing 35
conté sticks 34
fixing 35
hard pastels 34
Ingres paper 35
Jackie Simmonds 38
linear techniques 153
oil 35
paper 34–35
pastel pencils 34–35
pastel sticks 34
starter palette 35
tooth 34, 35

Paul and Ringo (Heinz Edelman) 150
Payne, William 77, 84
Pearce, Emma 12
pen and ink 107

pencils aquarelle 35
charcoal 35
coloured 30, 35, 152
graphite 152
pastel 34, 35
watercolour 35, 153

Perkin, William Henry 13, 58, 81
permanence 12–14, 16, 33, 35, 66, 70, 72, 74, 180
Perry, Chris 149
Persian Gulf 72
perspective 132
pewter 88
photography 150
phthalocyanine 54
Picasso, Pablo 53, 71, 84

pigment aniline 58, 81
arylide 14
black 76–83
bleeding 16
blue 50–53
brown 72–75
cadmium 14
characteristics 16–17
Chinese 12
chrome 13
cobalt 13
colour bias 16
drying rate 16
earth 12, 14, 72, 73, 144
Egyptians 12
flesh 90–93
granulation 16
Greeks 12
green 67–71
grey 84–85
Hansa yellows 14
history 2–14
inorganic 14
lake 12–13, 56
lightfastness 13–15, 16–17, 35, 66, 70, 84, 180
madder 58
natural 144–45
natural organic 14
opacity 16
orange 60–61
permanence 12–14, 16, 33, 35, 66, 70, 72, 74, 180
perylene 14
pyrrole 14
quinacridones 14
red 56–59
red lake 13, 56
Renaissance 12, 13
Romans 12
staining properties 16, 32
standards 16–17
synthetic iron oxides 14
synthetic organic 14
transparency 16
turquoise 54
violet 55
white 86–87
yellow 62–66
zinc 14

Pissarro, Camille 23
Plate of Fruit (Anon) 44-45
Pliny 57, 62
pointillism 23
poliment 89
Polke, Sigmar 23
polychrome sculpture 43
Pompeii 12, 67
poppy oil 37
Portrait Fragments (George Underwood) 113
Portrait of a Woman (Anon) 12
poster paints 34
Post-Impressionists 70
potash 13, 52
primary colours 25–27
printing 20
prism 24
process colours 20, 21, 23
projected light 25
pumice 37

Q
Quayside (Ray Balkwill) 100
quinacridones 14, 32, 59

R
rabbit-skin size 34
rainbow 24
realgar 60–61
Reay, John 96, 132–35
recycling 140–43

red Alizarin Crimson 14, 15, 30, 32, 57, 58, 59
aniline 58, 81
cadmium 59, 60, 64
Cadmium Red 13, 57, 58, 59
Cardinal Red 56
carmine 15, 58
chemical pigments 59
China 56
Chinese Red 58
Chrome Red 58
cinnabar 57
cochineal 15, 58
Colour Index 161–65
crimson 15, 58
Daemonorops draco 57
Dragon's Blood 57
dye 58
earth reds 56, 73–75
Egyptians 56
Fauves 59
fuchsin 58
fugitive 56, 58
Genuine Rose Madder 15
Greeks 56, 57
history 56–57
India 56
lightfastness 59
madder 58, 74, 75
Madder Lake 58
magenta 14, 21, 58
Mars Red 74
Mesopotamia 56
Middle Ages 56

Naphthol Red 59
Permanent Carmine 15
Permanent Madder 57
Permanent Rose 14
Perylene Red 59
pigment 56–59
primary colour 58
Pyrrole Red 59
realgar 56
red lake 13
red lead 12, 56, 62
red ochre 72
Renaissance 56
Romans 57
Rose Madder 57, 58
Rubia tinctorum 58
Scarlet Lake 58
symbolism 56–57
toxicity 56, 59
Vermilion 57, 59
wavelength 57
Winsor Red 57

red earth Alizarin Crimson 75
Burnt Sienna 72, 75
Burnt Umber 72, 75
hematite 73
Italian Earth 75
iron ores 73
Mars Red 74
pigments 74–75
Pozzuoli 75
Raw Sienna 72, 75
Raw Umber 72, 75
reddish browns 73
Rubens' Madder 75
Sinopia 73
Terra di Siena 75

red-hot poker 145
red lake 13
red lead 12, 56, 62
Red man crossed legs, leaning back (Tim Riddihough) 109
Red man, standing (Tim Riddihough) 106
red poliment 89
Red Tulips (Marina Yedigaroff) 38, 126–27
red wine 144
reflected light 25
Reinhardt, Ad 79
Rembrandt, Harmensz van Rijn 74, 79, 148
Renaissance 12, 34, 43, 50, 56, 75, 84
resin oil colours 31
retarding mediums 37
Richter, Gerhard 85
Riddihough, Tim 38, 96
Riley, Bridget 85
Romans 12, 43, 50, 57, 67, 74
Romney, George 24
rose hip 145
Rothko, Mark 59
Rowlett, George 38, 96, 114–17
Royal Talens 156, 180
Royal Watercolour Society 35
Rubens, Peter Paul 74
rue 67

S

safflower oil 31, 37
saliva 144
sand 37
sandstone 145
Sardinia 75
Scheele, Carl Wilhelm 68
Schmincke 156, 180
Schmincke, Herman 180
Schoenfeld, Dr Franz 180
Science of Art, The
  (Winsor & Newton) 15
secondary colours 25–27
Self-portrait aged 34 (Rembrandt) 79
Self-portrait with Yellow Waistcoat
  1994 (Desmond Haughton), 111
Sennelier 156, 180
Sennelier, Gustave 180
Sepia 74
Set Aside (Helen Dougall) 148
Seurat, Georges-Pierre 23
Seydelmann, Professor Jacob C 74
shades 27
Sheltered Moorings,
  (Ray Balkwill) 99
Shoreline, 2001
  (Judith Chestnutt) 38, 141
Siberian Red Lead 69
Siblings, 2001
  (Daphne Jo Lowrie) 129
Sicily 75
siderite 73
Siena 72, 75, 112
silk paints 33, 35
silver 88, 123
silver leaf 123
Simmonds, Jackie 38
Sinope 73
Sinopia 73, 112
six-colour division 26
skin tones – see flesh colours
Slade School of Fine Art 102
Smalt 12, 51, 52
'smike' (CMYK) 21
soot 145
South Africa 66
Southern Sun (Peter Graham) 28
Spain 72
special-effect colours 88, 178
special-effects mediums 37
spectrum 24
spontaneity 98, 100
stained glass 84
staining properties 16, 32
still life 44–45, 128–30
Still Life with Bottles
  (Daphne Jo Lowrie) 130
Still Life with Orange Flower
  (Daphne Jo Lowrie) 130
Straight paint (Tim Riddihough) 109
Stromeyer, Friedrich 13, 59
subtractive colour mixing 25, 26
Sudden Storm over Thames,
  Rotherhithe Pier, 1996
  (George Rowlett) 38, 115
sunflower oil 30, 37
sunlight 24

Sunlit Walmer Beach Deal Pier,
  Bathers and Crab Boat, 1997–98
  (George Rowlett) 115
Sunset on the Exe (Ray Balkwill) 99
suppliers 180
surface 124–27
synthetic oxides 74

T

tea 144
terracotta 145
Terre Verte 13, 67, 112
tertiary colours 27
textiles 30, 35, 51, 70, 118, 148–49
texture 36, 37, 123, 130, 150, 153
Thénard, Louis Jacques 13, 52
Theophrastus –
  The History of Stones 57
tints 27, 31, 32
tonalism 102–03
top tone 27
trade 13, 51
transparency
  16, 31, 32, 36, 37, 124–27
Tri-Art 156, 180
Trinidad 75
T-shirt designs 149
Turkey 54
Turner, Joseph Mallord William
  51, 180
turpentine 30, 31, 36
turquoise 54
twelve-colour division   26
Two Dragons (Sue Fitzgerald) 120–21
Tyrian Purple 12

U

underpainting
  84, 104, 110, 112–13, 132
undertone 27
Underwood (George) 113
USA 66

V

van Dyck, Sir Anthony   74, 75
van Gogh, Vincent 65, 71, 91, 180
vanilla 144
Vauquelin, Nicolas 64, 69
vegetable dyes 12
verdaccio 112
Vermilion 12, 57, 112
Verona 67
Vessels (Helen Banzhat) 148
Vesuvius, Mount 64
violet 55, 165–66
Virgin Mary 51, 83, 89
Vladimir Madonna, c.1125 (Anon) 89

W

walnut oil 37
washes 152
waste-paper collages 143

water-colour
artists' colours 156–79
atmosphere 98
boxes 32
brushes 100
Daphne Jo Lowrie 128–31
field boxes 32
glazing 32
granulation 32
gum arabic 37
mediums 37
mixed media 98–99
mood 98
opacity 32, 100
palettes 30, 40, 100
pans 32
paper 99, 100
pencils 35, 153
permanence 32
Ray Balkwill 38, 98–101
spontaneity 98, 100
staining 32
sticks 35
texture 100
transparency 32, 100
wet-in-wet 100

wavelength 24
wax crayons 35
'wet-in-wet' 37, 121
whelks 12

white
artists' 14
baryta white 87
bismuth white 87
blanc fixe   87
China 86
Chinese White 13, 86, 87
Colour Index 179
Cremnitz White 12, 86
Dutch White 86
Egyptians 86
Flake White 12, 86
glazing 86
ground work 86
history 86
Iridescent White 86
lead white 13
mica 86
Mixing White 86
oils 31
Permanent White 87
pigments 86
reserved white 87
resists 87
Titanium White 14, 31,67 86
underpainting 86
Underpainting White 86
watercolour 32
white lead 12, 86
Zinc White 31, 86

white light 24
white spirit 30, 36
Wilson, Douglas 38
Winsor & Newton
  13, 15, 58, 69, 70, 86, 156, 180
Winsor, William 64, 180
woad 50
Woven Basket (Anon) 42

Y

Yedigaroff, Marina 124–27

yellow
Antimony Yellow 64
Arsenic Yellow 62
Aureolin 64
azo dyes 64
Azo Yellow Medium 14
Cadmium Yellow 13, 64
Chinese Yellow 62
Chrome Lemon 64
Chrome Yellow 13, 64, 65
Cobalt Yellow 13
Colour Index 158–60
Crocus sativus 62
Earth Yellow 62
Egyptians 62
four-colour printing 21
Gamboge 63
Gamboge Genuine 65
gold 63
Golden Yellow 65
Greeks 62
Hansa 14, 64
Helios 63
history 62–63
India 63
Indian Yellow 14, 15,
  63, 65
King's Yellow 62
Leipzig Yellow 64
Lemon Yellow 14, 65
manuscript illumination
  62–63
Mars Yellow 62, 74
massicot 62
Mineral Yellow 62
Naples Yellow 13, 64, 146
ochre 72
orpiment 62, 63, 64
Oxford Ochre 66
Paris Yellow 64
pigments 62–65
'pinks' 64
prehistoric primary 62
realgar 63
saffron 62
Stone Age 62
symbolism 62
turmeric 62
van Gogh 65
Winsor Yellow 14, 64
Yellow Ochre 62, 65, 66

yellowing 36, 37
Young Bison (Abbé Breuil) 12
Young Scientist Anatomy Toy
  (Joustra/Humbrol Ltd) 43

Z

zinc oxide 14
Zuni Indians 54

Beige brick wall - White is some black & a little red.
a partic deep dark or coloured black - Phthalo Green +
                                          Quin Crimson
Favouritecolour - Naples yellow   AND
Chromium oxide green - dullish grey green   Crimsom Al
                                                        + Viridian
Green Earth - Terre Verte.
Viridian - wonderful 'cooler' of reds, greens, browns
         - useful for flesh tones

Olive Green - can obtain similar col by toning bright
             leaf green w a little orange
Earth colours - Raw & Bu Si, Raw & Bu Umber, Venetian Red,
              - Indian Red, yellow Ochre, Red Ochre,
              Terre Verte (green Earth), Vandyke Brown.

Titanium white - Best choice
              but opaque & can overwhelm more transpar
              colours.
* TRy MIXING WHITE in acrylics - transpar &
              mixes well to prod good transparent cols.
       Good for glazes + toning down of colours

WAT COL - DARKS - UBl + Bu Umb / Bu Si
                - Near Black - Viridian + sepia
       -